MIGRANTS AND REFUGEES IN EUROPE

Work Integration in Comparative Perspective

Edited by
Simone Baglioni and Francesca Calò

P

First published in Great Britain in 2023 by

Policy Press, an imprint of
Bristol University Press
University of Bristol
1–9 Old Park Hill
Bristol
BS2 8BB
UK
t: +44 (0)117 374 6645
e: bup-info@bristol.ac.uk

Details of international sales and distribution partners are available at
policy.bristoluniversitypress.co.uk

© Simone Baglioni and Francesca Calò 2023

The digital PDF and EPUB versions of this title are available Open Access and distributed under the terms of the Creative Commons Attribution-NonCommercial-NoDerivatives 4.0 International licence (https://creativecommons.org/licenses/by-nc-nd/4.0/) which permits reproduction and distribution for non-commercial use without further permission provided the original work is attributed.

British Library Cataloguing in Publication Data
A catalogue record for this book is available from the British Library

ISBN 978-1-4473-6451-1 paperback
ISBN 978-1-4473-6452-8 ePub
ISBN 978-1-4473-6453-5 OA PDF

The right of Simone Baglioni and Francesca Calò to be identified as editors of this work has been asserted by them in accordance with the Copyright, Designs and Patents Act 1988.

All rights reserved: no part of this publication may be reproduced, stored in a retrieval system, or transmitted in any form or by any means, electronic, mechanical, photocopying, recording, or otherwise without the prior permission of Bristol University Press.

Every reasonable effort has been made to obtain permission to reproduce copyrighted material. If, however, anyone knows of an oversight, please contact the publisher.

The statements and opinions contained within this publication are solely those of the editors and contributors and not of the University of Bristol or Bristol University Press. The University of Bristol and Bristol University Press disclaim responsibility for any injury to persons or property resulting from any material published in this publication.

Bristol University Press and Policy Press work to counter discrimination on
grounds of gender, race, disability, age and sexuality.

Cover design: Hayes Design and Advertising
Front cover image: Alamy/Nikreates
Bristol University Press and Policy Press use environmentally responsible
print partners.
Printed and bound in Great Britain by CMP, Poole

Contents

List of figures and tables		iv
Notes on contributors		vii
Acknowledgements		ix
1	Introduction *Simone Baglioni and Francesca Calò*	1
2	What do the numbers say about migration in European economies? *Christos Bagavos, Konstantinos N. Konstantakis, Panayotis G. Michaelides and Theocharis Marinos*	12
3	Legal frameworks *Veronica Federico*	38
4	Welfare regimes and labour market integration policies in Europe *Nathan Lillie, Ilona Bontenbal and Quivine Ndomo*	55
5	Civil society organisations and labour market integration: barriers and enablers in seven European countries *Dino Numerato, Karel Čada and Karina Hoření*	83
6	Social partners: barriers and enablers *Simone Baglioni, Tom Montgomery and Francesca Calò*	101
7	The 'back-stepper' and the 'career diplomat': turning points of labour market integration *Irina Isaakyan, Simone Baglioni and Anna Triandafyllidou*	120
8	The policy dimension: lessons learnt and ways forward *Maria Mexi*	138
Index		156

List of figures and tables

Figures

1.1	The multidimensional framework of analysis of migrant labour market integration proposed in the book	3
2.1	Changes (percentage) in the overall population size over the 2014–2019 period	14
2.2	Changes (percentage) in the size of the labour force between 2014 and 2020	17
2.3	Share of foreign nationals to total population (percentage), SIRIUS countries	20
2.4	Distribution of foreign nationals according to their educational attainment level (percentage), SIRIUS countries, 2008–2016	21
2.5	Mean activity rates of foreign nationals by educational attainment level (percentage), SIRIUS countries, 2008–2016	21
2.6	Participation of foreign nationals in the country's labour market (percentage), SIRIUS countries, 2008–2016	22
2.7	Mean employment rates of foreign nationals, by age group (percentage), SIRIUS countries, 2008–2016	22
2.8	Mean employment rates of foreign nationals by educational attainment level (percentage), SIRIUS countries, 2008–2016	23
2.9	Net migration rate, SIRIUS countries, 2008–2016	23
2.10	First time asylum seekers per 1,000 persons, SIRIUS countries, 2014–2016	24
2.11	Mean annual number of first instance decisions on asylum applications (per 1,000 persons), SIRIUS countries, 2008–2013, 2014–2016	25
2.12	Ratio of positive to total final decisions on asylum applications, SIRIUS countries, 2008–2013, 2014–2016	25
2.13	Mean annual number of first residence permits (per 1,000 persons), SIRIUS countries, 2008–2013, 2014–2016	26
3.1	Asylum seekers' labour market entry ban	44
3.2	Recognition of qualifications of third country nationals	45

Tables

2.1	Differences between foreign- and native-born population in their contribution to the overall population change and in their natural change (annual averages, per 1,000)	15
2.2	The components of the contribution of foreign- and native-born persons to the shifts in the size of the labour force (as percentage of the labour force in 2014)	18

List of figures and tables

2.3	Labour absorbing sectors	28
A.1	Classification of sectors of economic activity, NACE Rev. 2, 1-dig	31
A.2	Specialisation index of occupations, 2016	32
A.3	Classification of sectors of economic activity, NACE Rev. 2, 2-dig	32
A.4	Sectoral specialisation index, 2016	34
3.1	Vocational training and education	47
3.2	Unemployment benefits	48
3.3	Right to self-employment	49
4.1	Summary of the cases	75
6.1	Distribution of survey expert respondents by social partner categories (by country)	104
6.2	Respondents' perception of newcomers' skills by type of newcomers	105
6.3	Responses to the question 'What perception do you have of the skills levels of most migrants and refugees?'	106
6.4	Responses to the question 'Are migrants and refugees more of an asset or a burden for our societies?' by type of social partner	107
6.5	Responses to the question 'Has the arrival of migrants or refugees created tensions in the labour market in your country with native workers?'	109
6.6	Causes of tensions (this response item applied only to those who responded positively to the question on tensions in the labour market provoked by migrants)	110
6.7	Tools to mitigate competition between migrants and natives (this response item applied only to those who responded positively to the question about such a competition and multiple responses were allowed)	111
6.8	Responses to the question 'Do you think that the employment potential of migrants or refugees is fully realised?'	112
6.9	Responses to the question 'What are the most important factors that prevent the full realisation of migrants or refugees' employment capacities? (Please select every option that applies)'	113
6.10	Responses to the questions 'What are the most effective factors in facilitating labour market entry? (Please select every option that applies)'	113
6.11	Responses to the question 'Are policies effective in filling skills shortages?'	114
6.12	Responses to the question 'Do you think that the health and safety risks faced by migrants and refugees are higher than, the same as, or lower than the risks faced by the native workforce?'	115

6.13 Responses to the question 'Which factors prevent the development of opportunities for social dialogue (negotiation and consultation between organised workers and employers which can often include policymakers, for example, collective bargaining) on migration and labour migration (if more than one, please select the three most important)?' 116

Notes on contributors

Christos Bagavos is Professor of Demography at the Department of Social Policy, Panteion University, Greece. Christos' publications and research interests focus on methods and analyses of differentials in fertility, migration and health status and on the socioeconomic implications of demographic shifts.

Simone Baglioni is Professor of Sociology at the Department of Economics and Management, University of Parma, Italy. Simone's publications and research interests focus on employability, migration and social innovation.

Ilona Bontenbal is Project Researcher and PhD student in Social and Public Policy at the University of Jyväskylä, Finland. Ilona's publications and research interests focus on migration, social and economic remittances, and labour market integration.

Karel Čada is Researcher in the Department of Sociology, Faculty of Social Sciences, Charles University, Czech Republic. Karel's publications and research interests focus on poverty, social exclusion and migration.

Francesca Calò is Assistant Professor at the Department of Public Leadership and Social Enterprise, The Open University, UK. Francesca's publications and research interests focus on non-profit organisations, social innovation, migration and social enterprises.

Veronica Federico is Associate Professor of Public Comparative Law at the Department of Legal Studies, University of Florence, Italy. Veronica's publications and research interests focus on African comparative constitutional law, fundamental and human rights, citizenship and migration studies.

Karina Hoření is Researcher at Charles University, Czech Republic. Karina's publications and research interests focus on migration, ethnic relations, social and cultural history.

Irina Isaakyan is Senior Research Associate at Toronto Metropolitan University, Canada. Irina's publications and research interests focus on high skills and elite migrants, gender and identity and diaspora.

Konstantinos N. Konstantakis is Lecturer in Applied Economics at the National Technical University of Athens, Greece. Konstantinos' publications and research interests focus on econometrics, economic modelling and migration.

Nathan Lillie is Professor of Social and Public Policy at the University of Jyväskylä, Finland. Nathan's publications and research interests focus on trade union strategy, labour mobility and trade union relations with migrant workers.

Theocharis Marinos is Adjunct Professor at the School of Social Sciences of the Hellenic Open University, Greece and a Postdoctoral Researcher at the School of Applied Mathematical and Physical Sciences of the National University of Athens, Greece.

Maria Mexi is Senior Fellow at Geneva Graduate Institute, Switzerland. Maria's publications and research interests focus on employment and social policy, digital work and the platform economy.

Panayotis G. Michaelides is Associate Professor at the National Technical University of Athens, Greece. Panayotis' publications and research interests focus on econometrics, economic modelling and migration.

Tom Montgomery is Lecturer in Politics at Glasgow Caledonian University, UK. Tom's publications and research interests focus on youth unemployment, social innovation, social movements and the gig economy.

Quivine Ndomo is Project Researcher and PhD student at the Department of Social Sciences and Philosophy, University of Jyväskylä, Finland. Quivine's publications and research interests focus on labour market institutions and the migrant labour force.

Dino Numerato is Associate Professor at the Department of Sociology at the Faculty of Social Sciences, Charles University, Czech Republic. Dino's publications and research interests focus on the sociology of health and illness, civic engagement and activism, and migration.

Anna Triandafyllidou holds the Canada Excellence Research Chair on Migration and Integration at Toronto Metropolitan University, Canada. Anna's publications and research interests focus on migration, cultural diversity, policy and identity issues.

Acknowledgements

We would like to thank all the people that agreed to be involved in our research. We hope that our contribution will support the development of fairer and human-based migration policies in European countries and beyond. We are grateful to the anonymous reviewers for their helpful comments in revising the book.

We would also like to acknowledge the European Commission which funded our research through the European Union Horizon 2020 research programme – grant agreement 770515 (SIRIUS).

1

Introduction

Simone Baglioni and Francesca Calò

Decent and sustainable employment plays a significant role in the economic and social inclusion of people within society. This is also the case for migrants, refugees and asylum seekers (MRAs). Regardless of one's migrant or native background, employment provides income, social identity and social connections, and it enables individuals to contribute to the economy of the country. For decades, European governments have addressed migration primarily through border management and security policies, while the integration of new arrivals has remained an ancillary policy concern (Geddes and Scholten, 2016). Integration has become a policy taboo in some European countries following the peak in requests for asylum in 2015, and the instrumental use of migration by political entrepreneurs across the continent since the so-called 'refugee crisis' (Dennison and Geddes, 2018). Still, men, women and children continue to arrive in Europe, and the quality of the processes involved in their settlement in European societies, and the contribution that they make to the social and economic development of Europe, are inextricably linked to their prospects of finding and sustaining decent work. That is true regardless of the reasons motivating their journey, whether they are among us to seek employment and improve their living conditions, to join family members already living here, to seek asylum from persecution, or sanctuary from humanitarian or environmental disasters.

However, data and analyses of labour market integration of migrants depict an alarming situation. For example, Organisation for Economic Co-operation and Development (OECD) data show that in the EU27, in the last two decades (2002–2020), the employment rate of the foreign-born population has always been lower than that of the native-born population, highlighting a sharper decrease from 2019 onwards. Moreover, foreign-born workers are more likely to work at atypical times than native-born (OECD, 2021), evidencing that often migrants are employed or work in more precarious and insecure positions than native workers. In the last two years, the COVID-19 pandemic has worsened the scenario: the negative effects of the pandemic have contributed to the deterioration in the job (and life) quality of migrants, including refugees and asylum seekers (Baglioni et al, 2021). In fact, newcomers often work in sectors that have been badly hit by the pandemic, such as hospitality and leisure, or domestic work and care. COVID-19 quickly led to a drop in migrant employment in these sectors as a result of the policies implemented to contain the pandemic (OECD, 2021). The drop was twice that of native-born employment, for example in construction, where migrants often are employed more often than native workers as subcontractors (OECD, 2021), showing that COVID-19 created further inequalities and discrimination among people. However, on a positive note, in the sectors that were least affected by the crisis, such as scientific and technical activities (which have a lower share of migrant workers), migrants benefited more from employment growth than their native counterparts.

Such figures suggest that the integration of migrants via labour markets is not a straightforward task, due to the specific issues relating to migration and refugee/asylum statuses, but also due to the extent of heterogeneity apparent across contemporary labour markets in Europe (Könönen, 2019; D'Angelo et al, 2020; Federico and Baglioni, 2021; Calò et al, 2022). This heterogeneity (in economic structure, sectoral composition, labour force and demographic features, and so on), combined with the substantial, but also the uneven, legacy of the wider economic crisis on European labour markets, has created a highly differentiated economic and social environment across countries, and, consequently, the space for variations in policy implementation leading to the potential for a diverse range of outcomes for (non-EU) migrants, refugees and asylum seekers in terms of effectively integrating into their host societies.

Building on such premises, our book, a research output of the Horizon 2020 EU-funded project SIRIUS, understands the labour market integration of MRAs as being dependent on a pattern of concurring circumstances and features located at different analytical levels as explored in Figure 1.1: at the macro (legal framework and policy framework), at the meso (civil society organisations) and at the micro (individual) levels. Our book adopts then a multidimensional understanding of the 'labour market integration' in which an individual's capacity to seek (and retain) employment is determined by a concurrent set of factors located at three different analytical levels: at the macro (legal/institutional/policy), meso (organisational) and micro (individual) level (as presented in Figure 1.1).

From this perspective, the legal and political-institutional, societal and individual-related conditions function either as enablers or as barriers that affect the labour market access of non-EU MRAs in European countries. The chapters of our book reflect these analytical levels, providing a comparison of seven European countries (Czech Republic, Denmark, Finland, Greece, Italy, United Kingdom and Switzerland).

Figure 1.1: The multidimensional framework of analysis of migrant labour market integration proposed in the book

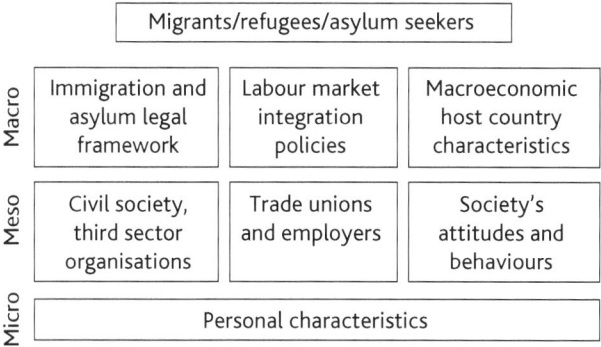

The macro level

At the macro level, integration depends on the characteristics of the labour market itself, on the specific policy/legal framework of asylum and migration, and the various labour market institutions facilitating or obstructing the labour market integration of non-EU MRAs. But macro-level features also include the institutional context of each country (for example, centralised versus decentralised, as labour market policy competences, as well as cognate policies – for example, housing, education, health – are sometimes devolved to the local or subnational levels), and therefore specific local/subnational policy may need to be considered along with the national and European level. Labour market institutions across member states are differently prepared to address the needs of MRAs and to support them adequately. There are uneven levels of experience and infrastructure for effective service provision including the financial resources necessary for programmes, but also there are variations in the readiness of countries to support MRAs. In Nordic countries, such as Denmark and Sweden, for instance, member states with long-standing and advanced policies, there is some existing evidence on the success or failure of different integration measures. In contrast, very little is known about integration schemes established in new destination countries in Central and Eastern Europe but also in Southern Europe. These countries seem to create policy as situations arise and often with little knowledge of their refugee population (Burnett, 2015), although countries such as the Czech Republic tend to adopt more systematically ad-hoc EU-grant driven schemes than other EU Central-Eastern member states (Drbohlav and Valenta, 2014; Kušniráková, 2014).

The selected countries (Czech Republic, Denmark, Finland, Greece, Italy, the United Kingdom and Switzerland) were selected because they vary considerably in terms of their political-institutional approaches towards unemployment and the labour market as well as their approaches towards welfare state provision more generally. On the one hand, there is evidence for a 'contingent convergence' (Eichhorst and Konle-Seidl, 2008) of instruments, goals and outcomes in labour market regulations, employment and social policies that have the common principal purpose of a 'work-first approach' (Triantafillou, 2011). On the other hand, there are differences in terms of policymaking dynamics and policy implementation that result in the establishment of diverse labour market and employment policy regimes (Gallie, 2007a, 2007b, 2007c; Rothgang and Dingeldey, 2009; Anxo et al, 2010). Finally, our countries also differ in terms of other relevant institutional dimensions that may affect the dynamics underpinning the integration of MRAs. Several studies have supported the idea that participatory and decentralised political contexts produce more responsive and redistributive policymaking (Calamai, 2009; Costa-i-Font, 2010), which sets the scene for a broader range of 'integration' related policies. Hence, we also consider how various countries differ in terms of political institutional opportunities offered to public and private actors to deal with integration. Countries like Switzerland, and to a certain extent also the United Kingdom, have an institutional design that supports subsidiarity as well as decentralisation and multilevel governance. Whereas countries like the Czech Republic maintain strong centralisation and a weak culture of governance. Three chapters in the book focus on the macro-level context.

Chapter 2, by Christos Bagavos, Konstantinos N. Konstantakis, Panayotis G. Michaelides and Theocharis Marinos, provides a macro-contextual overview of the countries, investigating labour shortages, skills needs and mismatches by examining skills and qualifications and their use in the labour market to assess the position of post-2014 MRAs in the workforce and identify barriers and enablers for their labour market integration. The chapter investigates the position of post-2014 MRAs in the workforce to build a comprehensive assessment of labour market barriers and enablers. The chapter presents cross-national comparative research at two levels. At the first level, it focuses on the characteristics (skills and qualifications) of post-2014 MRAs in each country under investigation, to evaluate the integration progress and determine the drivers behind unemployment and inactivity. At the second level, the chapter focuses on specific features of each country, including productive structure, employment composition by sector of economic activity, occupations and skills, labour flows, unemployment rates, level of skills as well as the overall macroeconomic situation.

Chapter 3, by Veronica Federico, assesses how far legal frameworks of migration and asylum work as enablers or obstructers of non-EU MRAs' integration in European labour markets across the seven countries studied in the book. It does so by gathering and critically analysing information on the political, legal and institutional context of migration governance for each country, and by comparatively discussing national situations. When legal issues are at stake, newcomers' integration heavily depends on the legal status that is attributed to them. In fact, entry and settlement in European countries are subject to strict limitations for non-EU nationals, but such limitations take different shades according to a given European country and a given migrant status.

Chapter 4, by Nathan Lillie, Ilona Bontenbal and Quivine Ndomo, discusses migrant labour market integration policies and services in the seven countries. The empirical work underpinning this chapter emanates from two main research tasks: policy discourse analysis; and assessment of existing policies and their outcomes. A policy discourse analysis was conducted to identify and analyse how issues of labour market integration are discussed by policymakers and policy actors. By analysing the findings of the discourse analysis together with the assessment of policies, which forms the second part of the chapter, the consistency between policy rhetoric and policy goals is evaluated. The second part of the chapter consists of a policy assessment in which the barriers to labour market integration and existing policies to remedy them are identified, categorised and evaluated. This was performed using a meta-analysis of the existing national literature, and interviews with policy experts, implementers and beneficiaries. The chapter suggests that welfare policy regimes play an important role in shaping labour market integration policy, but this is more due to the residual effect of having certain active labour policy structures and the existence of professional employment services rather than employer demands or a deep-set political consensus.

The meso level

At the meso level, integration depends on the availability of supporting infrastructure playing an 'enabler' role vis-à-vis the refugees and migrants themselves. This refers to ethnic networks and civil society organisations that enable migrants and refugees to access information about the labour market and how to enter it, which means access not only to legal knowledge but also practical issues (for example, where to find a potential employer but also accommodation). More specifically, civil society organisations and the reaction of local communities and non-governmental organisations are crucial players in ensuring integration to be effective (or, indeed, can be significant opponents to it). Frequent and meaningful interactions between migrants and member state citizens is considered to be a significant tool for opening societies for all migrants, but especially for refugees.

Given the lack of systematic research findings on the impact of refugees participation in associations and civil society organisations (see Garkisch et al, 2017, for a systematic review), our book fills a gap on what role civil society actors play in the integration of non-EU MRAs into society and the labour market. Moreover, and still at the meso level of analysis, the role played by social partnerships in the dynamics of labour market integration is explored. Studies reveal (for example, ILO, 2016) that particularly at the sectoral level, representative organisations for employers and workers are critical in assisting the integration process for migrants and refugees, through collective bargaining processes, and by alleviating the concerns of workers relating to wages and working conditions. Trade unions have an important role in respect of the provision of support services, including representing their rights in the workplace, and are organisations which have experience in being versatile in times of austerity and crisis (Gumbrell-McCormick and Hyman, 2019). Concurrently, recent studies (for example, OECD, 2016) show that many employers do not see an immediate business case for hiring refugees or asylum seekers. Studies cite several reasons for the slow uptake in the employment of refugees and asylum seekers, ranging from uncertainty about the rules governing refugees' and asylum seekers' rights, labour market access and uncertainty about their skills and qualifications, to lower productivity due to a lack of host-country language skills, at least initially, and public opinion that is sceptical about hiring refugees or asylum seekers. Against this background, our book aims to provide an in-depth comparative perspective on how the role of social partners facilitates or hinders the integration of post-2014 non-EU MRAs into the labour market. Two chapters focus upon the meso level.

Chapter 5, by Dino Numerato, Karel Čada and Karin Hoření, presents and discusses the role of civil society organisations in the labour market integration of MRAs. It examines the positions of civil society organisations and how they are perceived by newcomers by means of face-to-face interviews with both civil society organisations and migrants having made use of their services. The findings suggest that civil society organisations can work as important actors enhancing not only integration into the labour market but also integration through the labour market. Civil society organisations are important language course providers, and thanks to their social, legal and administrative guidance, they help migrants in overcoming ineffective administrative and legal structures. Several organisations also assist migrants with the recruitment process, providing courses and advice on how to prepare for an interview, how to write a CV or how to draft a cover letter. Furthermore, civil society also assists newcomers in their efforts to have their skills and qualifications recognised. Moreover, by providing mentorship, training programmes, volunteering or even direct employment, they contribute to the development of migrants' skills and competences and provide platforms to enhance their agency and autonomy. However, such a capacity is unevenly spatially distributed. Furthermore, civil society organisations help to mitigate and, often together with migrants, struggle against the hostile context of a widespread atmosphere of xenophobia.

Although the authors conclude that civil society organisations primarily work as enablers of newcomers' integration in the labour market, their critical analysis also suggests that civil society can in some nuanced ways also hinder labour market integration.

Chapter 6, by Simone Baglioni, Thomas Montgomery and Francesca Calò, discusses the role that social partners and social dialogue can play by enabling or not the integration of MRAs in the European labour market. It presents findings from a four-month process of fieldwork of interviews with social partners (gathering 123 interviews) complemented by an experts' survey which managed to collect responses from 293 additional social partners' representatives across the seven countries discussed. The experts' responses reveal that some of the key issues that had been discussed by extant studies, and in particular the dilemmas faced by unions vis-à-vis migrants, whether they should be approached as potential new members or whether they should be monitored to prevent salary dumping, are still relevant. Our data also show the social partners' awareness about the higher (than local workers') risks to migrants' health and safety due to the poor regulations of migration and asylum which often confine newcomers to employment in the irregular economy, or to jobs requiring lower skills. However, our study also reveals the appreciation that social partners have of newcomers' skills, of their potential for the wellbeing of our societies and economies, a potential which very often remains unrealised. What we can take from this analysis of social partners is the need for both policymakers at various levels of government and social partners to commit to create further social dialogue opportunities. Too few cases of social dialogue have occurred across our seven countries in the field of labour migration, but social dialogue seems to us a (if not the) fundamental tool to solve problems occurring in such a polarised domain of migration, and in what is even a more contentious one, that of labour migration.

The micro level

At the micro level, integration depends on the specific capacity of a given migrant/refugee, that is, her/his skills, education, language proficiency, age, psychological and physical wellbeing, entrepreneurial potential and so on. In order to understand the different ways in which migrants and refugees themselves experience labour market integration in their host societies, sociodemographic characteristics (age, gender, educational background) of the recent cohort of post-2014 non-EU MRAs should be explored, alongside their qualifications and their personal and professional profile. Moreover, at the micro level of analysis our book aims to target more specifically the needs and aspirations of post-2014 non-EU MRAs and what they consider as barriers and enablers to potential avenues for integration. Our book will explore those factors that are necessary to inform the design of integration policies and programmes in ways that are inclusive of our target groups' needs and voices. One chapter focuses upon the micro level of analysis.

Delving into everyday experiences of a range of migrants and hearing their voices, Chapter 7, by Irina Isaakyan, Simone Baglioni and Anna Triandafyllidou, discusses how newcomers exercise agency to seize opportunities offered by their country of settlement and mitigate the effect of the turbulent social, political and economic circumstances they are often met with. The micro-level research takes a closer look at the needs of migrants, with a specific focus on what migrants themselves consider to be barriers for and enablers of integration. To understand migrants' capabilities and agency, the authors not only looked at their lives over the last five years but also explored their more distant memories long before their migration. Analysis of their past experiences enables a better understanding of their motivation for emigration, of barriers and opportunities they were facing and of their individual capacity for change and resistance. Looking back into their past also favoured an in-depth analysis of the reciprocal relationship between their agency and the sociocultural context. The analytical accent was specifically placed on the turning points and emerging epiphanies of migrants' lives as well as on issues of intersectionality which heavily determine migration outcomes.

Conclusion

Labour market and social integration of non-EU MRAs have a key political bearing for the future of Europe. Decisions concerning whether or not to implement inclusion or integration policies also involve decisions over the allocation of resources. In a scenario where there is a limited capacity for public expenditure, the decision to utilise resources to facilitate labour market entry for migrants requires political leadership, as well as an evidence base for policy planning. This is particularly crucial when considering those citizens who are currently struggling to enter the labour market and who may feel challenged by decisions to allocate resources in order to ease the access of migrants to the same pool of jobs. Therefore, labour market integration policies cannot be isolated from the context of specific local or national labour market conditions and each and every decision must carefully consider the need to integrate both native and migrant workers.

At present, the current practice in many countries to limit the local labour market access of asylum seekers and refugees (at least before they are officially recognised) is highly problematic. These increased restrictions have been ineffective in avoiding or controlling the flows of refugees and other migrants; instead, we have continued to witness increased efforts by migrants to reach Europe, which in turn has exposed vulnerable migrants to even greater physical and other risks, as well as abuse, including abuses in the informal labour market where many migrants and refugees end up. For such reasons, a central aim of our book is to contribute towards developing a policy framework for an inclusive integration agenda, outlining an optimal mix of policy pathways for the labour market integration of native workers as well as non-EU MRAs.

The last chapter of our book, Chapter 8 by Maria Mexi, presents and discusses recommendations for an optimal policy mix to inform the design of policies and programmes that will provide post-2014 migrants, including refugees and asylum seekers, with greater protection through decent work in the years to come. The legal recommendations address, for example, the need to revisit the international and European frameworks responding to forced displacement, to better integrate the humanitarian, development and labour market perspectives. The lessons learned and best practices identified by earlier chapters allow, among other things, to measure the effectiveness of proactive employment policies targeting migrant cohorts, and evaluate the responsiveness of multistakeholder partnerships in terms of putting forward innovative policies and practices at national and local levels with a view to mitigating xenophobic attitudes and tensions. Responses that address the needs of both post-2014 migrants and host communities – whether through programmes targeting job creation, education, vocational training and skills development, social finance and cooperatives – are critical in ensuring that public discourses become more constructive and supportive. Chapter 8 also adds to the conceptual framework, discussed earlier in this chapter, to explain the role of concrete measures to make efficient use of the skills of migrants, the channels through which these affect the labour market integration of refugees and asylum seekers, as well as the combination and sequence of measures leading to the best outcome for a given group of beneficiaries.

References

Anxo, D., Bosch, G. and Rubery, J. (eds) (2010) *The Welfare State and Life Transitions: A European Perspective*, Cheltenham and Northampton: Edward Elgar.

Baglioni, S., Caló, F. and Lo Cascio, M. (2021) 'Covid-19 and labour migration: Investigating vulnerability in Italy and in the UK', *Quaderni di Economia del Lavoro*, 111: 109–130.

Burnett, K. (2015) 'Policy vs. practice: The effectiveness of refugee integration policies in the Czech Republic', *European Spatial Research and Policy*, 22(1): 121–133.

Calamai, L. (2009) 'The link between devolution and regional disparities: Evidence from Italian regions', *Environment and Planning*, 41(5): 1129–1151.

Calò, F., Montgomery, T. and Baglioni, S. (2022) 'You have to work ... but you can't!: Contradictions of the active labour market policies for refugees and asylum seekers in the UK', *Journal of Social Policy*. DOI: https://doi.org/10.1017/S0047279422000502 .

Costa-i-Font, I. (2010) 'Does devolution lead to regional inequalities in welfare activity?', *Government and Policy*, 28(3): 435–449.

D'Angelo, A., Kofman, E. and Keles, J.Y. (2020) 'Migrants at work: Perspectives, perceptions and new connections', *Work, Employment and Society*, 34(5): 745–748.

Dennison, J. and Geddes, A. (2018) 'Brexit and the perils of "Europeanised" migration', *Journal European Public Policy*, 25(8): 1137–1153.

Drbohlav, D. and Valenta, O. (2014) *Building an Integration System: Policies to Support Immigrants' Progression in the Czech Labor Market*, Washington, DC and Geneva: Migration Policy Institute and International Labour Office.

Eichhorst, W. and Konle-Seidl, R. (2008) 'Contingent convergence: A comparative analysis of activation policies', Working Paper, IZA DP No. 3905, Bonn: Institute for the Study of Labour.

Federico, V. and Baglioni, S. (eds) (2021) *Migrants, Refugees and Asylum Seekers' Integration in European Labour Markets*, Cham: Springer.

Gallie, D. (ed) (2007a) *Employment Regimes and the Quality of Work*, New York: Oxford University Press.

Gallie, D. (2007b) 'Production regimes, employment regimes, and the quality of work', in D. Gallie (ed), *Employment Regimes and the Quality of Work*, New York: Oxford University Press, pp 1–33.

Gallie, D. (2007c) 'The quality of work life in comparative perspective', in D. Gallie (ed), *Employment Regimes and the Quality of Work*, New York: Oxford University Press, pp 205–232.

Garkisch, M., Heidingsfelder, J. and Beckmann, M. (2017) 'Third sector organizations and migration: A systematic literature review on the contribution of third sector organizations in view of flight, migration and refugee crises', *Voluntas: International Journal of Voluntary and Nonprofit Organizations*, 28(5): 1839–1880.

Geddes, A. and Scholten, P. (2016) *The Politics of Migration and Immigration in Europe*, second edition, Thousand Oaks: SAGE.

Gumbrell-McCormick, R. and Hyman, R. (2019) 'Democracy in trade unions, democracy through trade unions?', *Economic and Industrial Democracy*, 40(1): 91–110.

Könönen, J. (2019) 'Becoming a "labour migrant": Immigration regulations as a frame of reference for migrant employment', *Work, Employment and Society*, 33(5): 777–793.

Kušniráková, T. (2014) 'Is there an integration policy being formed in Czechia?', *Identities: Global Studies in Culture and Power*, 21(6): 738–754.

ILO (International Labour Organization) (2016) *Towards a Framework for Fair and Effective Integration of Migrants into the Labour Market*, Geneva: ILO Publications.

OECD (Organisation for Economic Co-operation and Development) (2016) *International Migration Outlook 2015*, Paris: OECD Publications.

OECD (2021) *International Migration Outlook 2020*, Paris: OECD Publications.

Rothgang, H. and Dingeldey, I. (2009) 'Conclusion: The governance of welfare state reform', in H. Rothgang and I. Dingeldey (eds), *Governance of Welfare State Reform*, Cheltenham and Northampton: Edward Elgar, pp 238–250.

Triantafillou, P. (2011) 'Metagovernance by numbers – technological lock-in of Australian and Danish Employment Policies?', in J. Torfing and P. Triantafillou (eds), *Interactive Policy Making, Metagovernance and Democracy*, Colchester: ECPR Press, pp 149–166.

2

What do the numbers say about migration in European economies?

Christos Bagavos, Konstantinos N. Konstantakis, Panayotis G. Michaelides and Theocharis Marinos

Introduction

Within the context of pronounced demographic ageing and increasing migration flows in Europe, focus has been placed on the impact of migrants on overall population change and labour force as well as on their integration into the labour market. In this context, the present chapter presents and discusses: key demographic characteristics; labour market barriers and enablers; and employability opportunities for migrants, refugees and asylum seekers (MRAs) for a selected panel of EU economies, namely the Czech Republic, Denmark, Finland, Greece, Italy, Switzerland and the UK. The aforementioned economies have participated in the Horizon 2020 EU project, SIRIUS – Skills and Integration of Refugees, Migrants and Asylum Applicants in European Labour Markets. In the analysis that follows, the acronym SIRIUS is directly equivalent with a reference to these economies.

The first section of this chapter focuses on the demographic characteristics of the population in the SIRIUS economies. In this context, the chapter offers a comparative view between the native population and the foreign-born population of the SIRIUS economies. In addition, key demographic characteristics of the labour force of the SIRIUS economies are analysed, as well as the impact of post-2014 migration flows on these characteristics. The second section of the chapter presents key characteristics regarding the MRAs in the various SIRIUS economies. In addition, in this chapter, the employability opportunities of MRAs are assessed using relevant panel-data models. Finally, the third section of the chapter focuses on the economies that attract new workforce, that is, MRAs. In this context, a relevant methodological framework is put forward in order to econometrically detect the labour 'absorbing' economies as well as the labour 'absorbing' sectors in each economy. Additionally, two new composite indices are introduced to identify the sectors and the occupations, respectively, of an economy which have simultaneously high growth potential and required educational attainment level compatible to the MRAs' educational attainment level.

The estimates are disaggregated by sector of economic activity and by occupation for each country and analytical presentations will be offered to assess the current state of integration of international MRAs in the countries under investigation.

Migration, overall population change and labour force in the SIRIUS economies

Foreign-born population and overall population change

Over the recent period (2010–2020), international migration has become the main demographic component of population change in Europe (Coleman, 2008; van Nimwegen and van der Erf, 2010; Murphy, 2016; European Commission, 2020). In particular for the EU27 as a whole, during 2010–2020, population decline was prevented due to positive net migration, that is, the difference between inward and outward migration flows, which has compensated for the excess of the number of deaths over that of births, the so-called natural change. In addition, the contribution of international migration to an increasing population change results from migrants, either foreign nationals or foreign-born persons, when the migratory phenomenon is examined on the basis of the country of birth.

There are two main reasons for this. First, foreign-born population exhibits positive net migration, which contrasts with the negative net migration of natives. In other words, the direct effect of international migration on the overall population change is negative for the natives, given that outward exceed inward flows, whereas the net migration of foreign-born population leads to increases in population of the receiving countries (Bagavos, 2021). Second, in the majority of the European countries, the number of births and deaths to natives are very close, implying a limited or often negative natural change, and therefore a shrinking contribution of natives to the overall population change (Coleman, 2008; Salzmann et al, 2010). On the opposite, foreign-born population, because of its relatively young age structure, there is a higher number of births than deaths, which implies a positive indirect effect of foreign-born population on the overall population change.

There is an additional point which merits particular attention. In demographic terms, foreign-born population is not a typical population, since changes in its total size over time are solely determined by deaths and net migration, but not by births, which, by definition, are classified as native-born persons. Therefore, there is a significant difference between changes in the foreign-born population and contribution of the foreign-born population to the overall population size and growth. In practice, the difference between births and deaths to foreign-born population does not represent the natural change of foreign-born population but the natural change attributable to foreign-born population or, put differently, the natural change of the overall population of the receiving country attributable to the foreign-born population. Similarly, births and deaths of native-born population do not reflect the natural change of that population but its contribution to the overall natural change and therefore to the overall population change. Obviously, foreign-born population, through births to foreign-born (mothers) affects the size and the shifts in the native-born population.

Migration has its proper dynamic, but its impact on population change is additionally related to the demographic situation prevailing in the receiving countries (MacKellar and McNicoll, 2019). In that respect, given the current European context of low fertility settings and pronounced population ageing, the impact of foreign-born population on the size of the overall population of European countries is more pronounced than what would have been observed in a context of population growth. Consequently, there are strong reasons to believe that the foreign-born migration of the post-2014 period has had a relevant impact on population change in Europe, since it has occurred in a framework of stagnation and slowdown in the overall population growth.

Figure 2.1 displays the contribution of foreign- and native-born population to the overall population change in the seven countries involved in the SIRIUS project for the 2014–2019 period. It shows that the foreign-born population has been the driving force behind changes in the overall population as this population has attenuated overall population decline in Greece and Italy; or turned the expected population stagnation in Czech Republic and the UK into population increase and the expected population

Figure 2.1: Changes (percentage) in the overall population size over the 2014–2019 period

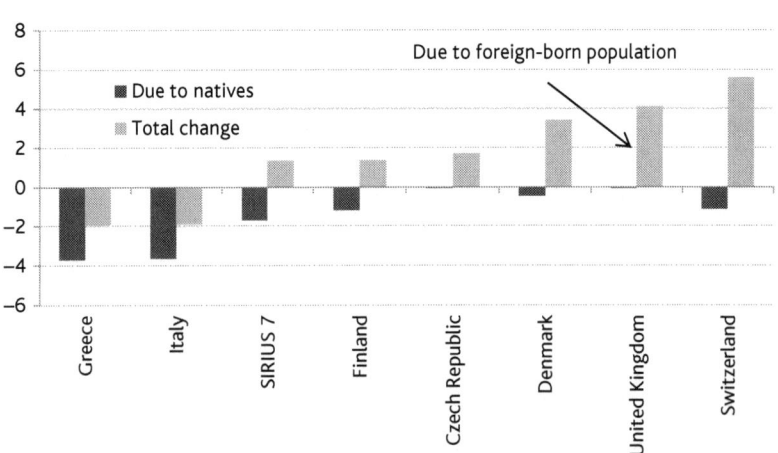

Source: First author's calculations based on Eurostat's data (Eurostat, 2021a, 2021b, 2021c, 2021d, 2021e, 2021f)

decline in Denmark, Finland, Switzerland and in the seven countries as a whole into population growth.

Differentials between foreign- and native-born population in the contribution to the overall population change mainly results from different schemes as regards net migration (Table 2.1). Indeed, results confirm that the net migration of the foreign-born population is of positive sign, which is in contrast with the negative figure occurring for the native-born. Pronounced diversities are additionally observed in terms of the natural change attributable to each population group. In contrast to what is observed for natives, where the corresponding contribution is, in the largest majority of cases, of a negative sign, the excess of births over that of deaths among foreign-born population implies an increase in the overall country's population. It is also worth noticing that the indirect effect of migration related to births and deaths of the foreign-born population is of relevant importance as it accounts for around 30 per cent of the total effect of foreign-born population on the overall population change. Seen in relation to the net migration of foreign-born population, the indirect effect implies that, for every 100 net foreign-born migrants, there are almost 45 persons added to the overall population through births and deaths to foreign-born population.

Findings plotted in Table 2.1 additionally challenge the idea that the contribution of migration to the overall population change, through its

Table 2.1: Differences between foreign- and native-born population in their contribution to the overall population change and in their natural change (annual averages, per 1,000)

	Contribution due to:						Difference in natural change due to the diversity in:		
	Natural change			Net migration					
	Foreign-born	Native-born	Overall natural change	Foreign-born	Native-born	Overall net migration	Fertility and mortality	Age structure	Total
Denmark	1.7	−0.5	1.2	4.7	−0.2	4.5	0.5	15.1	15.6
Greece	0.9	−3.8	−2.9	2.0	−2.3	−0.3	2.5	9.9	12.3
Finland	1.1	−1.5	−0.4	3.1	−0.5	2.6	3.9	15.7	19.6
Switzerland	3.1	−0.7	2.4	8.1	−1.2	6.9	3.0	8.8	11.8
United Kingdom	2.2	0.1	2.4	4.6	−0.2	4.4	2.2	14.2	16.3
SIRIUS 5	2.1	−0.5	1.6	4.6	−0.6	4.0	2.5	12.7	15.3

Note: Because of the low robustness of specific demographic data by country of birth, the Czech Republic and Italy are not included in this part of the analysis.
Source: First author's calculations based on Eurostat's data (Eurostat, 2021a, 2021b, 2021c, 2021d, 2021e, 2021f)

indirect effect, relies on the excess fertility of foreign- over that of native-born mothers. The results suggest that the difference in natural change attributable to each population group results mainly from the diversity in the age structure of foreign- and native-born population. In practice, the younger age structure of the foreign-born population as compared to that of natives implies diversity in terms of the corresponding contribution of each population group which surpasses any effect of the differences in fertility and mortality levels.[1] Overall, although, in demographic terms, the shares of foreign-born to the overall population are of relatively low levels – between 6 per cent and 28 per cent – the young age structure of foreign-born population drives the shifts towards positive natural change of a country's population.

Foreign-born population and shifts in the size of the labour force

Slowdown in population growth and population ageing are both phenomena that challenge Europe, and therefore SIRIUS economies as well, in terms of the subsequent shifts in the number of economically active persons as reflected in the labour force, that is, the number of employed and unemployed persons. In recent times, those demographic transformations have taken place in a context of increasing migration flows and stocks, which, along with current upward trends in the participation in the labour market of both native females and natives aged between 55 and 64 years, inevitably affect the size and the age structure of the labour force (Hilgenstock and Kóczán, 2018; Spielvogel and Meghnagi, 2018a, 2018b; Bagavos, 2019).

There are two dimensions affecting the total size of the labour force. The first one is of demographic nature and has to do with the size and the age structure of the working age population (most frequently defined as those aged 15 to 64). The second is socioeconomic and refers to the propensity of persons to participate in the labour market, or equally the wish to have a job, and it is reflected in the participation rates, that is, the ratio of the labour force to the working age population. Changes in the size of the labour force results from shifts in population and in the participation rates and, therefore, migration affects the labour force of the receiving country through those two components. The relatively young age structure of migrant population coupled with a relatively high share of migrants aged 15 to 64 compared to the total migrant population impact on the demographic dimension of the labour force. In addition migrants' shares compared to the overall population and their level of participation rates affects the overall participation rate, that is, the participation rate of the entire working age population (Cully, 2011).

What do the numbers say about migration?

Figure 2.2: Changes (percentage) in the size of the labour force between 2014 and 2020*

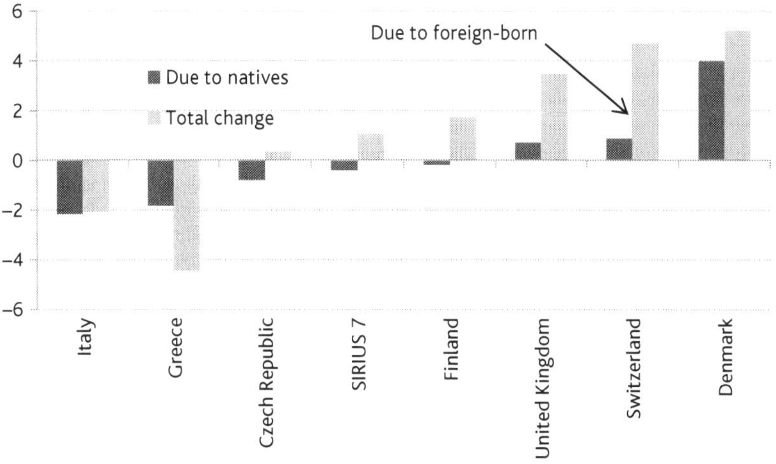

[Bar chart showing labour force changes by country (Italy, Greece, Czech Republic, SIRIUS 7, Finland, United Kingdom, Switzerland, Denmark) decomposed into "Due to natives", "Due to foreign-born", and "Total change"]

Note: *2019, rather than 2020, for the UK
Source: First author's calculations based on Eurostat's data (Eurostat, 2021g)

Changes in the size of the workforce from 2014 onwards have been largely affected by migration, in particular by the foreign-born population. Results plotted in Figure 2.2 show that in the large majority of countries, shifts in the overall labour force were mainly driven by foreign-born population as this population has accelerated overall labour force decline in Greece; or turned the expected decline in workforce into growth in the Czech Republic, Finland and in the seven countries as a whole; or accelerated labour force growth in Denmark. In addition, the foreign-born population has been the driving force behind the upward trend in the overall labour force in the UK and Switzerland. Italy seems to be an exception to that pattern as the impact of the foreign-born population on the total workforce has been negligible.

A decomposition exercise allows to detect the components behind the countries' diversity as regards the role of migration for the changes in the size of the labour force over time (Table 2.2). In general, there is a larger diversity among countries regarding the aforementioned impact of migration on the overall population change, than on the size of the overall labour force. In particular, the impact of foreign-born population on the labour force of the receiving countries is of demographic nature, as migrants' participation rates do not significantly vary over time (Table 2.2a). In addition, a further decomposition of the population effect plotted in Table 2.2a, by distinguishing the effect due to the size of the working age population and the one attributable to the age structure of the working age population (last two columns of Table 2.2b), shows that the population effect, for both migrants and natives, relies largely on changes in the size of the working

Table 2.2: The components of the contribution of foreign- and native-born persons to the shifts in the size of the labour force (as percentage of the labour force in 2014)

a. Population and participation effects

	Foreign-born			Native-born		
	Effects due to:			Effects due to:		
	Participation	Population	Total	Participation	Population	Total
Czech Republic	0.2	0.9	1.1	2.1	−2.7	−0.6
Denmark	0.5	0.7	1.2	2.7	1.2	3.9
Greece	−0.4	−2.3	−2.7	1.4	−3.3	−1.9
Italy	−0.7	0.8	0.1	1.9	−4.2	−2.3
Finland	0.3	1.6	1.9	3.4	−3.4	0.0
Switzerland	0.8	2.9	3.7	0.9	−0.1	0.8
United Kingdom	0.6	2.1	2.7	1.2	−0.6	0.6
SIRIUS 7	0.1	1.3	1.4	1.6	−2.2	−0.6

b. Effects related to migrants' origin, gender and the size of the working age population

	Foreign-born		Native-born		Foreign-born	Native-born
	Effect due to:		Participation effect		Effect due to the size of the working age population	
	EU27	Non-EU27	Men	Women		
Czech Republic	0.4	0.8	0.6	1.5	0.9	−4.2
Denmark	0.3	0.9	1.3	1.4	0.8	1.2
Greece	−0.6	−2.0	0.3	1.1	−2.4	−2.3
Italy	−0.3	0.4	0.4	1.4	0.7	−2.9
Finland	0.4	1.5	1.9	1.5	1.6	−3.8
Switzerland	2.6	1.2	0.2	0.7	3.2	0.0
United Kingdom	1.7	1.1	0.0	1.3	2.1	−0.5
SIRIUS 7	0.8	0.7	0.3	1.3	1.3	−1.7

Source: First author's calculations based on Eurostat's data (Eurostat, 2021g)

age population than on its age structure. We also note that the foreign-born population does not fully compensate for the decline or stagnation of the working age population of natives (second and fifth columns of Table 2.2a) with Switzerland, UK and, to a smaller extent, Finland. Practically, the foreign-born population effect is quite limited in the Czech Republic, Denmark and Italy, and largely negative in Greece. On the whole, the population component (foreign- and native-born population combined) tends to reduce the labour force in four countries, namely the Czech Republic, Greece, Italy and Finland, and in the seven countries as a whole.

Migrants' origin is an additional aspect of diversity among countries. Although for the countries as a whole the effect of migration on the overall workforce is equally provided by non-EU27 and EU27 migrants, the corresponding effect occurring in Switzerland and the UK is largely due to the EU27-born migrants and is driven by non-EU27-born in Finland and Greece (Table 2.2b).

In the meantime, the increasing participation of native women – but also of native men in Denmark and Finland – in the labour market (Table 2.2b) leads to an upward trend in the overall participation rates of natives[2] (Table 2.2a); with the noticeable exception of Switzerland and the UK, this implies a participation rate effect on the overall labour force which exceeds the one attributable to the migration effect (Table 2.2a). However, the overall labour force decreases in Italy and Greece, as the increase in the labour market participation of native women does not counterbalance native population decline and the migration effect is either negligible (in Italy) or negative (in Greece).

Labour market barriers and enablers

To determine, first, the position of post-2014 MRAs in the labour market of their host country, and, second, the main features of the host countries' labour markets focusing on the sectoral structure and the relevant skills and occupations, we conduct a comparative statistical analysis. In this context, the particular goals of this chapter as we have mentioned earlier are the investigation of: the MRAs flows for the SIRIUS countries and the MRAs' integration opportunities into the corresponding labour markets; the SIRIUS countries labour markets' sectoral and occupational specialisation; and the labour market determinants.

To investigate these goals, probabilistic panel data models have been employed to econometrically investigate how the flows of MRAs affect their employment opportunities in the labour market. Furthermore, dynamic panel data analysis has been undertaken to investigate the determinants of labour market dynamics for each economy.

Migrants, refugees and asylum seekers in SIRIUS countries: a comparative analysis

Switzerland retains by far the highest percentage share (24.96 per cent) of foreign nationals of all the SIRIUS countries. By foreign nationals we refer to people whose nationality is diffcrent from their country of residence. The United Kingdom, Italy, Denmark and Greece come next, while the Czech Republic and Finland are the countries with the lowest shares of foreign nationals (4.83 per cent and 4.43 per cent, respectively) (Figure 2.3).

Figure 2.3: Share of foreign nationals to total population (percentage), SIRIUS countries

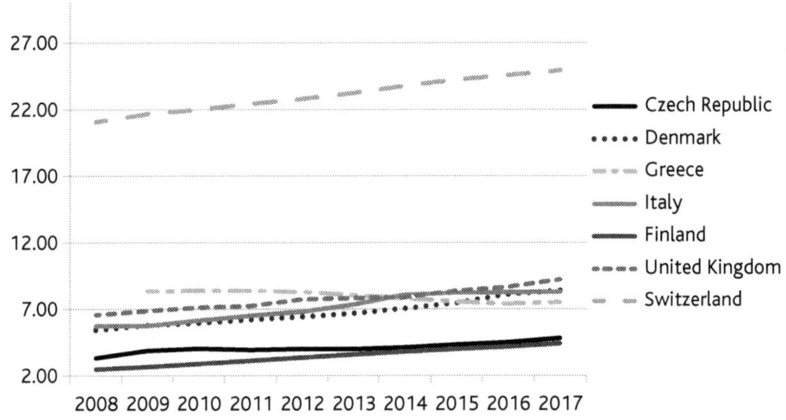

―― Czech Republic
••••• Denmark
– – Greece
▬▬ Italy
▬▬ Finland
– • – United Kingdom
– – Switzerland

Source: Eurostat (2018)

The United Kingdom, Denmark and Switzerland retain high shares of foreign nationals with a tertiary educational attainment level (42.13 per cent, 32.58 per cent and 31.03 per cent of the total foreign nationals population, respectively). In contrast, Greece and Italy are the countries with the lowest shares of foreign nationals who have attained tertiary education (10.37 per cent and 10.12 per cent, respectively). Interestingly, in the United Kingdom and the Czech Republic, foreign nationals of less than primary, primary or lower secondary educational attainment levels constitute only 17.52 per cent and 13.50 per cent of the total foreign population respectively (Figure 2.4). In addition, foreign nationals with tertiary education have higher activity rates than those that have attained upper or post-secondary educational levels who, in turn, have higher activity rates than foreign nationals with less than primary, primary or lower secondary educational attainment levels (Figure 2.5). The less noticeable differences in activity rates among foreign nationals of different educational attainment levels have been recorded in Greece. Indeed, in this country the mean 2008–2016 activity rate of foreign nationals with educational attainment levels 0–2 is 73.4 per cent, which is 1.87 per cent and 4.80 per cent lower than those of educational attainment levels 3–4 and 5–8, respectively.

With regard to the position of foreign nationals in the labour market of each country, in Switzerland foreign national employees represent, on average, 24.07 per cent of the country's total employees. Italy, the United Kingdom and Greece come next with 9.37 per cent, 9.25 per cent and 8.03 per cent, respectively. Finland and the Czech Republic rank last, in terms of the foreign nationals' participation in the country's labour market, with 2.47 per cent and 1.70 per cent, respectively (Figure 2.6).

Figure 2.4: Distribution of foreign nationals according to their educational attainment level (percentage), SIRIUS countries, 2008–2016

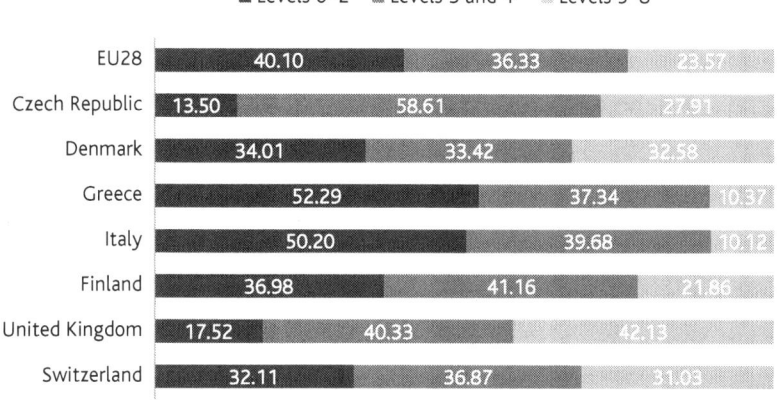

Source: Eurostat (2018)

Figure 2.5: Mean activity rates of foreign nationals by educational attainment level (percentage), SIRIUS countries, 2008–2016

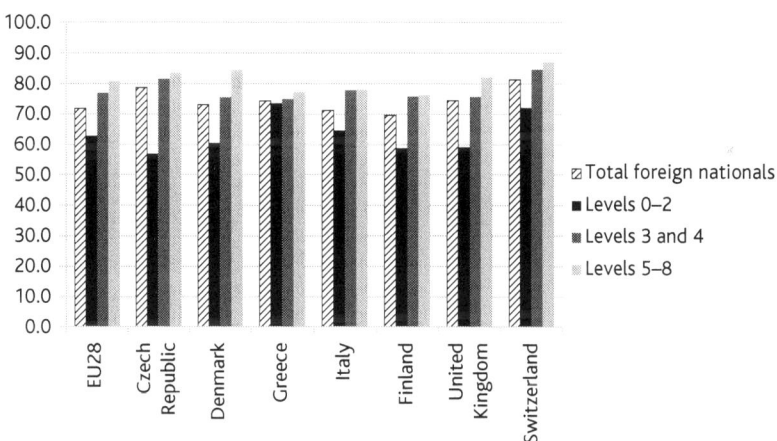

Source: Eurostat (2018)

Moreover, regarding the differentiation of employment rates, according to the age and educational attainment level, foreign nationals aged 35–39 and with educational attainment level 5–8 have, on average, the highest employment rates in all SIRIUS countries over the period 2008–2016 (Figures 2.7 and 2.8). Those aged 30–34 and with educational attainment levels 3 and 4 follow, while those aged 20–24 and with educational attainment levels 0–2 rank last. During the post-2014 migration period, an inflow of MRAs from various parts of the world passed through Greece and Italy and on to the Central

Figure 2.6: Participation of foreign nationals in the country's labour market (percentage), SIRIUS countries, 2008–2016

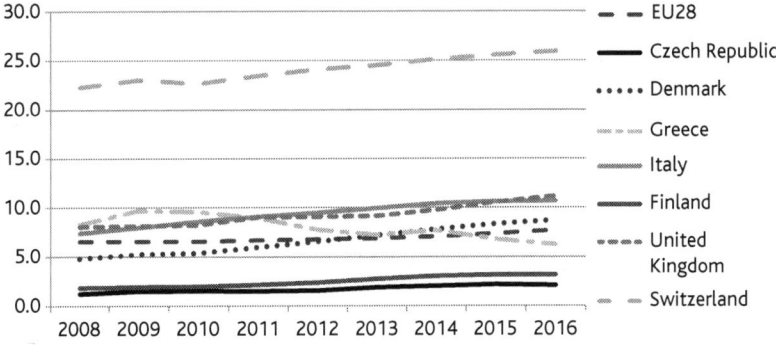

Source: Eurostat (2018)

Figure 2.7: Mean employment rates of foreign nationals, by age group (percentage), SIRIUS countries, 2008–2016

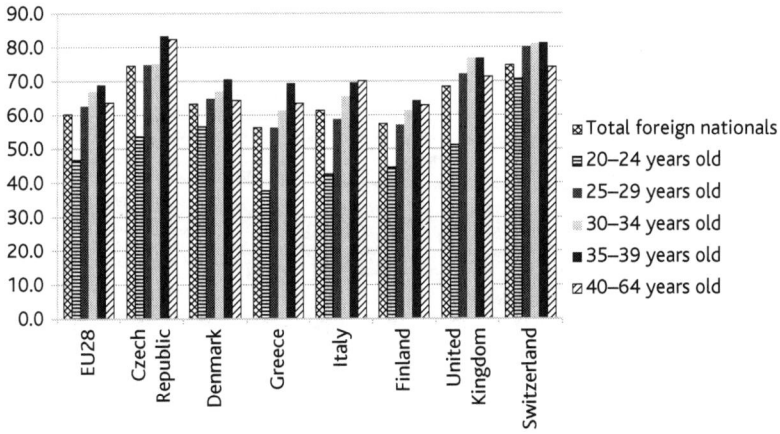

Source: Eurostat (2018)

and Northern parts of Europe. This inflow of third-country nationals was dispersed in most European countries, changing the already established migration flows.

With regard to the net migration rate of the SIRIUS countries, the highest increase was recorded in Finland, although it fell in 2016, breaking its 2012–2015 upward trend. Switzerland and Italy experience high net migration rates, with downward trends, though, while the UK's net migration rate records an almost 36 per cent increase in 2014 (compared to 2013) – which

Figure 2.8: Mean employment rates of foreign nationals by educational attainment level (percentage), SIRIUS countries, 2008–2016

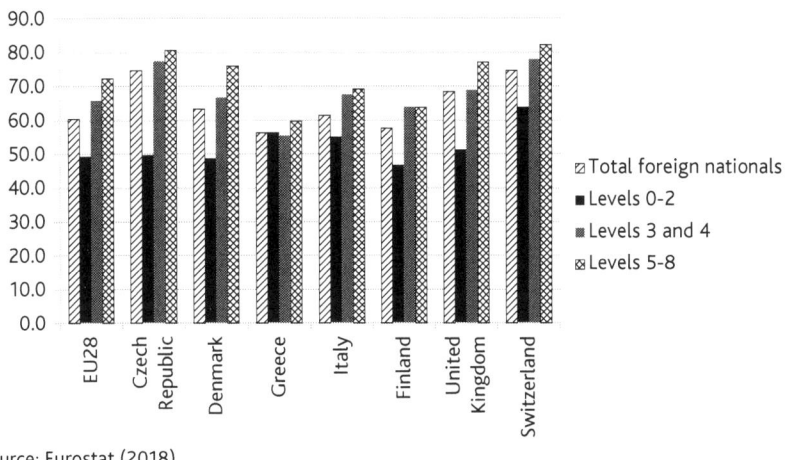

Source: Eurostat (2018)

Figure 2.9: Net migration rate, SIRIUS countries, 2008–2016

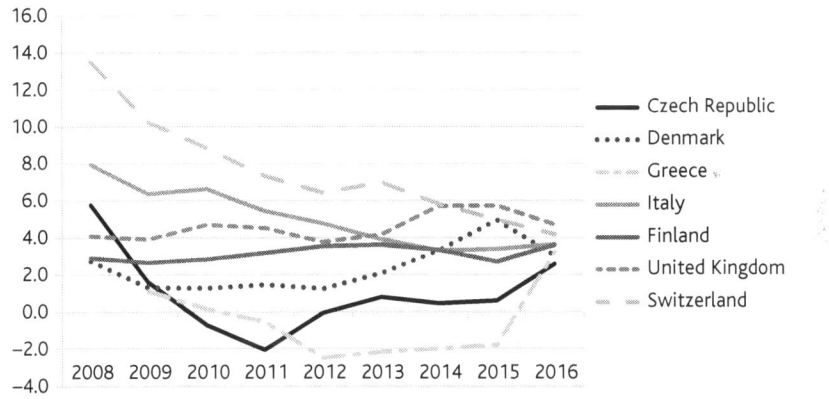

Source: Eurostat (2018)

remains in 2015 – before decreasing again in 2016. Finally, Greece and the Czech Republic retain smaller net migration rates over the examined period; both, however, increased in 2016. For Greece, in particular, its 2016 net migration rate was almost 280 per cent higher than its 2015 rate (Figure 2.9).[3]

As regards the asylum seekers per 1,000 persons, in 2015 Finland, Switzerland and Denmark faced, proportionally, the greatest inflow of asylum seekers among the SIRIUS countries (5.9, 4.6 and 3.7, respectively). Greece, on the other hand, faced an increase in 2016 (4.6 asylum seekers per 1,000 persons). The economies of UK and Italy received a relatively small inflow of asylum seekers, that is, 1.05 and 1.4, respectively. In contrast, the Czech

Figure 2.10: First time asylum seekers per 1,000 persons, SIRIUS countries, 2014–2016

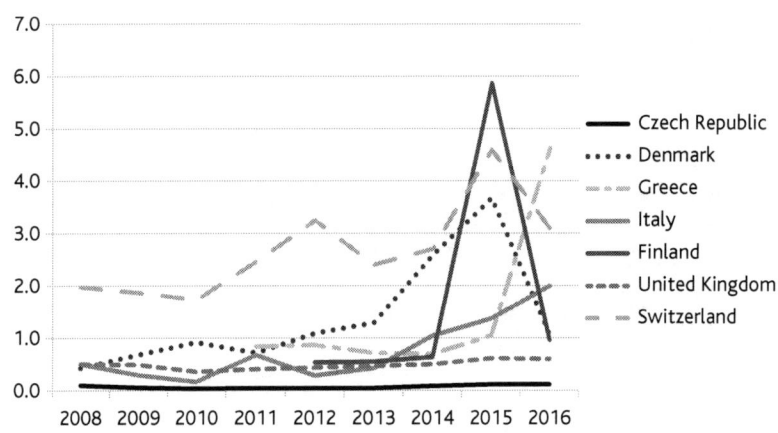

Source: Eurostat (2018)

Republic seems not to have been affected during the period 2014–2016 (Figure 2.10). The rise in the number of asylum seekers in the period 2014–2016 caused a respective increase in this period's mean annual number of first instance decisions on asylum applications (per 1,000 persons), compared with the period 2008–2013. In fact, all SIRIUS countries increased this number over the last period with the greatest increases recorded in Italy, Denmark and Finland (with a 197.14 per cent, 180.41 per cent and 176.31 per cent higher number of first instance decisions per 10,000 persons than in the previous period, respectively) (Figure 2.11).

The ratio of positive to total first instance decisions has also increased over this period (Figure 2.12).[4] Greece is the country with the highest percentage relative increase, namely 134.41 per cent.

Finally, in the Czech Republic, Denmark, Greece and Finland, there has been an increase in the mean annual number of first residence permits per 1,000 persons over the period 2014–2016, compared to the period 2008–2013. However, the highest number still remains in the United Kingdom (10.57 first residence permits per 1,000 persons), followed by Denmark and the Czech Republic with 7.24 and 5.82 residence permits respectively (Figure 2.13).

Various panel data models have been employed in an attempt to capture the determinants that directly influence, either positively or negatively, the employment opportunities of MRAs in the various labour markets. More precisely, using random effects panel data models and stepwise backward elimination we will uncover the fundamental determinants of employment opportunities for the MRAs. Next, using panel data probability models and stepwise backward elimination we will estimate the statistically significant factors that increase or decrease the probability of MRAs to integrate in the SIRIUS economies' labour markets through employment.

Figure 2.11: Mean annual number of first instance decisions on asylum applications (per 1,000 persons), SIRIUS countries, 2008–2013, 2014–2016

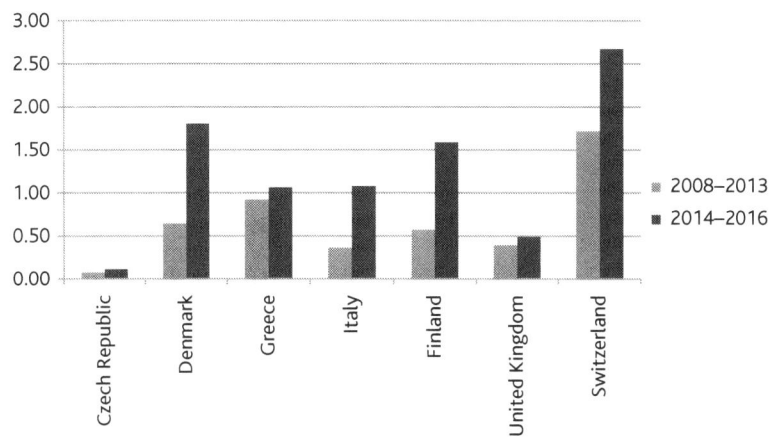

Source: Eurostat (2018)

Figure 2.12: Ratio of positive to total final decisions on asylum applications, SIRIUS countries, 2008–2013, 2014–2016

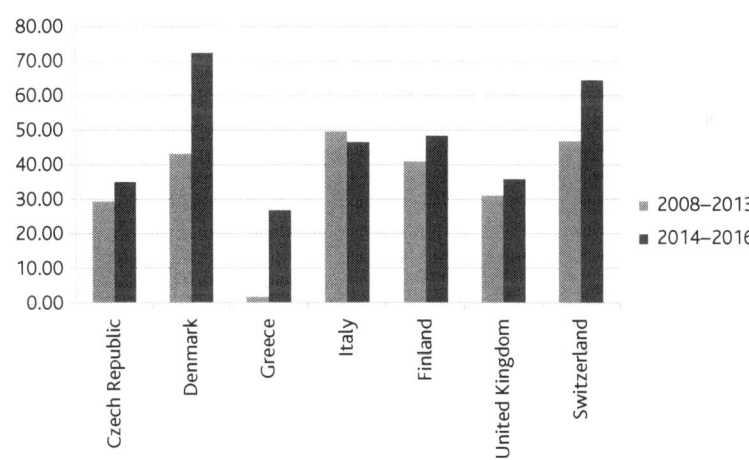

Source: Eurostat (2018)

Based on our empirical results, the gender of MRAs plays a statistically significant and positive role on the employment rate since male candidates have better chances of being integrated in the labour market. The same picture applies for the educational attainment level as well. In fact, an increased level of education is associated with an increased set of skills and competences for each individual. This, in turn, implies that a more educated MRA is more likely to adapt to the working conditions since she has a

Figure 2.13: Mean annual number of first residence permits (per 1,000 persons), SIRIUS countries, 2008–2013, 2014–2016

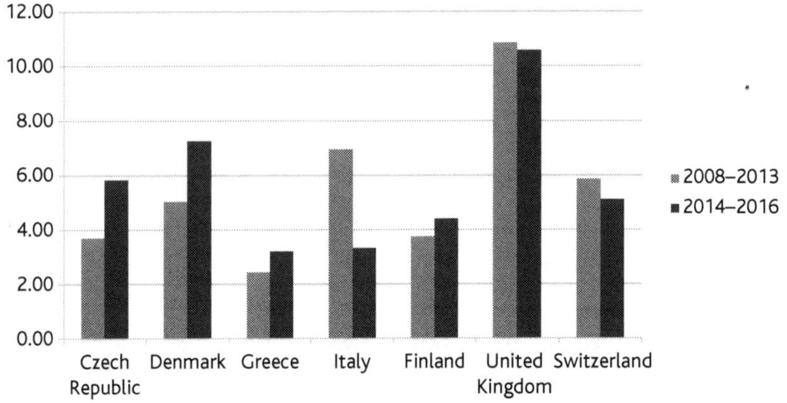

Source: Eurostat (2018)

steep learning-by-doing curve, based on economic theory, which leads to increased potential productivity compared to less educated MRAs. Therefore, more educated MRAs are more appealing to employees in all economies compared to less educated ones.

On the other hand, there are some low-skilled occupations that were found to have a negative and statistically significant impact on the employment rate. More precisely, based on our analysis, MRAs with occupations such as technicians and associate professions, service and sales workers, skilled agricultural, forestry and fishing workers, plant machine operators and assemblers and elementary occupations have statistically significantly decreased employment opportunities, since these professions are considered to be saturated in the various labour markets. As a result, a general finding is that SIRIUS labour markets prefer educated male MRAs that have significant occupational skills, such as managers, professionals, and so on.

Employability of migrants, refugees and asylum seekers in the SIRIUS economies

In this section, we analyse further the integration capabilities of the MRAs in the countries of interest (the Czech Republic, Denmark, Finland, Switzerland, the UK, Greece and Italy). We identify the SIRIUS economies and the sectors of economic activity that could be considered as being 'labour absorbing'. To do so, we proceed at multiple levels. Specifically, two complementary methodological frameworks have been used to investigate the aforementioned topic.

Employment opportunities for migrants, refugees and asylum seekers in the SIRIUS economies

First, to detect the labour 'absorbing' economies we need a modelling framework that can deal with both the interlinkages and spillovers among different economies. Therefore, following the related econometric literature (Pesaran et al, 2004) by using the Global Vector AutoRegressive (GVAR) model, we model the dynamic interlinkages and the potential spillover effects among the various SIRIUS economies. In this context, the results of the GVAR estimation pinpoint the labour absorbing economies in the dataset. Next, using the VAR/VEC framework, we investigate if there are any specific labour absorbing sectors, that is, primary, secondary, manufacturing and tertiary sectors, that correspond to the NACE Rev. 2 classification A, B-F, C, and G-U (see Table A.1 in the Appendix), respectively, for all the SIRIUS economies. The implicit assumption here is that there is labour mobility across the various sectors, but not necessarily across the various economies. Based on our two-step approach, the first step provides evidence for the total economy, whereas the second step provides evidence for the sectoral dimension of the economy. Therefore, a labour absorbing economy, identified in the first step, implies that the economy in total could attract more labour from the rest of the economies in order to increase its production. On the other hand, a labour absorbing sector, identified in the second step, implies that this specific sector could attract, independently, more labour from the rest of the sectors in order to increase its production. The fundamental difference in the second step is that the labour attracted by a sector comes directly from the labour force of the respective economy, whereas in the first step the labour attracted by an economy comes both from the rest of the economies, as well as from the respective economy.

A main finding is that the aggregate output of the UK has a statistically significant effect on the aggregate labour dynamics of the Czech Republic, Finland and Switzerland. This could be attributed to the strong interconnection between the UK and these economies mainly in terms of trade and financial relations. Another interesting finding is that the economies of the UK, Switzerland, Finland and the Czech Republic could be considered as being 'labour absorbing'. In other words, based on our econometric analysis, these economies can attract extra workforce from the other SIRIUS economies. In this context, in these economies any potential future migration flows have increased potential of being integrated into their labour markets.

Next, at a sectoral level, another main finding is that the economies of Switzerland and Greece have the highest 'labour absorbing' capability for MRAs in the sense that all their sectors are characterised as being 'labour absorbing'. Then, the economies of Finland and the Czech Republic have three labour absorbing sectors, namely primary, secondary and manufacturing for Finland, and primary, secondary and tertiary for the Czech Republic, whereas Denmark presents two, that is, primary and secondary sectors, and the UK only one labour absorbing sector, that is, primary sector. It should be noted that, with the exception of Italy, the primary sector[5] in all the economies could be considered as being 'labour absorbing'. This fact implies that in most economies there is an acute need for workers in the agriculture, forestry, fishing and other related activities sector. Finally, another interesting finding is the fact that the secondary sector is considered to be 'labour absorbing' for all the SIRIUS economies, with the exception of Italy and the UK, whereas the manufacturing and tertiary sectors are considered to be 'labour absorbing' for three out of seven SIRIUS economies, that is, Switzerland, Czech Republic and Greece. In other words, the econometric investigation undertaken at the sectoral level, with the results presented previously, showed that the SIRIUS economies have the capacity to reallocate their labour force between the various economic sectors in a way that would lead to an increase in their industrial production. Therefore, the MRAs that are integrated in the labour force of each economy have an increased potential of being employed in the specific sectors described in this section (see also Table 2.3).

Employability indicators: a structural analysis

In this section, a quantitative analysis is also presented based on two composite indicators, that is, SIRIUS 1 and SIRIUS 2. SIRIUS 1 and SIRUS 2 are used to identify the sectors and the occupations, respectively, of an economy which have simultaneously high growth potential and required educational attainment level compatible to the MRAs' educational attainment level. For the construction of both indicators, input-output analysis is used, which constitutes a widely used methodology appropriate for this type of investigation. The estimates are disaggregated by sector of economic activity

Table 2.3: Labour absorbing sectors

	Switzerland	Czech Republic	Denmark	Finland	Greece	Italy	United Kingdom
Primary sector	+	+	+	+	+		+
Secondary sector	+	+	+	+	+		
Manufacturing sector	+			+	+		
Tertiary sector	+	+			+		

and by occupation for each country and analytical presentations will be offered to assess the current state of integration of international MRAs in the countries under investigation.

For each SIRIUS country the most dynamic sectors and occupations are determined and the MRAs' integration potential is approached based on the similarity of their educational attainment level with the educational attainment level's demand, at the sectoral and occupational levels, respectively.

In this research, a methodology of estimating the employability of MRAs for an economy is proposed. Based on the proposed methodology, an efficient model for the simulation of the labour market will be used, providing a method for the matching of educational attainment level of MRAs across the sectors and the occupations of the economy, aiming at the optimisation of the integration process.

First, the investigation of the labour market structural characteristics of the Czech Republic, Denmark, Greece, Italy, Finland, United Kingdom and Switzerland focuses on the employment structure at the level of sectors, occupations and educational attainment level. Then, two composite indicators, focusing on the sectoral structure of employment and on the occupational structure of employment, respectively, are introduced: the Growth Indicator for Sectors (GIS), and the Growth Potential Indicator for Occupations (GIO). The estimation of the GIS and the GIO is based on important indicators. These indicators are connected, on one hand with the structure and growth of employment at the sectoral and occupational level, respectively, and on the other, with the multiplying effect of sectors and occupations in the examined economy. The multiplying effect of economic sectors and occupations is estimated based on Input-Output Analysis (IOA). Then, for the comparison of the educational attainment level of MRAs with the educational attainment level of the employment for each country, two indicators expressing the similarity level are introduced: the Sectoral Structure Similarity (SSS) and the Occupational Structure Similarity (OSS). Finally, two composite indicators are used to identify the priorities, at the sectoral and occupational level, for MRAs' integration in each economy: SIRIUS Indicator for Sectors (SIRIUS 1) and the SIRIUS Indicator for Occupations (SIRIUS 2).

Based on our findings, in the Czech Republic, the occupations with high employability potential are in the categories of elementary occupations, craft and related trades workers and clerical support workers. In Denmark, the occupations with high employability potential can be found in a wide range of occupations, such as craft and related trades workers, clerical support workers, service and sales workers. In Greece, the occupations with high employability potential are in the categories of skilled agricultural workers, plant and machine operators and assemblers, and elementary occupations. In Switzerland, the occupations with high employability potential are in the categories clerical support workers, plant and machine operators and assemblers, and elementary occupations. In the United Kingdom, the occupations with high employability potential are in the categories of professionals, technicians and associate professionals, and clerical support workers. In Finland, MRAs' integration potential is found in the services sectors and in the occupational categories of craft and related trades workers, skilled agricultural, forestry and fishery workers, and professionals. In Italy, MRAs' integration potential is found in manufacturing, services and primary sectors, and in the occupational categories of clerical support workers, service and sales workers, and professionals. All things considered, the uneven structure of each economy's labour market dictates the use of tailor-made policy actions that would differ considerably from country to country, depending on the inherent characteristics of each economy.

Conclusion

The main aims of this chapter were threefold. To begin with, the chapter presented the overall demographic situation in Europe by focusing on the economies participating in the SIRIUS project. In this context, the demographic role of post-2014 MRAs was assessed as well as their impact on these economies. The main demographic finding was that MRAs will significantly improve the labour force of the economies participating in the SIRIUS project, in terms of the working age population. Next, the chapter dealt with the barriers and enablers in the labour market of the economies participating in the SIRIUS project, acknowledging at the same time the key characteristics of the post-2014 MRA flows. In this context, the main findings were that the gender as well as the educational attainment level of MRAs are the most important factors that determine their employability opportunities. In other words, the analysis yielded that males with high educational level have increased opportunities to be integrated in the labour market of the SIRIUS economies. Finally, the chapter detected the labour absorbing economies and sectors in the countries participating in the SIRIUS project. Based on our findings, the economies of the UK, Switzerland, Finland and the Czech Republic could be considered as being 'labour absorbing', whereas the primary sector of each economy seems to be highly 'labour absorbing' in almost all the countries participating in the SIRIUS project.

Notes

[1] The population component of the differences in the contribution of foreign- and native-born population to the overall population change thought the natural change, refers to the share of women of reproductive age as compared to the total population of each population group and the age structure of women of reproductive age in each

population – which affect birth rates – and the age structure of each population group which affects death rates.
2 Results not presented here in detail indicate that this upward trend results from increasing participation rates of persons aged 55 to 64.
3 Part of this increase is due to the fact that asylum seekers are included in the 2016 inflows.
4 In all countries participating in the SIRIUS project, except Italy.
5 Note that the present chapter utilises official data on migration and labour without taking into consideration any irregular migration flows or irregular employment that could be present in the various economies.

Appendix

Table A.1: Classification of sectors of economic activity, NACE Rev. 2, 1-dig

A	Agriculture, forestry and fishing
B	Mining and quarrying
C	Manufacturing
D	Electricity, gas, steam and air conditioning supply
E	Water supply, sewerage, waste management and remediation activities
F	Construction
G	Wholesale and retail trade, repair of motor vehicles and motorcycles
H	Transportation and storage
I	Accommodation and food service activities
J	Information and communication
K	Financial and insurance activities
L	Real estate activities
M	Professional, scientific and technical activities
N	Administrative and support service activities
O	Public administration and defence, compulsory social security
P	Education
Q	Human health and social work activities
R	Arts, entertainment and recreation
S	Other service activities
T	Activities of households as employers, undifferentiated goods- and services-producing activities of households for own use
U	Activities of extraterritorial organisations and bodies

Source: Eurostat (2008)

Table A.2: Specialisation index of occupations, 2016

	Czech Republic	Denmark	Greece	Italy	Finland	United Kingdom	Switzerland
OC1	0.877	0.459	0.452	0.633	0.555	1.833	1.459
OC2	0.797	1.318	0.994	0.761	1.246	1.313	1.288
OC3	1.080	1.070	0.511	0.995	1.187	0.775	1.193
OC4	0.969	0.812	1.089	1.251	0.609	0.982	0.861
OC5	0.901	1.166	1.406	1.032	1.157	1.095	0.964
OC6	0.382	0.515	3.199	0.680	0.933	0.339	0.857
OC7	1.459	0.632	0.831	1.140	0.929	0.712	0.998
OC8	1.853	0.686	0.810	0.917	1.047	0.690	0.496
OC9	0.606	1.235	0.766	1.233	0.667	0.942	0.453
OC0	0.509	0.684	3.104	1.881	0.675	0.506	0.000

Source: Eurostat (2017)

Table A.3: Classification of sectors of economic activity, NACE Rev. 2, 2-dig

	Description
A01	Crop and animal production, hunting and related service activities
A02	Forestry and logging
A03	Fishing and aquaculture
B	Mining and quarrying
C10–C12	Manufacture of food products, beverages and tobacco products
C13–C15	Manufacture of textiles, clothing apparel and leather products
C16	Manufacture of wood and of products of wood and cork, except furniture; manufacture of articles of straw and plaiting materials
C17	Manufacture of paper and paper products
C18	Printing and reproduction of recorded media
C19	Manufacture of coke and refined petroleum products
C20	Manufacture of chemicals and chemical products
C21	Manufacture of basic pharmaceutical products and pharmaceutical preparations
C22	Manufacture of rubber and plastic products
C23	Manufacture of other non-metallic mineral products
C24	Manufacture of basic metals
C25	Manufacture of fabricated metal products, except machinery and equipment

Table A.3: Classification of sectors of economic activity, NACE Rev. 2, 2-dig (continued)

	Description
C26	Manufacture of computer, electronic and optical products
C27	Manufacture of electrical equipment
C28	Manufacture of machinery and equipment NEC (national electrical code)
C29	Manufacture of motor vehicles, trailers and semi-trailers
C30	Manufacture of other transport equipment
C31–C32	Manufacture of furniture; other manufacturing
C33	Repair and installation of machinery and equipment
D35	Electricity, gas, steam and air conditioning supply
E36	Water collection, treatment and supply
E37–E39	Sewerage; waste collection, treatment and disposal activities; materials recovery; remediation activities and other waste management services
F	Construction
G45	Wholesale and retail trade and repair of motor vehicles and motorcycles
G46	Wholesale trade, except of motor vehicles and motorcycles
G47	Retail trade, except of motor vehicles and motorcycles
H49	Land transport and transport via pipelines
H50	Water transport
H51	Air transport
H52	Warehousing and support activities for transportation
H53	Postal and courier activities
I	Accommodation and food service activities
J58	Publishing activities
J59–J60	Motion picture, video and television programme production, sound recording and music publishing activities; programming and broadcasting activities
J61	Telecommunications
J62–J63	Computer programming, consultancy and related activities; information service activities
K64	Financial service activities, except insurance and pension funding
K65	Insurance, reinsurance and pension funding, except compulsory social security
K66	Activities auxiliary to financial services and insurance activities
L68	Real estate activities
M69–M70	Legal and accounting activities; activities of head offices; management consultancy activities
M71	Architectural and engineering activities; technical testing and analysis
M72	Scientific research and development

(continued)

Table A.3: Classification of sectors of economic activity, NACE Rev. 2, 2-dig (continued)

	Description
M73	Advertising and market research
M74–M75	Other professional, scientific and technical activities; veterinary activities
N	Administrative and support service activities
O84	Public administration and defense; compulsory social security
P85	Education
Q	Human health and social work activities
R–S, T, U	Other service activities, activities of households as employers, activities of extraterritorial organisations and bodies

Source: Eurostat (2008)

Table A.4: Sectoral specialisation index, 2016

	Czech Republic	Denmark	Greece	Italy	Finland	United Kingdom	Switzerland
A01	0.61	0.58	3.04	0.92	0.71	0.23	0.75
A02	2.27	0.47	0.39	0.99	3.25	0.28	1.00
A03	0.72	0.00	5.60	1.19	0.00	0.62	0.00
B	2.20	0.36	1.03	0.41	0.41	1.01	0.29
C10–C12	1.10	0.94	1.52	0.94	0.66	0.58	0.76
C13–C15	1.23	0.28	0.84	1.77	0.26	0.43	0.23
C16	1.92	0.73	0.63	1.04	2.10	0.48	1.98
C17	1.65	0.57	0.70	1.30	2.56	0.63	0.59
C18	1.37	0.56	1.13	1.07	1.01	0.96	1.19
C19	1.07	0.00	1.39	1.25	1.73	1.11	0.00
C20	1.24	0.74	0.44	1.00	0.87	0.59	0.93
C21	0.78	2.92	1.20	1.09	0.49	1.12	1.94
C22	2.30	0.67	0.44	1.08	0.64	0.56	0.57
C23	2.34	0.90	0.52	1.26	1.03	0.51	0.61
C24	2.31	0.28	0.54	1.50	1.02	0.55	0.39
C25	2.31	0.78	0.59	1.46	1.04	0.50	0.96
C26	1.99	0.77	0.15	0.79	1.41	0.76	2.71
C27	2.53	0.68	0.46	1.33	1.18	0.37	1.06
C28	1.50	1.46	0.10	1.46	1.21	0.54	1.02
C29	3.02	0.08	0.03	0.64	0.20	0.43	0.06
C30	1.29	0.32	0.26	0.99	0.60	1.33	0.53

Table A.4: Sectoral specialisation index, 2016 (continued)

	Czech Republic	Denmark	Greece	Italy	Finland	United Kingdom	Switzerland
C31–C32	1.57	0.71	0.53	1.27	0.50	0.59	0.66
C33	1.33	0.62	0.33	1.13	1.20	1.25	0.56
D35	1.44	0.74	1.10	0.79	1.01	0.85	0.86
E36	1.34	0.52	1.02	0.87	0.56	1.07	0.18
E37–E39	1.22	0.77	0.74	1.53	0.56	0.87	0.53
F	1.12	0.82	0.60	0.92	1.08	1.08	1.01
G45	1.04	0.90	0.94	1.03	0.92	0.83	0.98
G46	0.79	1.35	0.90	1.01	1.05	0.70	1.33
G47	0.82	1.01	1.49	0.99	0.75	1.06	0.75
H49	1.47	0.75	0.90	0.88	1.14	0.89	0.81
H50	0.37	2.38	7.18	1.07	2.08	0.90	0.35
H51	0.64	0.89	1.19	0.53	1.13	1.19	1.47
H52	0.78	0.84	0.67	0.93	0.94	0.85	0.74
H53	1.07	0.98	0.54	1.07	1.01	1.35	1.09
I	0.73	0.89	1.92	1.27	0.73	1.13	0.87
J58	0.56	1.44	0.82	0.56	1.11	1.11	0.69
J59–J60	0.95	1.45	0.78	0.70	0.94	1.65	0.95
J61	1.05	0.89	1.54	0.98	0.93	1.17	1.18
J62–J63	1.04	1.56	0.43	0.87	1.69	1.38	1.31
K64	0.69	1.08	0.99	1.05	0.74	1.07	1.65
K65	0.70	1.12	1.08	0.92	0.78	1.34	2.22
K66	1.05	0.41	0.39	0.80	0.59	2.10	1.92
L68	0.89	1.38	0.19	0.75	1.15	1.37	1.24
M69–M70	0.60	0.75	1.16	1.22	0.76	1.29	1.57
M71	0.95	1.25	1.26	1.26	1.80	1.23	2.02
M72	1.06	1.00	0.34	0.70	2.29	0.98	1.37
M73	1.39	1.12	0.80	0.66	1.06	1.38	1.04
M74–M75	1.01	1.21	0.49	1.15	0.95	1.58	1.08
N	0.58	0.91	0.57	1.04	1.05	1.13	0.91
O84	0.93	0.79	1.31	0.81	0.66	0.88	0.67
P85	0.85	1.19	1.06	0.89	0.94	1.39	1.00
Q	0.63	1.61	0.54	0.74	1.54	1.20	1.27
R-S-T-U	0.81	1.23	0.76	1.04	1.36	1.26	1.14

References

Bagavos, C. (2019) 'The importance of foreign migration for shifts in the size of the labour force of European countries: Methodological insights and contemporary evidence from SIRIUS and from selected non-SIRIUS countries', Working Paper, No 2, SIRIUS Project.

Bagavos, C. (2022) 'How Much Does Migration Affect Labor Supply in Europe? Methodological Insights and Contemporary Evidence from the European Union and Selected European Countries', *International Migration Review*. Doi: 10.1177/01979183221115148

Coleman, D. (2008) 'The demographic effects of international migration in Europe', *Oxford Review of Economic Policy*, 24(3): 452–476.

Cully, M. (2011) 'How much do migrants account for the unexpected rise in the labour force participation rate in Australia over the past decade?', paper presented at the Australian Conference of Economists. Available at: https://www.homeaffairs.gov.au/research-and-stats/files/migrants-account-unexpected-rise-labour-force-rate-aus-2000-2010.pdf

European Commission (2020) *Report from the Commission to the European Parliament, the Council, the Economic and Social Committee and the Committee of the Regions on the Impact of Demographic Change*, Brussels COM(2020) 241 Final.

Eurostat (2021a) Population change: Demographic balance and crude rates at national level, Brussels: European Commission. Available at: https://ec.europa.eu/eurostat/cache/metadata/en/demo_r_gind3_esms.htm

Eurostat (2021b) Population on 1 January by age group, sex and country of birth, Brussels: European Commission. Available at: https://appsso.eurostat.ec.europa.eu/nui/show.do?dataset=migr_pop1ctz

Eurostat (2021c) Live births by mother's age and country of birth, Brussels: European Commission. Available at: http://appsso.eurostat.ec.europa.eu/nui/show.do?dataset=demo_facbc&lang=en

Eurostat (2021d) Deaths by age, sex and country of birth, Brussels: European Commission. Available at: https://data.europa.eu/data/datasets/ukwszrhxhlwj9tpvcz5idq?locale=en

Eurostat (2021e) Immigration by age group, sex and country of birt, Brussels: European Commission. Available at: https://appsso.eurostat.ec.europa.eu/nui/show.do?dataset=migr_imm3ctb&lang=en

Eurostat (2021f) Emigration by age group, sex and country of birth, Brussels: European Commission. Available at: https://appsso.eurostat.ec.europa.eu/nui/show.do?dataset=migr_imm3ctb&lang=en

Eurostat (2021g) Population by sex, age, country of birth and labour status, Brussels: European Commission. Available at: https://appsso.eurostat.ec.europa.eu/nui/show.do?dataset=lfsa_pgacws&lang=en

Hilgenstock, B. and Kóczán, Z. (2018) 'Storm clouds ahead? Migration and labor force participation rates in Europe', IMF Working Paper, WP/18/148.

MacKellar, L.F. and McNicoll, G. (2019) 'International migration: Approaches, issues, policies. Introduction to the online collection of articles', *Population and Development Review,* 45: e12246. https://doi.org/10.1111/padr.12246

Murphy, M. (2016) 'The impact of migration on long-term European population trends, 1950 to present', *Population and Development Review*, 42(2): 225–244.

Pesaran, M.H., Schuermann, T. and Weiner, S. (2004) 'Modeling regional interdependencies using a global error correcting macroeconometric model', *Journal of Business and Economic Statistics*, 22(2): 129–162.

Salzmann, T., Edmonston, B. and Raymer, J. (eds) (2010) *Demographic Aspects of Migration*, Wiesbaden: VS Verlag für Sozialwissenschaften.

Spielvogel, G. and Meghnagi, M. (2018a) 'The contribution of migration to the dynamics of the labour force in OECD countries: 2005–2015', Working Paper, No. 203, OECD Social, Employment and Migration Working Papers.

Spielvogel, G. and Meghnagi, M. (2018b) 'Assessing the role of migration in European labour force growth by 2030', Working Paper, No. 204, OECD Social, Employment and Migration Working Papers.

van Nimwegen, N. and van der Erf, R. (2010) 'Europe at the crossroads: Demographic challenges and international migration', *Journal of Ethnic and Migration Studies*, 36(9): 1359–1379.

3

Legal frameworks

Veronica Federico

Work, work, work ...

'Work, work, work ...' is the mantra of any integration plan and programme, of any public discourse on migration and, interestingly enough, it is also the mantra of most migrants I have met, interviewed and talked with in the last ten years of research activity in the migration domain.

'Work, work, work ...' because the demography of third country nationals (TCNs) in the European Union shows a population mainly concentrated in the working age (15–64 years old); because TCNs' propensity to work remains high; because the EU member states' labour markets need workforce, especially in those economic sectors that nationals tend to neglect, if they can; because the EU member states' welfare regimes need TCNs' contribution to resist the impact of an ageing native population; because the political discourse based on the paradigm 'integration through work' works in political terms, across the left/right divide; because evidence-based data of 'integration through work' show that it works, even though not as smoothly as political discourses depict it; because the dignity of people strongly depends on their capacity to be self-sufficient, to secure their livelihood and to support families and loved ones.

'Work, work, work ...', though, might be much more difficult than it may appear. First, because the labour market is not an open-access source for TCNs, who require a permit to work; second, because due to a number of reasons (fragmentation of labour markets, obstacles in skills and qualification recognition; national preference clauses, and so on) TCNs experience a mismatch between their competences and the job opportunities available to them much more often than nationals; third, because when they work, often their working conditions are worse than those of nationals. Therefore, more frequently than should be the case, TCNs are denied access to the labour market, they end up accepting unqualified jobs or resort to entering the informal labour market.

The aim of the chapter is to explore migrants, refugees and asylum seekers' integration legal framework in the European labour markets across several European countries, in the light of the notion of legal status, in order to critically discuss if and how the very way in which TCNs' legal statuses are designed by current migration law is intended to foster integration or, on the contrary, tends to create legal peripheries. Legal peripheries are not understood, for the purpose of current analysis, as geographical spaces, but rather as immaterial spaces where the actual enforcement of rights is at odds with the formal recognition of equality, dignity and fundamental rights. Legal peripheries are immaterial spaces defined by a series of unbalanced relations that cripple the empowering and emancipatory potency of rights and of the rule of law. As will be discussed, for certain categories of TCNs, the peripheral legal status has a 'ghetto effect' and does not allow the person to move from periphery to semi-periphery and centre, creating a vicious circle of legal rights downsizing. Under this perspective, the chapter intends to contribute to existing scholarship on migrants' integration in the labour market by advancing knowledge on legal statuses, a subject that has generally attracted scant attention coupled with labour market integration.

The data this chapter is based on have been collected in the Czech Republic, Denmark, Finland, Greece, Italy, Switzerland and the UK; at the time of the analysis, six countries were EU member states and one (Switzerland) a non-EU member. These countries represent diversity under several aspects crucial to the discussion of the chapter hypothesis. They mirror the diversity of European landscapes in terms of state structure, system of government, rights enforcement and litigation, the political system, and also migration flows and migration governance regimes, labour market structure and economic parameters, rules on labour market access and working conditions, as well as Europeanisation processes. The importance of the Europeanisation of both migration (either forced and non-forced migration, even though at different pace) and labour market rules is irrefutable. Nonetheless, with regard to non-forced migration, the European common immigration policy 'shall not affect the right of Member States to determine volumes of admission of third-country nationals coming from third countries to their territory in order to seek work, whether employed or self-employed' (Article 79(5), Treaty on the Functioning of the European Union [TFEU]). Forced migration, that implies people seeking protection in the EU, is, on the other hand, mainly disciplined, at the European level, with the legal instrument of the Directives, that leave quite a broad space of manoeuvre to member states. Moreover, the increasingly multilevel nature of European migration governance, that incorporates international, supranational, national, subnational and even local rules, coupled with a multiplicity of actors operating at (and often also across) each level, tends to mitigate the harmonisation effort of the common European immigration and asylum policies. And this is why, in this chapter, much space will be devoted to national legislation.

The chapter uses primarily the methodology of comparative law, favouring an approach open to other sciences and consistent with the 'methodological pluralism' (Scarciglia, 2015), which implies an integration of different research methods (functional, structural, systematic and critical method) in connection with the research question (Frankenberg, 2012). Consistently with the dynamic nature of the object, a multifactor analysis is proposed, carried out with a necessarily interdisciplinary methodological approach not only in the context of legal fields but also with other complementary social sciences (Hirschl, 2014).

The chapter starts with a brief introduction on the notion of legal status, its importance in migration law and in migration governance, to develop the analysis on TCNs' integration in European labour markets along two different steps in labour market integration: accessing the labour market and working under the same conditions as nationals (and Europeans). In the conclusion, some hypothesis on how to mitigate the legal status 'ghetto effect' will be advanced.

Legal status and the ghetto effect

In legal terms, legal status is the position that a person, an entity (association, company, institution, and so on) or a good has in the legal system and the set of mutual relations that exist between the person, entity or good and the legal system. That is to say that legal status defines the standing of the person, entity or good in the society from a legal point of view. It is a relational notion, that may vary over time, and it has a vertical dimension, defining the position of the person, entity, good vis-à-vis the state, and a horizontal one, that defines the multiple relations vis-à-vis the other subjects of the legal system.

The legal status of a person can be defined as 'her legal position or conditions', that is the aggregate of rights and duties attributed to a given person, as a subject of law, in a given community (Rescigno, 1973: 211). This means that there is a triangulation of relations that include the person, the state and the members of a given community in the definition and recognition of those rights and duties.

Reframing Eric Hobsbawm's renowned reflection on identities, legal statuses 'are not like shoes, of which we can only wear one pair at a time' (Hobsbawm, 1996: 171). 'We are all multi-dimensional beings', as Hobsbawm's quote continues, makes sense also in legal terms. Each person can be contemporarily, for example, a citizen, a full-time employee, a spouse, a parent, a shareholder, and so on, without any major conflict among those statutes. But when it comes to foreigners, and more specifically, to TCNs, the question becomes thornier and more complex.

To foreigners, legal status means 'the rights afforded or denied by the State' (Sohn, 2014: 371) depending on the foreigner's entry channel on the one hand, and 'upon the specific choices undertaken by each legal system with reference to: *a*) different kinds of legal status recognised to migrants; *b*) criteria which the migrant has to fulfil in order to obtain a specific legal status; *c*) rights and duties related to this status', on the other hand (Federico and Pannia, 2019: 18). When the overarching legal status is not the citizen one, the coexistence of several statuses may become limited or even impossible. TCN seasonal workers, for example, are often not recognised the right to family reunification in our case studies. Also, in Italy, beneficiaries of humanitarian protection (the national temporary protection regime that has undergone major changes in the last few years) cannot convert their permit into a working permit, even if they do have a job.

Moreover, in all the countries there is a 'proliferation of legal statuses' (Zetter, 2007: 175), a continuous trend towards the multiplication of extremely specific statuses, each tailored to fit a very narrowly determined case. Paradigmatic is the case of Italy, where more than 40 different legal statuses exist for foreigners. This creates a very complex 'set of requirements and rights, a normative labyrinth, which is extremely difficult to navigate' (Federico and Pannia, 2019: 32) for migrants first, but also for the multiple actors that populate the migration governance system and for the labour market actors, which quite often are hampered rather than facilitated by the legal system in the process of inclusion of TCNs in the labour market.

A further characteristic of legal statuses in all the countries we have been studying, except Finland, is their rigidity, that is to say that passing from one to another may be long, heavy in terms of documents to be attached and costly, therefore TCNs tend to remain captured in the status allocated them when they first enter the country (obviously this does not apply to the asylum seeker status, that is a transitional status that shall 'naturally' change either into a protection status or into an expulsion order), thus limiting the possibility of profiting from opportunities of advancing in the social (and legal) ladder.

Legal statuses, in fact, are not on the same level, but rather organised in a hierarchy in terms of number and wideness of rights (Federico and Baglioni, 2021). At the top, in all countries, there are refugees, beneficiaries of subsidiary protection; at the bottom, asylum seekers and short-term economic migrants, whose uncertain (for the former) and extremely temporary (for the latter) relation with the state and the community heavily impacts on the set of rights and duties coupled with their status: their family reunification rights are very limited (for asylum seekers) or totally denied (for short-term economic migrants), they rarely fully benefit from unemployment allocation (Italy and Switzerland are the two countries that are more generous towards those categories of TCNs) and tend to be excluded from education and vocational training (that are even more limited for short-term economic migrants). At the very bottom, with almost no rights except the fundamental human rights, lie undocumented migrants, whose position is extremely vulnerable, even when, as in the case of irregular caregivers and domestic workers, their contribution to the economic and welfare system is crucial (Ambrosini, 2010; Triandafyllidou, 2013; Mullally and Murphy, 2014).

As we will argue in the concluding reflections, the intertwin between narrowness, rigidity, hierarchy creates a legal 'ghetto' effect: TCNs are captured into legal categories that are ill-suited to favour their integration into Czech, Danish, Finnish, Greek, Italian, Swiss and British labour markets and relegate them to marginal positions. Furthermore, such a vicious intertwine may also come at odds with TCNs' fundamental rights and mark a regression of the whole legal system to a pre-modern era, when a multiplicity of statuses allocated to people according to their socio-economic corporative conditions prevailed over the broader empowering status of citizens.

Rights, work and integration

If, when and how migrants, asylum seekers and refugees integrate into the labour market determines their prospects for integrating socially and economically into European societies, and it is needless to spend additional words on what literature and empirical evidence has already widely proved (Ruiz and Vargas-Silva, 2017, 2018; Marbach et al, 2018; Zwysen, 2019; Brell et al, 2020). If, when and how depend on many factors, pertaining on the one hand to external factors (economic system, legal and policy framework, trade unions and third sector activism, and so on) and, on the other, to individual ones (psychological attitude, skills and capacities, gender and gender roles in both origin and hosting societies, social capital, and so on). The legal framework, while belonging naturally to the external factors category, bridges the two levels, as it allows certain individual factors to get transposed and become relevant for the external one (through the recognition of qualifications and skills, for example). This transposition largely relies on the TCN's legal status, as her/his legal status depends a wide range of employment-related conditions and rights.

First, the very access to the labour markets. Here, the data gathered in the SIRIUS research clearly point to a major barrier that determine a crucial cleavage between national and European workers, on the one hand, and TCN ones, on the other; and other cleavages among TCNs themselves. Nationals and Europeans have free access to EU member states' labour markets, whereas TCN workers are required to have a permit to work that depends on labour markets needs for economic migrants (it is up to each member state to determine the 'volumes' of admissions that Article 79(5) of the TFEU refers to) and on their legal status in the case of forced migrants. Refugees, beneficiaries of subsidiary protection and their family members enjoy a full right to work, and this limits the barriers to access the labour markets to other factors that are discussed in other chapters of the volume (see Chapters 4 and 7). The same applies to beneficiaries of national forms of temporary protection, but with some further restrictions: in Switzerland they must have an additional permit to work and in Italy, when the protection status expires, they cannot convert their permit to stay and work into a working permit. Much more complex is the position of asylum seekers. As already mentioned, the asylum seeker's status is necessarily time-limited and transitional (all TCNs' statuses are time-limited except for permanent residents, but they are not transitional) and this could, somehow, justify a restricted access to the labour market (the state is given the time to scrutinise the application and either grant protection or deny it and expel the TCN, before letting them enter the labour market). Decisions on asylum applications, however, may take a long time and, as already highlighted, early integration in the labour market is desirable to foster integration in European societies, to alleviate the pressure on public expenditure, and it can also contribute to address labour markets shortages (UNHCR, 2013), therefore it is reasonable that asylum seekers are able to enter the labour markets as soon as possible, and as smoothly as possible.

Asylum seekers experience time limitations in all our countries (Greece was the only exception until December 2019, when asylum seekers were allowed to work as soon as they lodged their application. But since January 2020 the new International Protection Act L.4636/2019 has introduced a six-month employment ban for asylum seekers). Some allow asylum seekers to work after a short period (Italy after 60 days, Switzerland after three months, Denmark and Greece after six months), while others prevent them accessing the labour market for at least one year (the Czech Republic and the UK – in the latter, the one-year ban from the labour market stretches for even longer periods given that only those applicants who possess high skills can enter after one year and the rest have to wait until their claim is assessed, which can take up to two or even more years). In Finland there are two different options: asylum seekers can work three months after lodging their application if they travel with valid identification documents, or after five months if they do not possess such documents. Even though not central to the reasoning of the chapter, this brief overview of the time limitations on asylum seekers accessing employment nourishes some considerations concerning harmonisation at the EU level: six (at the time of the research) EU jurisdictions present six different time limits for asylum seekers to access domestic labour markets, as clearly illustrated in Figure 3.1, with obvious impacts on the harmonisation of the integration processes.

Entering the labour market, however, can be obstructed also regardless of TCNs' statuses. In several countries the national preference clause, which may have a constitutional recognition as in the case of Article 4 of the

Figure 3.1: Asylum seekers' labour market entry ban

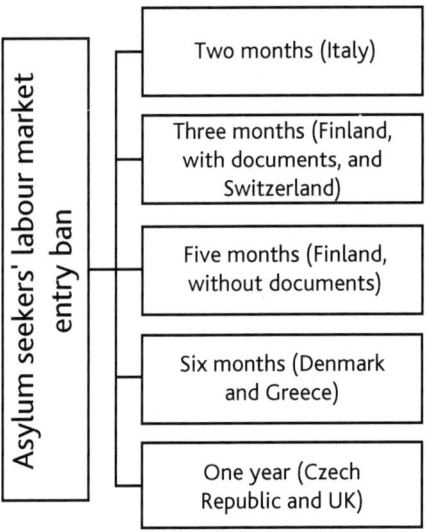

Italian constitution, or may be entrenched by specific laws, as is the case in Switzerland and in Finland, establishes that nationals and EU citizens shall have priority in accessing the labour market. This clause goes beyond the labour market test that, as already noted, is a guiding principle for granting the permit to stay and work to economic migrants, and grants that, in case of competition, nationals and EU citizens shall prevail over foreigners. Citizens first.

Accessing the labour market does not mean that TCNs are offered the job they are qualified for, or the one they strive for. As existing literature has widely demonstrated, TCNs tend to be relegated into dirty, dangerous and dull jobs that nationals and European workers try to avoid (Favell, 2009; Lim, 2021). This phenomenon is the output of a multiplicity of interrelated causes (segmentation of labour markets, discrimination, low skills, national preference clause, and so on), three of which relate to the legal framework and legal statuses: the recognition of qualifications (illustrated in Figure 3.2) and the possibility of attending both language courses and vocational training.

Only Denmark, Switzerland and Italy (with the exception of asylum seekers who are excluded from recognition in Denmark and have to provide formal evidence of their qualifications in Italy) are open to the recognition of foreign titles and qualifications, even though in Italy the recognition process is often long and complex. The UK recognises exclusively qualifications from selected countries of origin, based on a common table of conversion. In the Czech Republic and in Greece, the formal equalisation of qualifications is substantially undermined by the requirement of the official certificates issued

Figure 3.2: Recognition of qualifications of third country nationals

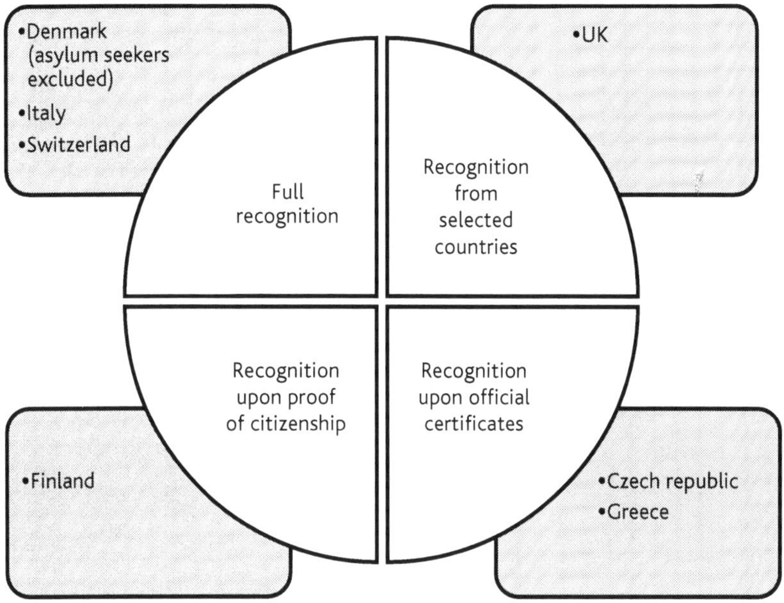

- Denmark (asylum seekers excluded)
- Italy
- Switzerland

- UK

Full recognition

Recognition from selected countries

Recognition upon proof of citizenship

Recognition upon official certificates

- Finland

- Czech republic
- Greece

by competent authorities. Of course, this may be considered fair towards economic migrants, who, in principle, can plan their migration trajectory, whereas forced migrants will hardly bring proof of their diplomas, and presenting them to national authorities. In between lies Finland, where not diplomas but proof of citizenship is required to allow for fair conversions. Noticeably, in all countries where this is allowed, TCNs must apply for recognition through specific administrative proceedings. In the most favourable of cases, as in Finland, this is done during the application process. Understand and being understood in the host society is of paramount importance for integration, and surely for accessing and remaining in the labour market. It goes without saying that in no country there are barriers to admission-with-fee courses, but what happens to destitute TCN workers? Language courses are not offered for free everywhere. In this field, much space is left for collaboration with non-state entities, both non-profit and for-profit companies. Attending language courses is rarely a duty imposed on non-EU foreign workers, and where there is no duty, the state has no responsibility in organising free language courses. The duty exists solely in those countries where attending civic integration programmes is compulsory: in Denmark for all forced migrants, and as a requirement for those economic migrants applying for permanent residency; in Finland for refugees, beneficiaries of subsidiary protection as well as for short- and long-stay economic migrants some welfare benefits, such as unemployment benefits, are conditional on participation in integration programmes that include language courses. De facto this creates a duty, whereas it is not compulsory for asylum seekers. In Italy language proficiency is requested for both integration agreements (for refugees and beneficiaries of the national short-term protection regime) and integration programmes (for long-staying economic migrants), whereas for asylum seekers some reception centres impose a duty on language course attendance. No duty exists in the Czech Republic, Greece, Switzerland (except for short-term economic migrants in those cantons where signing an integration convention is required to access social assistance) and the UK.

Vocational education and training is a relevant component of current active labour market policies, a useful tool to facilitate migrants, refugees and asylum seekers' integration into their host societies (Flisi et al, 2016). Vocational qualifications can be particularly valuable for skilled refugees and economic migrants to find adequate employment, while for illiterate and poorly educated refugees and migrants, long-term vocational programmes could be a strategic target for emancipation and advancement in the social ladder. In Greece and Finland, all migrants except undocumented people can access vocational training on the same basis as Greek and Finnish citizens (see Table 3.1). In Italy and in Switzerland, in addition to the undocumented migrant exception, asylum seekers may be restrained from vocational training either because there are no courses available in the reception centres (the Italian case), or because the course's length exceeds the asylum seeker's temporary permit to stay. In Denmark, only refugees, beneficiaries of subsidiary protection and of the Danish national form of temporary protection are entitled to vocational training, from which economic migrants are excluded, whereas in the UK, even though not formally entitled to by specific legal provisions, vocational training is open to refugees and beneficiaries of subsidiary protection (that in the UK is named humanitarian protection). By contrast, asylum seekers are excluded, but not in Scotland, where devolved legislation opens the door of vocational training also to them. Economic migrants may benefit from these measures, but with limits due to the type of visa they hold. Finally, in the Czech Republic neither asylum seekers nor short-term economic migrants nor beneficiaries of national forms of temporary protection can access vocational training, that is open to refugees, beneficiaries of subsidiary protection and long-term economic migrants, who, in case of unemployment, can participate in the retraining schemes available to nationals.

Again, this is a rather diverse scenario across countries and across statuses, that makes it more difficult, for certain categories of TCNs, to fully make good use of their eventual capacities, skills and competences. Legal barriers tend to strengthen social prejudices and contribute relegating TCN workers to unskilled, low-paid occupations. An additional brick in the wall of the 'ghetto effect'.

Table 3.1: Vocational training and education

	Refugees	Subsidiary protection	National protection	Asylum seekers	Short-term economic migrants	Long-term economic migrants	Undocumented
Czech Republic	Yes	Yes	No	No	No	Yes	No
Denmark	Yes	Yes	Yes	No	No	No	No
Finland	Yes	Yes	Yes	Yes	Yes	Yes	No
Greece	Yes	Yes	–	Yes	Yes	Yes	No
Italy	Yes	Yes	Yes	Depending on time limits	Yes	Yes	No
Switzerland	Yes	Yes	Yes	Depending on time limits	Yes	Yes	No
UK	Yes	Yes	Yes	No (yes in Scotland)	Yes (depending on visa)	Yes (depending on visa)	No

Once in the labour market, the countries considered here enforce the joint principles of equality in working conditions and benefits and of non-discrimination for all, regardless of their citizenship or length of stay in the country. In the field of non-discrimination, several European directives (Directive 2000/43/EC against discrimination on grounds of race and ethnic origin; Directive 2006/54/EC on equal opportunities and equal treatment of women and men in employment and occupation; Directive 2007/78/EC against discrimination at work on grounds of religion or belief, disability, age or sexual orientation) have played a crucial role in harmonising legislation in the different jurisdictions (Gropas, 2021). Therefore, no legal discriminations exist with reference to the principle of 'equal pay for equal jobs'. But legal statuses, nonetheless, maintain their importance for granting several connected rights, which have a very significant impact on how people work and on the 'inclusion through work' paradigm.

The first testbed of this is the right to receive unemployment benefits, summarised in Table 3.2. Switzerland and Italy are the countries that present fewer restrictions in accessing unemployment benefits: all are entitled as nationals are, except, in Switzerland, asylum seekers not allowed to work, but asylum seekers can qualify for unemployment allowances after two years of contributions – which is a tricky condition to impose on people with a temporary status. In Denmark, only refugees and long-term economic migrants holding a permanent residency permit can receive unemployment benefits. In Finland, unemployment benefits are made conditional upon permanent residency, which entails that neither asylum seekers nor short-term economic migrants are included. In Greece, refugees, beneficiaries of subsidiary protection and long-term economic migrants can access the unemployment register and receive all benefits and services as Greek citizens do, whereas asylum seekers

Table 3.2: Unemployment benefits

	Refugees	Subsidiary protection	National protection	Asylum seekers	Short-term economic migrants	Long-term economic migrants	Undocumented
Czech Republic	Yes	Yes	No	No	No	Yes	No
Denmark	Yes	No	No	No	No	Yes (but with permanent residency)	No
Finland	Yes	Yes	No	No	No	Yes (but with permanent residency)	No
Greece	Yes	Yes	N/A	Yes (after application)	No	Yes	No
Italy	Yes	Yes	Yes	Yes	Yes	Yes	No
Switzerland	Yes	Yes	Yes	After two years of contribution	Yes	Yes	No
UK	Yes	Yes	Yes	No	No	Yes (but with permanent residency)	No

can do so only after having completed the application procedure. The situation in the UK is not so different, since refugees and beneficiaries of subsidiary protections are equalised to British citizens, but long-term economic migrants must be granted indefinite leave to remain in the UK in order to claim benefits. Similarly, in the Czech Republic, solely refugees, beneficiaries of subsidiary protection and long-term economic migrants are entitled to benefits.

Similarly, retirement benefits are not granted to all TCN workers in all the countries: asylum seekers are denied retirement benefits in all countries except in Greece, Italy and Switzerland (where they are entitled to receive the part of their contribution if they had contributed to the retirement fund). Refugees, beneficiaries of subsidiary protection and of the national forms of temporary protection are recognised retirement benefits on the same basis as nationals, even though under some conditionalities. In Finland, three-year residence in the country is required, for example. Full retirement benefits are granted also to long-term and short-term economic migrants (with the three-year residence condition in Finland), except in the UK, where solely long-term economic migrants can claim pension benefits.

A third domain in which to explore the importance of legal statuses to discuss the 'integration through work' paradigm is the enforcement of the right to self-employment. This is a quite interesting domain: in self-employment

Table 3.3: Right to self-employment

	Refugees	Subsidiary protection	National protection	Asylum seekers	Short-term economic migrants	Long-term economic migrants	Undocumented
Czech Republic	Yes	Yes	Yes	No	No	Yes	No
Denmark	Yes	Yes	Yes	No	Yes (but with a specific visa)	Yes	No
Finland	Yes	Yes	Yes	Yes	Yes (but with a specific visa)	Yes	No
Greece	Yes	Yes	N/A	No	Yes	Yes	No
Italy	Yes	Yes	Yes	Yes (but de facto no)	Yes (but not seasonal workers)	Yes	No
Switzerland	Yes	Yes	Yes	No	Yes (but with a specific visa)	Yes	No
UK	Yes	Yes	Yes	No	Yes (but with a specific visa)	Yes	No

the rhetoric of the 'job-stealer foreigner' works differently, as it also has a different effect on the process of social and cultural integration through the labour market, and therefore we could expect a different pattern of rights across legal statuses (as laws are the product of political mechanisms that quite often, especially in the field of migration, respond more to perceptions of the reality than to evidences [Maggini, 2021]). In all jurisdictions refugees and beneficiaries of subsidiary and national temporary protection can work as self-employed, and the same applies to long-term economic migrants, as it can be observed in Table 3.3. The strongest restrictions exist for asylum seekers and short-term economic migrants. In the Czech Republic, also short-term economic migrants are permitted to be self-employed, whereas in Denmark, in the UK and in Switzerland, asylum seekers cannot, and for short-term economic migrants the right to self-employment is only accessible to those who have been granted a visa specifically for starting a business in Denmark, the UK or Switzerland. In Finland, self-employment is open to asylum seekers under the same conditions of employee work: after three months of residence for those who have valid travel documents, and five for those that have not. Short-term economic migrants who go to Finland to set up an enterprise need to apply for the residence permit for self-employed persons. Greece limits self-employment only to asylum seekers, whereas in Italy there is no specific restriction for asylum seekers, but a number of corollary rules that limit asylum seekers range of rights de facto severely undermine this right, and foreign seasonal workers are not allowed to be self-employed.

Particularly interesting is the position of short-term economic migrants: in principle they are not denied the right to self-employment, that is to say that setting up a business, even for a short period, is generally welcomed in the countries discussed, but this shall be decided in advance, before the migration journey, and authorised *ex ante* by the hosting state. On the one hand, this responds to the trivial understanding that setting up a business requires a good deal of preparatory activities, but, on the other, especially in the field of small artisan businesses or care and cleaning businesses, the rigidity of legal statuses impede short-term TCN workers to become self-employed, unless undergoing a brand-new permit request. And this may lead them to prefer to turn to the irregular labour market.

To conclude: how to transform legal status into enablers?

In the previous section, solely the most common and broad legal statuses have been discussed, but, as highlighted, in each country, especially in the fields of non-forced migration and of the national forms of temporary protection, a plethora of narrow statuses exist, so that, for example, babysitters have a different status, with different rights, benefits and duties attached, than au pairs or caregivers.

If legal status is a 'technique through which the law differentiates the individuals' (Alpa, 1993: 3), and it is legitimate in principle, as it ensures that each person, entity or good is attributed a clear and peculiar position in the legal system, this differentiation shall be reasonable and fairly applicable, as all legal instruments shall. What happens to legal statuses applied to TCNs, on the contrary, is that borders between them are hard and difficult to overcome, and they are static instruments, deemed to provide for the governance of one of the most fluid and dynamic social phenomena. Not surprisingly, 'the close and static nature of legal status complicates and stiffens the migration processes, narrowing the room for social mobility and integration opportunities' (Federico and Pannia, 2019: 34). This phenomenon exacerbates the fragmentation and the sectorialisation of the TCN's position in society.

What is even more critical is that legal statuses are not equalised, but rather hierarchically structured. 'If we compare legal statuses across types of migrants, in all the countries examined here we can see the creation of a hierarchy in terms of access to rights and therefore in terms of capacity and opportunity of integration' (Federico and Baglioni, 2021: 16). As it clearly emerges from the analysis of the previous section and as anticipated in the introduction, refugees and, to a lesser extent, beneficiaries of subsidiary protection and long-term economic migrants are at the top of the hierarchy, endowed with the broader and stronger sets of rights, whereas at the bottom of the hierarchy we find asylum seekers, and just above them, short-term economic migrants, both categories of migrants with the most restrictive access to rights and entitlements allowing them to enter an integration path. The different layers of the hierarchy, however, are inversely populated in relation to rights' broadness and strength. The lower layers of the legal and social pyramid are the most populated, and the top the least, which means that the large majority of TCNs living in the Czech Republic, Denmark, Finland, Greece, Italy, Switzerland and the UK are entrapped in a legal relation with the other members of the community and with the state that hinders their integration opportunity.

Legal processes have resulted in many forms of clustering, as this is the way the law defines the position of people, entities and goods, as already mentioned. But the dividing lines between those clusters should be porous and allow for legal and social mobility, otherwise clustering becomes segregation, and this creates ghettos. As geographers and social scientists show, '[s]egregation is the process by which a population group … is forced to cluster in a defined special area. … Segregation is the process of formation and maintenance of a ghetto' (Marcuse, 2005: 16). 'Customarily, the ghettos were enclosed with walls and gates and kept locked at night' and on particular occasions, as the *Britannica* encyclopaedia tells us. Our research seems to suggest that something similar happens with legal statuses, as they become non-spatial *loci* where TCNs are enclosed with gates made by the legal denial of certain rights, whose recognition, by contrast, would allow them to work as nationals and Europeans do. Against the aspiration of living a decent life, the ghetto effect created by the narrowness and rigidity of legal statuses contributes to pushing TCNs into irregularity, with detrimental consequences for people and communities.

Out of the hierarchy, irregular migrants are excluded from the discourse of integration via labour markets. They do not have the right to have rights, except for the very fundamental ones recognised to every human being in democratic systems. In certain countries like Italy, however, when they work, irregular TCNs are also entitled to workers' rights. Their irregular position should not exempt employers from providing fair working conditions, but we know too well that this very seldom happens and that there is an almost direct causal relation between irregularity and exploitation (Triandafyllidou and Bartolini, 2020).

SIRIUS research data clearly shed light on the critical aspects of contemporary legal statuses attributed to TCNs in the Czech Republic, Denmark, Finland, Greece, Italy, Switzerland and the UK, but at the same time they equally clearly suggest possible strategies to mitigate those criticalities.

First, simplifying and reducing the number of statuses, making each of them more comprehensive and also more easily knowable and applicable by both migrants themselves (building on TCNs' agency in determining the legal status they strive for) and migration governance actors in EU member states. Navigating the complexity of migration laws and authorities is already a challenge (Federico and Pannia, 2021; Pannia, 2021); evidence shows that adding the intricacy and involution of legal statuses creates more barriers than enablers (Federico and Baglioni, 2021).

Second, making the transition from one legal status to another simpler, less costly in terms of fees, time and competences required, and subject to more limited conditions. Personal, social and economic factors change, and they do so even more rapidly for people involved in migration processes. If legal statuses accompany rather than hinder those transformations, the gap between how migrants could contribute to host societies and how they actually do so can be reduced, with benefits for migrants' personal wellbeing as well as for society.

Making more employment-connected rights available to a larger number of categories of people impacts on integration processes, but also on the democratic quality of our countries and of the EU. Living in the 'age of rights' (Bobbio, 1990) means recognising that democratic systems depend on people's rights.

References

Alpa, G. (2013) *Status e capacità, la costruzione giuridica delle differenze individuali*, Roma-Bari: Laterza.

Ambrosini, M. (2010) *Richiesti e respinti: l'immigrazione in Italia: come e perché*, Milan: Il Saggiatore.

Bobbio, N. (1990) *L'età dei diritti*, Turin: Einaudi.

Brell, C., Dustmann, C. and Preston, I. (2020) 'The labor market integration of refugee migrants in high-income countries', *Journal of Economic Perspectives*, (34)1: 94–121.

Britannica, 'Ghetto', Available at: https://www.britannica.com/topic/ghetto

Favell, A. (2009) 'Immigration, migration, and free movement in the making of Europe', in J. Checkel and P. Katzenstein (eds), *European Identity*, Cambridge: Cambridge University Press, pp 167–189.

Federico, V. and Baglioni, S. (2021) 'Europe's legal peripheries: Migration, asylum and the European labour market', in V. Federico and S. Baglioni (eds), *Migrants, Refugees and Asylum Seekers' Integration in European Labour Markets: A Comparative Approach on Legal Barriers and Enablers*, Cham: Springer, pp 1–18.

Federico, V. and Pannia, P. (2019) 'Migrants' legal statuses in contemporary Italy: First attempts of conceptualization', *Percorsi Costituzionali*, 1: 17–36.

Federico, V. and Pannia, P. (2021) 'The ever-changing picture of the legal framework of migration: A comparative analysis of common trends in Europe and beyond', in S. Barthoma and A.O. Cetrez (eds), *RESPONDing to Migration: A Holistic Perspective on Migration Governance*, Uppsala: Acta Universitatis Upsaliensis, pp 15–43.

Flisi, S., Meroni, E.C. and Vera-Toscano, E. (2016) 'Educational outcomes and immigrant background'. Available at: https://publications.jrc.ec.europa.eu/repository/handle/JRC102629

Frankenberg, G. (2012) 'Comparative constitutional law', in M. Bussani and U. Mattei (eds), *The Cambridge Companion to Comparative Law*, Cambridge: Cambridge University Press, pp 171–190.

Gropas, R. (2021) 'Migrant integration and the role of the EU', in V. Federico and S. Baglioni (eds), *Migrants, Refugees and Asylum Seekers' Integration in European Labour Markets: A Comparative Approach on Legal Barriers and Enablers*, Cham: Springer, pp 73–93.

Hirschl, R. (2014) *Comparative Matters: The Renaissance of Comparative Constitutional Law*, Oxford: Oxford University Press.

Hobsbawm, E. (1996) 'Language, culture, and national identity', *Social Research*, 63(4): 1065–1080.

Lim, D. (2021) 'Low-skilled migrants and the historical reproduction of immigration injustice', *Ethical Theory and Moral Practice*, 24(5): 1229–1244.

Maggini, N. (2021) 'Between numbers and political drivers: What matters in policy-making', in V. Federico and S. Baglioni (eds), *Migrants, Refugees and Asylum Seekers' Integration in European Labour Markets: A Comparative Approach on Legal Barriers and Enablers*, Cham: Springer.

Marbach, M., Hainmueller, J. and Hangartner, D. (2018) 'The long-term impact of employment bans on the economic integration of refugees', *Science Advances*, (4)9: 1–6.

Marcuse, P. (2005) 'Enclaves yes, ghettos no', in P. Varady (ed), *Desegregating the City: Ghettos, Enclaves, and Inequality*, Albany: State University of New York Press, pp 15–30.

Mullally, S. and Murphy, C. (2014) 'Migrant domestic workers in the UK: Enacting exclusions, exemptions, and rights', *Human Rights Quarterly*, 36(2): 397–427.

Pannia, P. (2021) 'Tightening asylum and migration law and narrowing the access to European countries: A comparative discussion', in V. Federico and S. Baglioni (eds), *Migrants, Refugees and Asylum Seekers' Integration in European Labour Markets: A Comparative Approach on Legal Barriers and Enablers*, Cham: Springer, pp 49–71.

Rescigno, P. (1973) 'Situazione e status nell'esperienza del diritto', *Rivista Diritto Civile*, I: 211–212.

Ruiz, I. and Vargas-Silva, C. (2017) 'Are refugees' labour market outcomes different from those of other migrants? Evidence from the United Kingdom in the 2005–2007 period', *Population, Space and Place*, (23)6: 1–15.

Ruiz, I. and Vargas-Silva, C. (2018) 'Differences in labour market outcomes between natives, refugees and other migrants in the UK', *Journal of Economic Geography*, (18)4: 855–885.

Scarciglia, R. (2015) 'Comparative methodology and pluralism in legal comparison in a global age', *Beijing Law Review*, 6(1): 42–48.

Sohn, J. (2014) 'How legal status contributes to differential integration opportunities', *Migration Studies*, 2(3): 369–391.

Triandafyllidou, A. (2013) *Irregular Migrant Domestic Workers in Europe: Who Cares ?*, London: Routledge.

Triandafyllidou, A. and Bartolini, L. (2020) 'Irregular migration and irregular work: A chicken and egg dilemma', in S. Spencer and A. Triandafyllidou (eds) *Migrants with Irregular Status in Europe*, Cham: Springer, pp 139–163.

Zetter, Z. (2007) 'More labels, fewer refugees: Remaking the refugee label in an era of globalization', *Journal of Refugee Studies*, 20(2): 172–192.

Zwysen, W. (2019) 'Different patterns of labor market integration by migration motivation in Europe: the role of host country human capital', *International Migration Review*, (53)1: 59–89.

4

Welfare regimes and labour market integration policies in Europe

Nathan Lillie, Ilona Bontenbal and Quivine Ndomo

Introduction

Migrant labour market integration (LMI) is widely regarded as important both to the migrants themselves, and to the economic and social welfare of the host countries. Because migrants, for a variety of reasons, tend to be less successful in host country labour markets than natives, governments often offer various kinds of support to migrants in finding employment. Migrant integration is often equated with LMI, and policy tools to promote LMI are a form of active labour market policy (ALMP). LMI policies and services consist of practical measures aiming to help migrants, refugees or asylum seekers find employment, or to improve their prospects for finding a job matching their career goals and potential. The form and extent of the offered support varies greatly between countries, with some offering few government services, or services narrowly targeted to small groups (in some cases relying on the third sector), while others have well-resourced bureaucracies offering systematically designed services. The extent and character of LMI policy regimes reflect their embeddedness in broader national welfare regimes, and the role of ALMP in it.

We define LMI policy inductively, based on the active labour market assistance that we find offered to migrants, refugees and asylum seekers in the host countries we investigate. We focus on assistance specifically offered due to their status as migrants seeking to join the job market of their new host state, although many of the policy tools, such as vocational education programmes, are also used to assist native job seekers. Others, such as language courses, are specifically targeted to migrant needs.

We find that integration policies embed deep contradictions, reflecting the way a particular host country engages with migrants generally. While, in general, host countries seek to limit access to welfare state services, including ALMP services, by non-citizens, they also seek to exploit migrants' labour power and skills. LMI services, like ALMP generally (Greer et al, 2017), tend to be caught between a political imperative to punish and control, and a functional imperative to assist. Well-functioning LMI promises to channel less employable migrants towards employment, an idea that, in concept at least, has broad political support. Nonetheless, xenophobic political sentiment and poorly designed policies following from these have, in some of the analysed countries, undermined the goals of LMI policies, as well as made them more punitive towards migrants in intent and outcome. Likewise, there is often a tension between migration management systems, which through various mechanisms function to keep migrants precarious and therefore cheap and highly exploitable, and the stated goals of LMI policies, which often seek to recognise and develop migrants' human capital.

We rely on seven national empirical case studies of the policy enablers and barriers to migrant LMI conducted under the auspices of the SIRIUS project (see Bontenbal and Lillie [2019] for the seven national reports). The seven countries in focus are the Czech Republic, Denmark, Finland, Greece, Italy, Switzerland and the United Kingdom. In the cases of Greece, Italy, the Czech Republic and the UK, low levels of aggregate ALMP spending correspond with poorly funded, narrowly targeted and/or uncoordinated LMI support for migrants. Responsibility for integration shifts to individual migrants, refugees and asylum seekers and their networks, and to civil society actors. Finland and Denmark have a more top-down approach with national level policies guiding national and local approaches to LMI. Switzerland has decentralised LMI policy to the cantons, who manage it through intensive civil society engagement, consistent with how the Swiss welfare state and society is organised. Finland and Denmark have the best funded LMI policies, although restrictive immigration policies, particularly in Denmark, work counter to LMI policy goals.

The text is organised in six sections. The next section summarises relevant literature and the theoretical framework of the chapter, followed by a brief section on methodology. Next is a case-by-case characterisation of LMI policy environment and actual policies in the seven research countries. The following section offers a discussion of findings, while the final section wraps up the chapter with concluding remarks.

Welfare, active labour market policy and migrant labour market integration

In this chapter, we will introduce the framework that guides our analysis, namely the classification of states into various taxonomies according to their citizenship models and welfare models. Based on previous literature we will illustrate how these models shape migrants' LMI. LMI does not operate in a vacuum, but rather is embedded in national welfare regimes (as a social service to workers), capitalist production regimes (as a service to employers) and citizenship regimes (because of its interaction with migration policy). We will first describe the logics behind different typologies. After this, we will summarise the logics behind different types of welfare regimes, with an eye to how these relate to ALMP. Decommodification is central to welfare regime analysis, and this concept has a problematic relation to ALMP, and therefore also to LMI policy. By this reasoning, ALMP and therefore LMI should be marginal and stigmatised in less decommodifying regimes, but less so in social democratic regimes. Based on our analysis, it is not apparent, however, that this is the case.

Welfare regimes and labour market integration policies

Within many areas of social sciences, there have been attempts to classify national states into various typologies, based on stylised macro characteristics thought in some way to describe a nation's institutional setting or cultural milieu. Despite the well-known pitfalls of reifying nation states (Chernilo, 2011), typologies remain a fundamental comparative tool, because our global society is organised into nation states which share many characteristics, but can also be compared and contrasted on others. A major foundation stone of such approaches is that there are certain patterns of institutional relations which occur in some countries but not others. For example, some countries have industry level collective bargaining, while others do not. Some have contributory unemployment systems, while others do not. These characteristics form interconnected national institutional subsystems, which are interdependent, in the sense that changes to a subsystem reverberate throughout all the subsystems. This means the subsystems work together to create path dependencies and tendencies towards equilibrium states which are different for different countries.

There is not one settled typology, but how nations are categorised depends on the characteristics of the different subsystems, and different scholarly concerns. Thus, we have varieties of capitalism (Hall and Soskice, 2001), and national business systems (Morgan, 2007), which are concerned with structural incentives to economic actors. Welfare state regimes depend on political histories and class compromises (Esping-Andersen, 1990). Within migration and citizenship studies, integration has long been supposed to depend on national citizenship models, such as the exclusionist, assimilationist and multicultural models, which reflect the way in which national societies respond to the introduction of 'others' (Finotelli and Michalowski, 2012).

However, as Carrera (2006) points out, models based on conceptions of citizenship have to some extent eroded and they no longer explain integration policies (Carrera, 2006). In fact, migration regimes in Europe have become more similar, partly due to common regulation within the European Union (Koslowski, 1998; Helbling and Kalkum, 2018). Simultaneously also local governance appears to be rising in importance (Doomernik and Bruquetas-Callejo, 2016: 72–73). In fact, we see historical trajectories which reflect in part the policy failures of these models. In particular, we see the inability of exclusionist regimes to prevent long-term settlement of guest workers, the inability of assimilationist regimes to overcome the social exclusion of migrants, and the inability of multicultural regimes to prevent a right-wing populist backlash against migration.

Besides citizenship models, there has also been a good deal of discussion in the literature on welfare states on how models of welfare state shape immigration policy, insofar as states admit or refuse migrants, and the rights migrants have access to (Forsander, 2004). Models of welfare regime have, for example, been shown to shape women's levels of labour market integration, both in terms of labour market participation and career outcomes (Anxo et al, 2007). However, it is important to note that efforts to neatly plug migrant social rights into a 'world of welfare capitalism' taxonomy can sit uncomfortably with the real-world outcomes, because migrants do not automatically receive all the social benefits citizens are entitled to (Geddes, 2003). On the other hand, there are sometimes programmes and entitlements designed especially for them. In the first instance, state institutions are likely to fall back on existing policies or create new ones with analogues to those already in use; for example, a social democratic welfare state is associated with professionalised social workers, who apply their professional ethos and working methods to the problem of migrant integration (see, for example, Valtonen, 2001, 2016).

Welfare state 'regimes', like the other forms of stylised national archetypes used in comparative political economy, rely on historical institutionalist tracing of the rise of various class-based interest formation (Esping-Andersen, 1990), taking into account the timing of when particular events occur, and institutions arise (Therborn, 1984). Path-dependency is caused by the institutionalisation of interactions between the state, civil society and capital, and these tend towards certain equilibrium points, or regimes, each following its own logic. For example, Esping-Andersen lays out the liberal, conservative and social democratic welfare regimes, and his analysis shows that the political histories of the countries he places in these respective categories do indeed lead to sets of social welfare outcomes that correlate quite well to their respective welfare regimes.

The welfare regime shapes the LMI policy options and service offerings of each country case. A central characteristic of welfare regimes, defining a state's position within the taxonomy, is the degree of decommodification of labour, meaning the degree to which workers' standard of living is independent of labour market earnings, due to access to transfer payments and free services. If workers have access to non-labour income streams, such as social benefits can provide, this can raise their 'reservation wage', meaning the wage below which they would rather be unemployed than work. Social democratic regimes have the highest level of decommodification, with extensive benefits, and relatively less emphasis on means-testing and personal contributions. This means that workers are not required to be destitute to receive benefits, and that the level of benefits is relatively high regardless and not closely tied to contributions to benefit funds. This regime is universalist, in that it seeks to provide a decent living standard to all, independent of the market. 'All', in this context, however, refers to citizens, with migrants being potentially or actually excluded from universalist programmes, depending on their migration status. Denmark and Finland's welfare systems largely correspond to Esping-Andersen's social democratic welfare regime.

Conservative welfare regimes, compared to social democratic regimes, have a lower level of decommodification, because benefits tend to be tied to contributions, which relate to earnings. Thus, income transfers between social classes are less important because of the importance of occupational social insurance programmes that reproduce status differentials. There are fewer publicly provided services, particularly for families, a male-breadwinner bias in both tax and transfer systems, and a tendency to devolve authority over delivery and implementation of social policy to non-state actors. Italy's welfare state meets many of these criteria (D'Apice and Fadda, 2003). Additionally, family and relatives assume the central role in providing social buffer against social emergencies such as unemployment and disability, 'allowing' minimal state spending on social services including ALMP and service transfers (Lynch, 2009: 93). From the country cases selected for our research, the Greek system is frequently characterised in this way (see, for example, Ferrera, 1996; Katrougalos, 1996; Kallinikaki, 2010). The system designates the family as the main source of social provision even though the state invests minimally on family social welfare as well as ALMP. The Church also plays a significant role in shaping welfare policies, especially pertaining to the family, as well as directly delivering social services to seriously vulnerable groups (Kallinikaki, 2010: 122).

The UK is an archetypical example of the liberal regime especially concerning England, given that Scotland, Wales and Northern Ireland have own policies which make their welfare regimes different from the English one. This implies there is a 'residual' social welfare state. A minimal social welfare net is provided, but primarily to the destitute, so means-testing is important for programme eligibility. Services are often of poor quality and there is a stigma attached to using them. Switzerland is considered as a 'transitional' regime between liberal and conservative (Trampusch, 2010). The Czech welfare regime has been described as 'post-socialist', but developing into a conservative regime (Aspalter et al, 2009; Aspalter, 2011), which, however, is underfunded and therefore in practice functions as a liberal regime (Saxonberg and Sirovátka, 2009).

Welfare regimes encompass the size, capacity and generosity of the welfare state, but more than that they also determine who pays for it, and who receives benefits. There is therefore also a normative dimension, as the more tightly means-tested a service is, the more likely beneficiaries are to be stigmatised. Since ALMP and LMI programmes rely on employer acceptance of their beneficiaries, stigma is a problem.

Active labour market policy stigma and employer participation

Welfare regimes set the context in terms of the size of welfare state, how it is financed, who receives benefits, and how extensive those benefits are. While social democratic regimes are more universalist, and therefore provide a higher level of services to broader categories of people than conservative or liberal regimes, nonetheless, all differentiate between categories of recipients in terms of their 'deservingness' to receive benefits and services. A survey study conducted by Van Oorschot across 23 European countries finds that natives regard immigrants and refugees at the bottom of a hierarchy of 'deservingness' to receive benefits. There is remarkably little variation across countries, and it is true for universalist welfare states, as well as more marginal ones (van Oorschot, 2006). Active labour market measures, however, serve as a partial exception to this, and the reason is that ALMP is not an unambiguous benefit, but rather includes services, benefits and obligations designed to 'activate' the recipient. This means it is not (necessarily) decommodifying, but also involves commodifying elements.

ALMP programmes, similarly to other welfare state services, tend to be stigmatised if they are targeted exclusively at the destitute. ALMP programmes targeted exclusively towards marginal labour market participants risk being regarded by employers as substandard. Employer views on the programme determine whether they improve participants' labour market opportunities. Employers that have a favourable view of refugees as potential employees also tend to regard LMI programmes for refugees favourably (Fossati and Liechti, 2020). ALMP has been found to function better in systems where it is more universal and 'mainstream', and less well in systems where it is marginal and stigmatised. This is due to the fact that employer opinions about the quality of ALMP programmes and the workers participating in them is a key factor in determining whether those workers will be hired. It is therefore plausible that LMI would exhibit much the same dynamics.

ALMP use micro-level interventions to attempt to remove obstacles for labour market participation by marginal groups, upskill workers to better fill high demand jobs, and increase the efficiency of job searches for employers and job seekers. The core types of ALMP include one or more elements of the following: classroom or on-the-job training, job search assistance or sanctions for failing to search, subsidised private sector employment, and subsidised public sector employment. Passive elements might be designed to supplement the active ones, but without some form of active element, it is not an ALMP. ALMPs can be implemented by governments, including municipalities, or outsourced to private actors (Greer et al, 2017).

Within the welfare regimes literature, ALMPs hold an ambiguous position. ALMPs offer services free of charge, which workers in some cases find useful, but they are also very much oriented towards encouraging and enabling labour market participation. They tend also to have coercive elements, with the availability of passive income maintenance benefits being to some degree dependent on ALMP participation. They therefore can also be considered as commodifying elements, which in theory should not fit well into decommodifying social democratic welfare regimes, but do fit well into liberal regimes. On the other hand, since integration programmes are generally only targeted at the unemployed, there generally needs to be a mechanism in place to ensure the income of migrants during the training. 'Decommodification' is therefore not a straightforward metric for LMI policies.

As Martin and Swank (2004) show, however, ALMPs appear in different kinds of regimes, but they are fitted to the local regime, meaning that despite similar rhetoric and superficially similar policy design, their effects are different in different contexts. In Martin and Swank's analysis, Danish ALMP programmes fit well to the universalist Danish welfare state, while in the UK they tend to be characteristically more minimalist and narrowly aimed at the less well off. This has been identified as a problem for activation policies in the UK, for example, where employers perceive that lower quality workers participate in such programmes, in contrast to Denmark where employers see it as more of a mixed bag (Martin and Swank, 2004). Welfare state ideologies, as well as the various bureaucratic instruments and institutions which spring therefrom, give European host countries certain familiar tools to address the challenges posed by the perceived need to integrate new migrants. The functioning of these tools is not only related to the bureaucratic state apparatus, but also to private actors such as employers whose views on state policies can be key to their success. This insight can also be extended to the role of the third sector, which, as we will see in what follows, is a major actor, perhaps even *the* main actor in all our non-social democratic regime cases.

Methodology

This chapter applies qualitative meta-synthesis techniques to synthesise and summarise policy relevant conclusions from seven discrete and interconnected reports on the barriers and enablers to post-2014 migrants' LMI in the EU (Sandelowski et al, 1997; Zimmer, 2006). Specifically, the chapter develops a typology of the structure, and implication of migrant LMI policies implemented in the Czech Republic, Denmark, Finland,

Greece, Italy, Switzerland and the UK. The core material reviewed consists of seven scientific reports, based on empirical research conducted by seven national teams participating in an international research consortium – Skills and Integration of Migrants, Refugees and Asylum Seekers in European Labour Markets (SIRIUS), based in the seven countries (see Bontenbal and Lillie, 2019). Together, the seven reports constituted the main deliverable of the third work package of the SIRIUS project, which focused on the policy barriers and enablers to migrant LMI. Additionally, the chapter draws on the research project's national reports focusing on the role of civil society in the integration of migrants, asylum seekers and refugees and reports focused on individual enablers and barriers, as individual migrants and civil society emerge as central actors in migrant integration in all case countries (see Numerato et al, 2019; Baglioni and Isaakyan, 2020). The three sets of work package reports at the core of this meta-synthesis were based on qualitative interview data with migrants, asylum seekers and refugees and varied integration stakeholders, as well as relevant secondary data, mainly discourse and policy analysis. The chapter also draws on relevant literature external to the SIRIUS project, especially literature illuminating the theoretical framework applied to the analysis. Thus, our analysis borrows heavily from theoretical work on welfare regimes, and ALMPs.

Country characterisations

In this section, we will go over the country cases selected for our research, keeping in mind the previously introduced welfare regimes. We will analyse how the selected countries fit into these taxonomies of welfare states and their ALMPs, by describing the position of migrants in the labour market and the services that exist to induce LMI in each country.

Czech Republic

The Czech Republic migration regime is based almost entirely on ensuring a fully commodified and exploitable source of labour for its overheated labour market, while minimising the state's obligations to provide services to migrants, and satisfying populist political demands for anti-migrant policies. In recent years, the Czech labour market has experienced labour shortages, so that migrants are generally able to quickly find work, albeit at very low pay levels, and under very poor conditions. Migrants are for the most part seen as a disposable resource, and not encouraged in their career development. This situation suites the Czech authorities, leaving little reason to develop LMI policies.

The Czech government also offers the weakest level of support for migrant integration, entirely focused on integration training for the very small number of refugees the Czech Republic is persuaded to take in. Of the countries characterised in this research, the Czech Republic has the lowest number of migrants (5.5 per cent in 2019) among its population (European Website on Integration, 2019). The Czech Republic only uses 0.46 per cent (2018) of its gross domestic product on ALMPs, which is the lowest among the analysed countries (OECD Stats, 2021), so it would also not have the resources for LMI policy, were it to develop one.

Migration policy in the Czech Republic is highly focused on labour migration and the government promotes a vision of labour migration being mainly short-term and regulated according to the economic needs of the country akin to the guest worker era of the 1960s and 1970s (Gheorghiev et al, 2020). Thus, most migrants come to the Czech Republic with a specific job in mind which is typically in the so-called secondary labour market, in labour-intensive, difficult and sometimes dangerous, low-paid jobs (Drbohlav and Janurová, 2019). Moreover, migrants are often employed through agencies rather than directly by the employer, resulting in a pattern of precariousness (Hoření, 2019). For third country nationals, labour market testing is used, and they are thus allowed to take up job offers only when no applications from Czech or other EU citizens have been made (Drbohlav and Janurová, 2019).

It is important to note how the centrality of labour migration impedes the development of specific LMI policies for all migrant groups in the Czech Republic. For instance, migrants who have short-term residence permits or visas are expected not to stay in the country without work and are therefore not provided any assistance related to skills and career development (Gheorghiev et al, 2020). Although most migrants have the right to use Labour Office services, in practice, these services are not always helpful, since the Labour Office has limited knowledge of the specific needs of migrants and does not offer services or training schemes for foreigners with low language proficiency (Hoření, 2019). There is a State Integration Programme, which is a voluntary one-year assistance programme for asylum holders and holders of subsidiary protection, that has been running since 1994. The programme also includes job counselling (Hoření, 2019). Although most eligible individuals participate in these programmes, the total number of participants remains small since the Czech Republic has traditionally not been an asylum country and the overall number of refugees is small compared to most European countries (Drbohlav and Janurová, 2019). For example, in 2015 only 450 people were eligible for the integration programme (Hoření, 2019). Thus, the integration services are not used by the majority of migrants in the country.

There are also Centres for Support of the Integration of Foreigners in the different regions of the country, funded by the European Commission, which offer language courses, sociocultural courses, and legal and social counselling (Hoření, 2019). However, in practice, there is a chronic lack of language courses (Numerato et al, 2019), which hinders the integration process. Migrants themselves report that the lack of Czech language skills especially undermines their access to better-paid employment (Gheorghiev et al, 2020).

Filling the gap left by the state, non-governmental organisations (NGOs) have a significant role in offering integration services, such as individual social and legal counselling, language courses, and the organisation of social events (Hoření, 2019; Hoření et al, 2019). However, funding for NGO-driven integration services is project-based and short-term. This partly explains why NGOs' assisting programmes have been found, in practice, to have a limited penetration capacity, with many economic migrants not even being aware of the existence of such programmes (Gheorghiev et al, 2020).

While there is little support for LMI, since 1 January 2021, foreign nationals have had to take a compulsory four-hour 'adaptation and integration course' organised by the Centres for Support of the Integration of Foreigners. This course is compulsory for foreign nationals who are issued a long-term residence permit and foreign nationals who are issued a permanent residence permit within one year of the date of collecting their residence permit. This does not apply to European Union citizens and their family members (Ministry of the Interior of the Czech Republic, 2021).

Denmark

Denmark is a social democratic welfare state with universalist institutions, and this fact is reflected in its extensive and well-resourced ALMP bureaucracy, which is also used for the LMI of migrants. Danish politics, however, have become increasingly anti-immigrant, and this fact is reflected in coercive elements in the way ALMP is applied to migrants. In particular, the 'employment first' element devalues migrant skills through excessive emphasis on finding employment, at the expense of career development. In 2020, 12.30 per cent of the Danish population were foreign born. A comprehensive Act of Immigration has been implemented since 1998 (Jørgensen, 2014), and of the countries characterised in this research, Denmark spent the most of its GDP on ALMP – 2.87 per cent in 2018 (OECD Stats, 2021). This reflects the importance of the 'flexicurity' model of employment activation policy for which Denmark is known.

In Denmark, success in integration is only measured by employment. The Danish discussion on migration is highly polarised, and integration policy reflects the contradictions internal to this political consensus. High-skilled individuals and their family members are perceived as beneficial to the Danish state. Asylum seekers, refugees and their families, on the other hand, are seen as unskilled (regardless of their actual level of skill) and as a burden

(Sen et al, 2019: 177, 183). This policy discourse reflects in the very limited number of services targeted at highly skilled migrants, who are considered to easily integrate into the labour market, whereas most available services are targeted at speedily pushing refugees and their family members into the first available employment. However, despite the central place of asylum seekers in the political discussion, they and their dependents constitute a very small percentage of the entire migrant population in Denmark. In 2020, of all the residence permits granted in Denmark, only circa 1 per cent were granted based on asylum and circa 8 per cent based on family reunification (Statista, 2021). Most third country national migrants enter Denmark on the basis of a work permit issued in relation to a particular job, in which case they are already employed and do not use LMI services.

The three-year integration programme is the core of the Danish integration policy. During the integration programme migrants are offered civic education, Danish language classes and job activation. Job activation includes activities such as counselling, skills-upgrading courses, internships and sometimes subsidised employment. For unemployed migrants, the programme is mandatory and non-participation can lead to the withdrawal of introduction benefits (European Commission Integration Information, 2021). The Danish integration is managed top-down and the main responsibility of implementing the integration programme lies with the municipalities, which often contract NGOs and private organisations to implement the activities (see Sen and Pace, 2019). Asylum centres provide basic education and language lessons to individuals awaiting a decision on their asylum application.

During the integration process refugees and their family members are expected to take on any job from day one, without questioning the type of job, or the suitability of it to the migrants' skills, qualifications or aspirations. Especially since the 'employment first' integration policy was implemented in 2015, municipal authorities have been 'pushing' migrants to take on any kind of job (Sen et al, 2019). From the perspective of migrants, this leads to devaluation of their skills and qualifications as well as being forced to reconsider their professional aspirations (Bjerre et al, 2020: 69). Furthermore, since 2019, the focus regarding refugees has shifted from integration to return, that is, the aim is to send refugees back to their country of origin as soon as conditions allow it (European Commission Integration Information, 2021). This also signals the fact that in Denmark the topic of integration is highly politicised (Jørgensen, 2014).

Finland

Like the Danish system, Finland's LMI is embedded in a well-developed ALMP infrastructure. While many migrants experience being pushed towards certain high-demand occupations, and needing to reskill as a result, Finland does not have the same 'employment first' emphasis as Denmark. Nonetheless, employment discrimination often in the end has similar effects – taking the first available job, because highly educated migrants choose to take unskilled jobs because employers in their field do not hire workers of their ethnicity. This is particularly common among members of visible minorities (Ndomo and Lillie, 2020). However, this is not a problem created by the *employment services*, but rather a reflection of employer attitudes and societal racism. Similar to the other Nordic countries, Finland spends comparatively highly on ALMP – 2.21 per cent of GDP in 2018 (OECD Stats, 2021). Most migrants in Finland come from neighbouring countries, such as Russia and Estonia. Labour migrants and family migrants form the largest stream, whereas asylum seekers and refugees form a significantly smaller stream of migrants. Of the countries characterised in this chapter, Finland has the second lowest number of migrants among the population (circa 7 per cent).

Compared to the other countries in the study, Finland's integration efforts are in many ways the most comprehensive; they are grounded in a coherent set of legislation, receive stable funding from the state, and offer a variety of services to migrants, refugees and asylum seekers. Integration services in Finland are delivered through an elaborate bureaucracy of state actors at both national and local level. As with the Danish integration policy, the Finnish integration policy is also very much focused on getting migrants into gainful employment and employment is considered synonymous to integration. This means employed migrants do not have access to most state-provided integration services such as free language courses. In Finland, all unemployed job seeking migrants or migrants that are considered to be living permanently (all migrants except those on a visa, or B permit for studies) can participate in integration training for up to 3–5 years after migration, and during this time they can receive income support. This does, however, exclude migrants who are students, and who are thus not considered unemployed, and asylum seekers, who are not considered to live in Finland permanently. In practice, however, both groups can take up employment, within specific regulations, and will therefore also experience unemployment and in-between job periods. Students have to rely on services offered by their education institutions and by NGOs, while asylum seekers mainly rely on services provided by the asylum reception centres, as they do not fit the migrant group targeted by most NGO service providers (see Bontenbal and Lillie, 2019).

The cornerstone of Finland's LMI policy is the integration training which is a component of the official integration programme. Integration training is in principle individualised based on the unique characteristics and needs of a migrant or refugee, although in practice this seems not to work as well as it should. Typically, it features a wide variety of discrete services such as language courses, labour market skill training, vocational training, internships, as well as compulsory education components such as reading and writing courses for special groups. Compared to the 'official' integration training, the courses offered by asylum reception centres for asylum seekers are far less comprehensive; once an asylum seeker receives a positive decision, however, LMI services become available.

The structure of the Finnish integration system is top-down, meaning that all levels of the state bureaucracy are involved and play a major role in implementation of services (see Bontenbal and Lillie, 2019). Employment offices (TE-offices) that spread across municipalities have a central role. Together with other municipality bodies, they are solely responsible for designing individual integration plans for migrants and for arranging integration training. The non-profit sector, on the other hand, has a limited and supplementary role to the state, also in terms of those policies and processes surrounding the integration of migrants (Bontenbal and Lillie, 2021). However, often course implementation is outsourced to learning institutes and NGOs.

Taking part in integration training is not compulsory for migrants. However, income support benefits may be reduced due to not taking part in the planned integration activities. There is no integration test. For those applying for citizenship there is a language test.

Greece

In Greece, LMI lags behind reception and immigration control as a policy priority, and there is no singular coherent LMI policy for migrants, refugees and asylum seekers (Bagavos et al, 2019). A unique dichotomy between pre- and post-2014 migration trends characterised by changing migrant demographics and host country context shape migrant LMI needs and outcomes in Greece. Pre-2014 migration featured widespread irregular migration practices, encouraged by an inefficient and ineffective bureaucratic residence permit and visa system, and overlooked to sustain a stream of economic migrants integrated solely through a labour market in need of labour (Bagavos et al, 2019). Post-2014 migration (of refugees and asylum seekers) faced greater LMI challenges owing to lingering adverse economic effects of the 2008 recession and budding informal labour market practices institutionalised by prior migration trends. The country also struggles with balancing resources between reception and integration for a population that was often not interested in integrating in Greece in the first place, seeing it rather as a transition point to other European countries (Bagavos and Kourachanis, 2020). Additional features of the Greek welfare system are divisions between the mainland and islands and urban and rural territories which usually undermine access of the islands and rural areas to social services. Of the seven countries compared in the chapter, Greece has the third largest migrant population, constituting circa 12.58 per cent of its entire population in 2020.

Despite stark LMI challenges, migrants' potential economic contribution as labour is desired, due largely to a declining native workforce and an established taste for cheap, malleable labour among employers in specific sectors such as agriculture. However, anti-migrant and xenophobic sentiment is present and shapes both political discourse and implementation of specific migrant integration policies exemplified, for example, by the botched implementation of a special work permit for irregular workers (Bagavos et al, 2019: 322).

Labour markets for migrants are strongly segmented by nationality-ethnicity, placing many migrants in informal and precarious work situations (Bagavos and Kourachanis, 2020). The conservative-corporatist nature of Greece's welfare regime therefore ensures that migrants are only minimally decommodified. This, coupled with weak ALMP spending generally, means that state-managed services are few, although there is a decentralised system with strong participation of local communities in governance, and civil society in implementation. Greece's welfare regime is commonly classified as conservative, but with a stronger role for families in social provision and with social contributions, it provides differential social protection that tends to favour the male 'breadwinner figure'. Since women are the main carers for children and the elderly, this welfare model hinders their labour market participation, a phenomenon that impacts migrant single-parent families (the common situation) even more severely (Bagavos and Kourachanis, 2020). However, alternatively, the availability of cheap migrant labour for care work functionally compensates for a lack of state support, by allowing families who can afford it to hire private caregivers more cheaply.

Lacking a dedicated migrant integration programme, LMI policy in Greece is grounded in the general 2018 National Integration Strategy. The strategy adopts a social integration model, thus prioritising access to education, the labour market and public services as pathways to integrate migrants and beneficiaries of international protection in Greece. The strategy also designates local communities as central actors in developing and delivering LMI services, with oversight from the central government administration. However, civil society organisations deliver most LMI services, and migrant and refugee associations, NGOs and UN agencies are the main providers of actual reception and integration services in Greece. LMI services in Greece are co-financed by international organisations and are exclusively available in mainland Greece while excluding asylum seekers arriving in the Greek islands after March 2016. However, the national integration strategy lacks a dedicated implementation framework and there is no evidence that it is being implemented at all as of 2021 (Bagavos and Kourachanis, 2020: 148).

In addition to a limited capacity, civil society integration services are however not obligatory, and migrants can opt out of services, which they often do, guided by their view of Greece as a transition and not settlement country.

All legal residents of Greek municipalities enjoy 'equal access' to available social welfare services, health clinics and employment services, meaning that no services are tailored specifically for migrants. Municipalities operate community centres that provide the services. The centres also run the Public Employment Service (OAED) that provide unemployment services including unemployment benefits, subsidised vocational training programmes and employment counselling as well as family allowance, maternity allowance or day nurseries – indicative of ALMP trends (see Bagavos et al, 2019). However, many migrants are unable to access the scarce OAED and its services and turn instead to private employment agencies which often direct migrants into the 'migrant' labour market and occupations rife with informality and discrimination (Bagavos and Kourachanis, 2020).

Since 2017 there has been some progress in Greek LMI, especially the development of a more organised and systematic reception and identification system for asylum seekers (Bagavos and Kourachanis, 2020), in addition to legislative procedures simplifying and devolving residence permit issue and renewal processes to combat informal work (Bagavos et al, 2019). However, myriad LMI barriers withstand. The most significant shortfall is the lack of clear, coherent and enforced LMI policy, and the will and mandate for actors to develop one (Bagavos and Kourachanis, 2020: 143). Second is the sustenance of informal economy practices grounded in a robust history of ethnicity-nationality based discrimination and exploitation of migrant labour. Third is the complete absence of a national mechanism for recognition of foreign qualifications and skills, resulting in more migrants being routed to unskilled and informal work. Lastly, the extent to which integration services are targeted to specific migrant groups undermines migrant LMI. In Greece, integration services are predominantly mere extensions of generic public socioeconomic services rather than tailored services for migrants, refugees and asylum seekers. Where some targeting is done, refugees and asylum seekers in mainland Greece are the dominant beneficiaries, while migrants and asylum seekers in the islands are largely excluded. The result is that historical strata are likely to reproduce even with regards to the new population of migrants, refugees and asylum seekers in Greece.

Italy

Italy operates multiple fragmented LMI policies, implemented through a poorly coordinated and poorly financed network of actors spread across different levels of government – national and local – and sectors – public and private. As with the Greek policy, LMI outcomes reflect the highly segmented nature of the Italian labour market, between formal and informal sectors, with many migrants drawn into the informal sector to provide the cheap, exploitable labour on which much economic activity depends. Italian migration policies serve to reinforce the informal migration system which provides labour willing to accept precarious jobs. Migrants with formal status are assisted (or not) by the same labour market services and decommodifying welfare rights as Italian citizens, but nonetheless tend to face pay discrimination and undervaluation of their skills (Collini and Pannia, 2020). In Italy, LMI services are well targeted towards migrants' needs but fragmented and under-resourced. Civil society organisations have a central role in the running of LMI services, which are mainly targeted at refugees. Outcomes for migrants who arrived for international protection are shaped by LMI policies, while those who arrived for other reasons rely more heavily on personal networks and family contacts.

The dominant political narrative template on migration and migrants in Italy today, best evidenced by the 2018 elections, securitises migration to promote deterrent policy instruments such as the 'Salvini decree' for the stricter management of immigration. Although seemingly marginal, Italy's nascent politically driven anti-immigration rhetoric undermines the policies at the heart of its integration service delivery – the Sistema di Protezione per Richiedenti Asilo e Rifugiati (SPRAR) network, renamed as SAI (Sistema di Accoglienza e Integrazione) in 2020.

Historically underdeveloped state-run public social service infrastructure coupled with administrative competence vested only in local institutions of regions and municipalities (Lynch, 2009: 104) reflects in the apparatus of Italy's main migrant LMI policy implementer – the SAI network. This consists of a network of local actors from across the public and the private sector including municipality institutions, civil society actors such as NGOs and corporative associations, and companies who are the primary integration service providers in Italy (Maggini and Ibrido, 2019). The SAI network draws together a number of actors in collaboration, but only targets beneficiaries of international protection and unaccompanied minors.

Newly arrived post-2014 migrants, disproportionally consisting of asylum seekers and refugees, draw little benefit from LMI policies. Poor funding equals limited or non-existent integration services for asylum seekers in tier one reception centres where most new arrivals are concentrated (Maggini and Ibrido, 2019). However, second tier reception centres run by the state-funded SAI network provide comprehensive integration services including language training, upskilling, health and legal support, and employment services, albeit only to beneficiaries of international protection and unaccompanied minors (Maggini and Ibrido, 2019: 216). Integration services target confirmed 'stayers', excluding asylum seekers who have yet to receive a decision on their status.

Economic and family migrants are not the central target of LMI programmes in Italy but have access to public social services in education, health and employment 'equal' to citizens, although equality here is defined narrowly in terms of access, not outcomes. Economic migrants have 'integration agreements', which are not labour market focused but include compulsory learning of Italian language, ethics and fundamental principles of the Italian constitution, but lack of funding for this programme hampers implementation. Economic migrants' residential status is tied to this obligation to learn Italian language, ethics and fundamental constitution principles. Unemployed refugees and asylum seekers are exempt from paying all or part of healthcare costs upon registering with the Public Employment Service. Asylum seekers stay in reception centres while unemployed or when employed with earnings below 5,889 euros annually. The extremely low earnings ceiling threatens to exclude from the reception centres many who would be unable to afford housing in the external market, effectively pushing them to informal sector work and undermining other integration policies combating the informal market in Italy (Maggini and Ibrido, 2019: 422). In general, limited finances from national public funds and Asylum, Migration and Integration Funds undermine ALMP programmes such as Employment Services in Italy.

At the national level, welfare benefits are available exclusively for long-term residents in dire need. Specifically, healthcare is guaranteed only for urgent and essential needs, while access to social housing is reserved for legally resident migrants temporarily unable to afford their own accommodation and subsistence needs. Separately, the Ministry of Labour – through the Agency Italia Lavoro Spa – supports projects delivering socio-occupational integration services for vulnerable migrant groups (pregnant women, children and elderly) through individualised integration plans. Asylum seekers and refugees are also legislatively considered vulnerable groups in Italy with regards to training internships.

The outcome of migrant LMI programmes in Italy is a mix of successes and shortfalls. A success is the SAI network, which epitomises best practices in LMI through its comprehensive integration services and outstanding performers such as training internships and public–private collaboration in integration service delivery.

> The area dedicated to training and job orientation is one of the most developed, and most important within the association [network] itself. Pairing this with targeted internships and training in cooperation with local enterprises, results successful integration of large numbers of migrants in the local job market, with many now having stable contracts. (Maggini and Collini, 2019: 152–153)

On the contrary, skills and qualifications of migrants largely go unrecognised formally or in practice, evidenced by migrants, asylum seeker and refugee narratives of underemployment, and are poorly rewarded in terms of remuneration (Collini and Pannia, 2020: 187). In turn, migrants in Italy remain vulnerable and susceptible to exploitation in both the formal and informal labour market, furthering existing labour market segmentation and occupational differentiation patterns (Maggini and Ibrido, 2019: 427). Additionally, migrants, asylum seekers and refugees who pass through the national and subnational integration programmes fall short of achieving social integration or autonomy as graduates of the system struggle to manoeuvre the labour market for a job and society for accommodation on their own once out of the system.

Switzerland

Switzerland is sometimes portrayed as a 'liberal' welfare state, but a coordinated market economy; some scholars consider it as a conservative Central European welfare state, as a result of the heavy participation of civil society actors in managing public policies. Trampusch (2010: 58) refers to it as a 'post-liberal' welfare state, which is 'right on the divide between liberal and conservative welfare states'. Policymaking is heavily decentralised to cantons, and very much embedded in the agreements negotiated between the social partners. The canton-centric nature of the policy is reflected in the way refugees are randomly distributed among cantons, which is a political solution to share the burden among the cantons, but which is not helpful for migrant LMI (Mexi et al, 2021). This random resettlement system takes no account of the refugee's existing language skills, which means that a French-speaking refugee might be placed in a German-speaking canton, resulting in a more difficult integration process (Auer, 2018). Also, there is a tendency to try to shift responsibilities between government levels: municipal, canton, federal, as well as between civil society actors and the state (Russi et al, 2020: 221). According to the Federal Statistics Office, more than one-third of the Swiss population has an immigrant background, while over one-quarter of the population over 15 years old living permanently in the country was born abroad (FSO, 2018: Mexi, 2021).

Civil society organisations are involved most often as state-policy implementers of integration policies, but this is up to the canton which is the primary shaper of integration policy. This way of organising policy reflects Switzerland's close relations between political institutions and organised civil society, so that unions, employer organisations, civil society organisations and local political structures are cooperatively involved in both policymaking and implementation. Thus, Caritas, for example, is a primary player in integration programmes for refugees in Geneva, but this is different in each locality.

There are also some civil society orgnisations that fill gaps in services not provided by government policy. Swiss law places the main responsibility for LMI on 'established frameworks', or mainstream unemployment, welfare or education services. However, often these do not meet the needs of specific categories of migrants, because of low language skills, or lack of time to invest in particular programmes or because the services offered do not meet their needs. The specialised programmes of the cantons therefore aim to fill these gaps (Russi et al, 2020: 221–222).

As with our other case countries, in Switzerland, migrants' skills and diplomas are often undervalued due to prejudices and assumptions made about certain nationalities and ethnicities. As in the Finnish case, it is often employer attitudes more than migrant skills that require improvement. As one Swiss stakeholder points out: "Integration projects need to break down those prejudices by showing through examples, that migrants have the capacity to work and to integrate" (SIRIUS Switzerland Work Package 3, Stakeholder Representative 9). Difficulties both in having diplomas formally recognised as well as in having foreign diplomas and suitability for skilled positions valorised by employers characterise migrant experiences. Discrimination is a common experience, as well as difficulties in coping with Swiss bureaucracy; migrants commonly do not fit into the necessary categories.

United Kingdom

The United Kingdom is a liberal market economy (Hall and Soskice, 2001) with a liberal welfare state model (Esping-Andersen, 1990). This implies that the labour market is minimally regulated, so that entry to low-wage, precarious work is relatively easy for migrants. On the other hand, welfare state support is at a low level and intended primarily for the truly destitute. This means strict means-testing for access to benefits and programmes, which is reflected in programme access. Consistent with liberal market ideology, responsibility for integrating is almost entirely on the migrant. Aside from special government programmes for refugee resettlement, there is little in the way of ALMPs for migrants. Government programmes for job seekers such as Job Centre are available, but with the same well-documented limitations and problems which arise for natives, including heavy-handed disciplinary regimes enforced through the threat of benefit cuts, and programme metrics which incentivise taking easy-to-place clients and ignoring those who need support (see Greer et al, 2017, for a discussion of these). Civil society organisations are used for the delivery of public services for migrant integration, and this forms part of a general government tendency towards privatisation and marketisation of services, allowing government to capture the third sector to turn it into a not-very-effective welfare service arm. ALMP budget cuts have, however, reduced the role of third sector organisations in providing labour market services to migrants (Calò et al, 2021).

Even more than the other SIRIUS countries, the UK has an explicit 'hostile environment' policy towards foreign nationals (and certain of its own nationals), which serves as an impediment to integration (Lidher et al, 2020). The hostile environment policies are inconsistently applied policies, nominally designed to target 'illegal' immigration, but which through seemingly deliberate incompetence, serve the purpose of making life as difficult as possible for migrants. This is reflected in the gap between LMI policymakers and implementers: policy implementers in the UK tend to regard policymakers as deliberately obstructing LMI of migrants. At the UK level, policymakers do not regard LMI as a host-state responsibility (Calò et al, 2022).

Specifically, there is a refugee resettlement scheme, which is regarded as well-designed for assisting in LMI of refugees (Calò et al, 2022), but which was targeted only at certain refugees, and therefore not broadly accessible. Related to this, a major limitation for job market access for asylum seekers is that there is a lengthy period for reviewing applications, during which the asylum seeker does not have a right to work. The work ban on asylum seekers, particularly when combined with sometimes years-long asylum application periods has a major impact on the quality of life and career development of refugees. While in principle the time could be spent in learning activities, fragmentation and low funding levels for language courses and other programmes for integrating migrants mean that these programmes are inadequate in availability and quality (Calò et al, 2022).

While the UK is in principle a unitary state, its constituent components have in some cases received greater responsibilities through devolution, and this is most noticeable in Scotland, which has taken a different approach from the central government in being more welcoming towards migrants, in terms of taking a more careful and evidence based approach to programme design, and also in not engaging in 'hostile environment' types of rhetoric (Calò et al, 2019: 567). Despite the existence of various programmes and services, the UK's LMI policy regime can be characterised as incoherent. There is no universal programme; the programmes that do exist are either narrow (that is, refugee resettlement), or minimalist and stigmatised (that is, Job Centre). Thus, integration does de facto become the responsibility of the migrant.

Summary of cases

A summary of the cases can be found in Table 4.1.

Southern European countries, such as Italy and Greece, found themselves with inadequately developed policy frameworks to meet the challenges

Table 4.1: Summary of the cases

	Welfare regime	ALMP spending	ALMP-LMI organisation	Eligibility for core LMI services	Other remarks
Czech Republic	Conservative/ liberal	Low	Fragmented, NGO-managed	Only refugees for state services, limited availability for others	Tight labour market, migrants as disposable resource
Denmark	Social democratic	High	Highly coercive/well resourced	Broad but especially targeted at refugees	'Jobs first', segmentation reinforcement
Finland	Social democratic	High	Mildly coercive service oriented/well resourced, top down	Broad, not only specific migrant groups: based on labour market status	Down-skilling and reskilling to migrant dominated professions
Greece	Conservative	Low	Fragmented, NGO-managed	Low capacity, limited availability	Informal labour market, segmentation
Italy	Conservative	Medium	Fragmented, NGO-managed	Low capacity, limited availability	Informal labour market, segmentation
Switzerland	Conservative/ liberal	Medium	Decentralised, corporatist	Only for refugees	Managed by cantons with strong NGO and social partner participation
UK	Liberal	Low	Fragmented, outsourced to NGOS	Refugees	'Hostile environment', tight labour market

brought on by migration. In these two, large economic sectors such as agriculture and home care have become dependent on migrant labour working informally. A common character of the Southern European integration policies has been that they have generally been elaborated from the bottom up. In Greece and Italy, NGOs play a very significant role in the implementation of integration policy, which suffers from a lack of central government funding. Integration policies thus started from the local and regional level, which is also why policies have been different from one area to another. Since the 2000s, however, efforts have been made to produce centralised national frameworks (Doomernik and Bruquetas-Callejo, 2016: 61–63).

In Central and Eastern European countries, the number of immigrants has been relatively small and so have the policy responses. Policy initiatives are largely EU-driven and accession to the EU has pushed countries to develop their policies in this area (Doomernik and Bruquetas-Callejo, 2016: 64, 71). Of the SIRIUS countries, Czech policy can be characterised in this way. However, the Czech Republic, due to economic growth and labour shortages, now hosts large numbers of labour migrants, whose integration prospects suffer from a lack of integration programmes. Formal publicly funded integration programmes in the Czech Republic are on a small scale, and targeted only at refugees. The UK is similar in that official anti-migrant hostility is combined with an economic need for migrants. The division between liberal (UK) and conservative (Czech) regimes is quite blurred in terms of LMI policy.

In Denmark, Finland and Switzerland, LMI policies are organised in a more 'top-down' manner, with state and quasi-state actors at the centre. The basic framework is set out by legislation in Denmark and Finland, and by multistakeholder canton-level initiatives in Switzerland. These policies are then implemented by bureaucracies in Finland and Denmark, and by a variety of quasi-state actors in Switzerland. Actors, such as NGOs and employers, are involved in implementation in all three countries, but the policy can be said in some sense to be state-driven. Although Finland's and Denmark's systems and policy context are broadly similar, Denmark's more punitive 'employment first' policy shows that policy intentions matter: policies that are deliberately cruel by design unsurprisingly have negative effects on their target groups, even if the programmes are well-funded and efficiently implemented.

Conclusion

We focus on migrant integration as public policy, which means that government activities are at the centre of the analysis, although the implementers of these policies are sometimes private or third sector organisations (see Numerato et al, 2019). Our analysis suggests that welfare policy regimes play an important role in shaping LMI policy, but this is more due to the residual effect of having ALMP structures, norms and policies in place, than employer demands or a deep-set political consensus.

According to Esping-Andersen (1990), central characteristics for classifying welfare regimes relate to how decommodifying and how universal they are. ALMP is not centrally about either commodification or decommodification, per se, although ALMP policies can be put to such use. LMI policies are by nature targeted at a special group – unemployed migrants – but can be more or less universal in terms of which migrants have access, and types of services provided. In this respect, LMI policy goals can be divided into two categories: helping migrants to find employment (that is, reducing their rate of unemployment), and helping migrants to achieve their career goals. Either can involve skill, language and job market training, or job brokerage, and the goals can complement each other. However, they differ insofar as the first is more about reducing social welfare budgets, and providing employers with workers, and the second more about granting migrants greater agency in navigating the host country job market. Migrants are a diverse group; from the ALMP perspective an individual's 'distance' from the labour market, and the kind of work he or she can realistically seek, is important in evaluating the type of support that should be offered. Seeking to upskill migrants, or to place highly skilled migrants in highly skilled jobs is more consistent with universalist welfare state aspirations, while pushing migrants, regardless of their skills, quickly into menial positions is more characteristic of a remedial welfare state.

However, from our cases, we find this is partly the situation in Finland where there is an aspiration to universalism in the LMI policy intent, but in Denmark, where high skilled migrants are deliberately pushed into low skill employment, universalism seems to be reserved for Danish nationals. As welfare regime theory predicts, the UK, as a liberal regime, lacks coherent national policies, and the policies it does have are small scale, and targeted to only the worst off. Similarly, the conservative regimes (Italy and Greece) also have smaller scale policies than those under social democratic regimes, due to less generous state funding, because such regimes de-emphasise wealth transfers between insiders and outsiders. Services are therefore more targeted and less universal. Switzerland and the Czech Republic are, in the literature, sometimes classified as liberal and sometimes as conservative, but for LMI policies it makes little difference as both conservative and liberal regimes are characterised by small, targeted 'resettlement' programmes for refugees and an important role for civil society organisations. The welfare regimes and ALMP literature suggests that participation in narrowly targeted LMI policies might carry a stigma, particularly among workers in liberal welfare states, but the interview data of the analysed reports did not give us a definitive answer on this topic. While there were indications from the interviewees in Denmark, and to a lesser extent in Finland, that they felt the LMI process demeaned them and devalued their skills, this is precisely the opposite of what we would expect. More detailed information, in particular from employers, would be needed to resolve this anomalous finding. We conclude that welfare regimes are clearly important in shaping terms of state capacities for LMI, but might be more usefully described in terms of state capacities. Furthermore, just as important is the politics of migrant inclusion and exclusion, which inform how, and for whom, those capacities are used.

References

Anxo, D., Fagan, C., Cebrian, I. and Moreno, G. (2007) 'Patterns of labour market integration in Europe: A life course perspective on time policies', *Socio-Economic Review*, 5(2): 233–260.

Aspalter, C. (2011) 'The development of ideal-typical welfare regime theory', *International Social Work*, 54(6): 735–750.

Aspalter, C., Jinsoo, K. and Sojeung, P. (2009) 'Analysing the welfare state in Poland, the Czech Republic, Hungary and Slovenia: An ideal-typical perspective', *Social Policy & Administration*, 43(2): 170–185.

Auer, D. (2018) 'Language roulette: The effect of random placement on refugees' labour market integration', *Journal of Ethnic and Migration Studies*, 44(3): 341–362.

Bagavos, C. and Kourachanis, N. (2020) 'Greece', in S. Baglioni and I. Isaakyan (eds), *Integration of Migrants, Refugees, and Asylum Seekers: Individual Barriers and Enablers*, SIRIUS WP6 integrated report. Available at: https://www.sirius-project.eu/sites/default/files/attachments/Individual%20Barriers%20and%20Enablers.pdf

Bagavos, C., Lagoudakou, K., Kourachanis, N., Chatzigiannakou, K. and Touri, P. (2019) 'Greece', in I. Bontenbal and N. Lillie (eds), *Integration of Migrants, Refugees and Asylum Seekers: Policy Barriers and Enablers*, SIRIUS WP3 integrated report. Available at: https://www.sirius-project.eu/sites/default/files/attachments/WP3%20Integrated%20report%20D3.2.pdf

Baglioni, S. and Isaakyan, I. (eds) (2020) *Integration of Migrants, Refugees, and Asylum Seekers: Individual Barriers and Enablers*, SIRIUS WP6 integrated report. Available at: https://www.sirius-project.eu/sites/default/files/attachments/Individual%20Barriers%20and%20Enablers.pdf

Bjerre, L., Pace, M. and Sen, S. (2020) 'Denmark', in S. Baglioni and I. Isaakyan (eds), *Integration of Migrants, Refugees, and Asylum Seekers: Individual Barriers and Enablers*, SIRIUS WP6 integrated report. Available at: https://www.sirius-project.eu/sites/default/files/attachments/Individual%20Barriers%20and%20Enablers.pdf

Bontenbal, I. and Lillie, N. (2019) *Integration of Migrants, Refugees and Asylum Seekers: Policy Barriers and Enablers*, SIRIUS WP3 integrated report. Available at: https://www.sirius-project.eu/sites/default/files/attachments/WP3%20Integrated%20report%20D3.2.pdf

Bontenbal, I. and Lillie, N. (2021) 'Minding the gaps: The role of Finnish civil society organizations in the labour market integration of migrants', *Voluntas*. DOI: https://doi.org/10.1007/s11266-021-00334-w

Calò, F., Montgomery, T. and Baglioni, S. (2019) 'United Kingdom', in I. Bontenbal and N. Lillie (eds), *Integration of Migrants, Refugees and Asylum Seekers: Policy Barriers and Enablers,* SIRIUS WP3 integrated report. Available at: https://www.sirius-project.eu/sites/default/files/attachments/Individual%20Barriers%20and%20Enablers.pdf

Calò, F., Montgomery, T. and Baglioni, S. (2021) 'Marginal players? Third sector and employability services for migrants, refugees and asylum seekers in the UK', *Voluntas*. DOI: https://doi.org/10.1007/s11266-020-00306-6

Calò, F., Montgomery, T. and Baglioni, S. (2022) 'You have to work … but you can't!: Contradictions of the active labour market policies for refugees and asylum seekers in the UK', *Journal of Social Policy*. DOI: https://doi.org/10.1017/S0047279422000502

Carrera, S. (2006) 'A comparison of integration programmes in the EU: Trends and weaknesses', Challenge Papers No. 1, March 2006. Brussels: Center for European Policy Studies (CEPS).

Chernilo, D. (2011) 'The critique of methodological nationalism: Theory and history', *Thesis Eleven*, 106(1): 98–117.

Collini, M. and Pannia, P. (2020) 'Italy', in S. Baglioni and I. Isaakyan (eds), *Integration of Migrants, Refugees, and Asylum Seekers: Individual Barriers and Enablers*, SIRIUS WP6 integrated report. Available at: https://www.sirius-project.eu/sites/default/files/attachments/Individual%20Barriers%20and%20Enablers.pdf

D'Apice, C. and Fadda, S. (2003) 'The Italian welfare system in the European context', *Review of Social Economy*, 61(3): 317–339.

Doomernik, J. and Bruquetas-Callejo, M. (2016) 'National immigration and integration policies in Europe since 1973', in Garcés-Mascareñas, B. and Penninx, R. (eds), *Integration Processes and Policies in Europe*, Cham: Springer, pp 57–76.

Drbohlav, D. and Janurová, K. (2019) 'Migration and integration in Czechia: Policy advances and the hand brake of populism', Migration Policy Institute. Available at: https://www.migrationpolicy.org/article/migration-and-integration-czechia-policy-advances-and-hand-brake-populism

Esping-Andersen, G. (1990) *The Three Worlds of Welfare Capitalism*, Princeton: Princeton University Press.

European Commission Integration Information (2021) 'Governance of migrant integration in Denmark'. Available at: https://ec.europa.eu/migrant-integration/governance/denmark

European Website on Integration (2019) 'Situation of foreigners, migration and integration in the Czech Republic 2019'. Available at: https://ec.europa.eu/migrant-integration/librarydoc/situation-of-foreigners-migration-and-integration-in-the-czech-republic-2019

Federal Statistic Office (FSO) (2018) Enquête Suisse de la population active (ESPA), Neuchâtel: Office Fédéral de la Statistique.

Ferrera, M. (1996) 'The "southern model" of welfare in social Europe', *Journal of European Social Policy*, 6(1): 17–37.

Finotelli, C. and Michalowski, I. (2012) 'The heuristic potential of models of citizenship and immigrant integration reviewed', *Journal of Immigrant & Refugee Studies*, 10(3): 231–240.

Forsander, A. (2004) 'Social capital in the context of immigration and diversity: Economic participation in the Nordic welfare states', *Journal of International Migration and Integration/Revue de l'integration et de la migration internationale*, 5(2): 207–227.

Fossati, F. and Liechti, F. (2020) 'Integrating refugees through active labour market policy: A comparative survey experiment', *Journal of European Social Policy*, 30(5): 601–615.

Geddes, A. (2003) 'Migration and the welfare state in Europe', *The Political Quarterly*, 74(1): 150–162.

Gheorghiev, O., Švarcová, M., Numerato, D., Hoření, K. and Čada, K. (2020) 'Czech Republic', in S. Baglioni and I. Isaakyan (eds), *Integrated Report on Individual Barriers and Enablers*, SIRIUS WP6 integrated report. Available at: https://www.sirius-project.eu/sites/default/files/attachments/Individual%20Barriers%20and%20Enablers.pdf

Greer, I., Breidahl, K.N., Knuth, M. and Larsen, F. (2017) *The Marketization of Employment Services: The Dilemmas of Europe's Work-first Welfare States*, Oxford: Oxford University Press.

Hall, P.A. and Soskice, D. (2001) 'An introduction to varieties of capitalism', in P.A. Hall and D. Soskice (eds), *Varieties of Capitalism: The Institutional Foundations of Comparative Advantage*, Oxford: Oxford University Press, pp 1–68.

Helbling, M. and Kalkum, D. (2018) 'Migration policy trends in OECD countries', *Journal of European Public Policy*, 25(12): 1779–1797.

Hoření, K. (2019) 'Czech Republic', in I. Bontenbal and N. Lillie (eds), *Integration of Migrants, Refugees and Asylum Seekers: Policy Barriers and Enablers*, SIRIUS WP3 integrated report. Available at: https://www.sirius-project.eu/sites/default/files/attachments/WP3%20Integrated%20report%20D3.2.pdf

Hoření, K., Numerato, D., and Čada, K. (2019) 'Czech Republic', in Numerato, D., Hoření, K. and Čada, K. (eds), *Civil Society Barriers and Enablers*, SIRIUS WP4 integrated report.

Jørgensen, M. (2014) 'Decentralizing immigrant integration: Denmark's mainstreaming initiatives in employment, education and social affairs', Migration Policy Institute. Available at: https://www.sirius-project.eu/sites/default/files/attachments/Civil%20society%20enablers%20and%20barriers%20D4.1.pdf

Kallinikaki, T. (2010) 'Gender, children and families in the Greek welfare state', in M. Ajzenstadt and J. Gal (eds), *Children, Gender and Families in Mediterranean Welfare States*, Dordrecht: Springer, pp 181–202.

Katrougalos, G.S. (1996) 'The south European welfare model: The Greek welfare state, in search of an identity', *Journal of European Social Policy*, 6(1): 39–60.

Koslowski, R. (1998) 'European Union migration regimes established and emergent', in C. Joppke (ed), *Challenge to the Nation-state: Immigration in Western Europe and the United States*, Oxford: Oxford University Press, pp 153–188.

Lidher, S., McIntosh, M. and Alexander, C. (2020) 'Our migration story: History, the national curriculum, and re-narrating the British nation' *Journal of Ethnic and Migration Studies*, 47(18): 4221–4237. DOI: 10.1080/1369183X.2020.1812279.

Lynch, J. (2009) 'Italy: A Christian democratic or clientelist welfare state?', in K. van Kersbergen and P. Manow (eds), *Religion, Class Coalitions, and Welfare States*, Cambridge: Cambridge University Press, pp 91–118.

Maggini, N. and Collini, M. (2019) 'Italy', in D. Numerato, K. Čada and K. Hoření (eds) *Civil Society Enablers and Barriers*, SIRIUS WP4 integrated report. Available at: https://www.sirius-project.eu/sites/default/files/attachments/Civil%20society%20enablers%20and%20barriers%20D4.1.pdf

Maggini, N. and Ibrido, R. (2019) 'Italy', in I. Bontenbal and N. Lillie (eds), *Integration of Migrants, Refugees and Asylum Seekers: Policy Barriers and Enablers*, SIRIUS WP3 integrated report.

Martin, C. and Swank, D. (2004) 'Does the organization of capital matter? Employers and active labor market policy at the national and firm levels', *American Political Science Review*, 98(4): 593–611.

Mexi, M., Russi, P.M. and Guzman, E.F. (2021) '"Fortress" Switzerland? Challenges to integrating migrants, refugees and asylum-seekers', in V. Federico and S. Baglioni (eds), *Migrants, Refugees and Asylum Seekers' Integration in European Labour Markets*, pp 213–233. Available at: https://www.sirius-project.eu/sites/default/files/attachments/WP3%20Integrated%20report%20D3.2.pdf

Ministry of the Interior of the Czech Republic (2021) 'Adaptation-integration courses'. Cham: Springer. Available at: https://www.mvcr.cz/mvcren/article/adaptation-integration-courses.aspx

Morgan, G. (2007) 'National business systems research: Progress and prospects', *Scandinavian Journal of Management*, 23(2): 127–145.

Ndomo, Q. and Lillie, N. (2020) 'Finland', in S. Baglioni and I. Isaakyan (eds), *Integration of Migrants, Refugees, and Asylum Seekers: Individual Barriers and Enablers*, SIRIUS WP6 integrated report.

Numerato, D., Čada, K. and Hoření, K. (2019) *Civil Society Enablers and Barriers*, SIRIUS integrated report.

OECD Stats (2021) 'Public expenditure and participant stocks on LMP'. Available at: https://stats.oecd.org/Index.aspx?DataSetCode=LMPEXP

Russi, P., Fischbach, A. and Mexi, M. (2020) 'Switzerland', in S. Baglioni and I. Isaakyan (eds), *Integration of Migrants, Refugees, and Asylum Seekers: Individual Barriers and Enablers*, SIRIUS WP6 integrated report.

Sage, D. (2015) 'Do active labour market policies promote the well-being, health and social capital of the unemployed? Evidence from the UK', *Social Indicators Research*, 124(2): 319–337.

Sandelowski, M., Docherty, S. and Emden, C. (1997) 'Qualitative metasynthesis: Issues and techniques', *Research in Nursing & Health*, 20(4): 365–371.

Saxonberg, S. and Sirovátka, T. (2009) 'Neo-liberalism by decay? The evolution of the Czech welfare state', *Social Policy & Administration*, 43(2): 186–203.

Sen, S. and Pace, M. (2019) 'Denmark', in D. Numerato, K. Čada and K. Hoření (eds), *Civil Society Enablers and Barriers*, SIRIUS WP4 integrated report.

Sen, S., Bjerre, L. and Pace, M. (2019) 'Denmark', in I. Bontenbal and N. Lillie (eds), *Integration of Migrants, Refugees and Asylum Seekers: Policy Barriers and Enablers*, SIRIUS WP3 integrated report. Available at: https://www.sirius-project.eu/sites/default/files/attachments/WP3%20Integrated%20report%20D3.2.pdf

Statista (2021) 'Number of residence permits granted in Denmark 2020, by reason', Statista Research Department, 19 March. Available at: https://www.statista.com/statistics/1171279/number-of-residence-permits-granted-in-denmark-by-type/

Therborn, G. (1984) 'Classes and states welfare state developments, 1881–1981', *Studies in Political Economy*, 14(1): 7–41.

Trampusch, C. (2010) 'The welfare state and trade unions in Switzerland: An historical reconstruction of the shift from a liberal to a post-liberal welfare regime', *Journal of European Social Policy*, 20(1): 58–73.

Valtonen, K. (2001) 'Social work with immigrants and refugees: Developing a participation-based framework for anti-oppressive practice', *British Journal of Social Work*, 31(6): 955–960.

Valtonen, K. (2016) *Social Work and Migration: Immigrant and Refugee Settlement and Integration*, London: Routledge.

van Oorschot, W. (2006) 'Making the difference in social Europe: Deservingness perceptions among citizens of European welfare states', *Journal of European Social Policy*, 16(1): 23–42.

Zimmer, L. (2006) 'Qualitative meta-synthesis: A question of dialoguing with texts', *Journal of Advanced Nursing*, 53(3): 311–318.

5

Civil society organisations and labour market integration: barriers and enablers in seven European countries

Dino Numerato, Karel Čada and Karina Hoření

Introduction

Civil society organisations (CSOs), conceived here as formal as well as informal social groups with an internal organisational structure and regularity of operations (Salamon et al, 2003), play an active role in labour integration and cover a wide range of services or roles; they assist migrants, refugees and asylum seekers (MRAs) in their entry to the labour market, increase their linguistic and working skills, and help them to deal with problematic situations (Greenspan et al, 2018; Ruiz Sportmann and Greenspan, 2019), extending the provision of services concerning the labour market integration offered by the state (Matikainen, 2003; Sunata and Tosun, 2018; Mayblin and James, 2019; Vandevoordt, 2019). CSOs might be involved in collective actions by participating in decision-making processes and advocating for the rights of MRAs (for example, Jaworsky, 2016; Rother and Steinhilper, 2019; Schrover et al, 2019). Moreover, CSOs are involved in public, political and legal advocacy (Garkisch et al, 2017). They can operate as actors who help in setting standards and developing and testing knowledge (Dunleavy and O'Leary, 1987). Finally, CSOs can provide expert knowledge and evidence often rooted in international contexts from which the local policy is disconnected (Čada and Ptáčková, 2014).

The role of CSOs has been even more reinforced amidst and following the so-called migrant crisis in 2014, and at the time of writing, during the ongoing Ukrainian crisis. The post-2014 era contributed to a higher diversification of CSOs and to the evolution of more independent transnational solidarity movements (Pries, 2018; Vandevoordt and Verschraegen, 2019). The relatively autonomous position of solidarity movements allows them to provide creative, flexible solutions when facing the challenge of integration, thus opening new innovative integration pathways (Galera et al, 2018).

Although the existing research was primarily focused on the capacity of CSOs to stress the sociocultural and human rights dimensions of integration, several scholars suggested that the role of CSOs cannot be idealised and that their positive impact on integration cannot be taken for granted. In this vein, CSOs not only assist MRAs on the labour market or with broader, societal integration, but they also contribute to (a subtle) reproduction of otherness, especially in those national contexts where MRA involvement in CSOs is rather weak. As a consequence, by approaching refugees and asylum seekers as recipients of services in need of assistance, CSOs do not necessarily develop MRAs' agency and autonomy; risking thus developing or deepening the dependence and passivity of MRAs (Szczepaniková, 2009). In fact, although CSOs act as cultural and linguistic mediators, they cannot fully substitute the voice of migrants (Lester, 2005). Furthermore, some authors have recently suggested that the label 'CSO' does not necessarily embrace the non-governmental ethos and that the post-2014 crisis has 'attracted a growing number of un-experienced and sometimes self-interested actors, including conventional enterprises and organisations that use the legal forms of the third sector in an opportunistic way' (Galera et al, 2018: 31).

This chapter analyses the role of CSOs in labour market integration. Emphasis was given to the perspective of MRAs. The aim was thus to understand both the demand and supply expected from and provided by CSOs in labour market integration services. In other words, in our research, we focused not only on how CSOs react to the needs of MRAs but also on what MRAs expect and get from them. The chapter is intended to discuss the role of CSOs in labour market integration, to identify the main agenda of CSOs, to capture the diversity of CSOs, and to analyse the main enablers of and barriers to CSO engagement in labour market integration.

Methods

Our analysis draws on extensive empirical evidence and is focused on seven European countries, more specifically on Denmark, the Czech Republic, Finland, Italy, Switzerland (Canton of Geneva), the United Kingdom and Greece. This focus allowed us to cover heterogeneity of migration as well as the variety of welfare regimes and the tradition of the third sector across different national contexts. Countries with a strong level of marketisation are represented by the United Kingdom (Zimmermann et al, 2014; Han, 2017), Nordic countries (Denmark and Finland) are representatives of welfare co-production (Evers, 2005; Saukkonen, 2013; Henriksen et al, 2015) where the boundaries between the state and civic society are often blurred (Alapuro, 2005), and countries with a weak civil society are represented by the Czech Republic and Greece (Fagan, 2005; Kalogeraki, 2019).

The research study draws on 302 semi-structured qualitative interviews with both MRAs (180) and representatives of CSOs (128). Confrontation of both perspectives shows the changing dynamics of the relationship between migrants and CSOs. Our focus was on CSOs favourable to integration and therefore we did not take into consideration the role of CSOs who embrace perspectives opposing integration. The post-2014 context contributed to the emergence of CSOs with anti-migration perspectives and which would explicitly resist any integration effort.

The primary aim here is to provide an overview of the barriers and enablers explored and identified in the seven analysed European countries. In line with the qualitatively driven nature of the research, the objective is to capture their emergence. In other words, enablers and barriers of CSOs discussed in this chapter are not necessarily present in all national contexts and do not function with the same significance. However, they appear to influence MRAs integration.

Civil society organisations and labour market integration: enablers and barriers

CSOs can work as important actors enhancing not only integration *into* the labour market but also integration *through* the labour market. More specifically, CSOs are important language course providers, and thanks to their social, legal and administrative guidance, CSOs help MRAs in overcoming ineffective administrative and legal structures. Several CSOs also assist MRAs with the recruitment process, providing courses and advice on how to prepare for an interview, how to write a CV or how to draft a cover letter. Furthermore, CSOs also assist MRAs in their efforts to have their skills and qualifications recognised. Moreover, by providing mentorship, training programmes, volunteering or even direct employment, CSOs contribute to the development of MRAs' skills and competencies and provide platforms to enhance the agency and autonomy of MRAs.

However, such a capacity is unevenly spatially distributed – it is rather rare in the Czech Republic and Denmark, it is somewhat developed in the United Kingdom, and more strongly presented in Finland, some areas of Italy, among the solidarity movement organisations of Greece, and in the Canton of Geneva in Switzerland. Moreover, CSOs frequently raise the problematic situation of illegal practices on the part of employers, exploitation, human trafficking or underpaid wages. Furthermore, CSOs help to mitigate and, often together with MRAs, struggle against the hostile context of a widespread atmosphere of xenophobia.

Civil society organisations and labour market integration: enablers

Empirical evidence from all observed countries suggests CSOs potentially work as important enablers of MRAs labour market integration, especially in those areas not covered by public policies. The following sections provide a more in-depth account of key external and internal enablers enhancing the role of CSOs in labour market integration and, consequently, the chances, opportunities and integration of MRAs on the labour market.

External enablers facilitating civil society support for labour market integration

There are three main structural enablers facilitating CSOs labour market integration: (1) state policies and funding; (2) national and transnational networks among CSOs; and (3) cooperative and social entrepreneurship culture.

When it comes to the material and financial support of CSOs, one of the most important external enablers facilitating labour market integration initiatives are state policies and funding. More specifically, national states in all the seven examined national contexts significantly financially support counselling and educational services provided by CSOs.

In addition to national state support, CSOs commonly benefit from funding and expert-driven support from transnational governmental and intergovernmental institutions. In this regard, important roles are played by the Asylum, Migration and Integration Fund and the European Social Fund as well as by country offices of the International Organization for Migration and the UN High Commissioner for Refugees. Similarly, the European Migration Forum and the Section for Employment, Social Affairs and Citizenship at the European Economic and Social Committee sometimes enable national initiatives.

The second type of external enablers are the existing and newly emerging horizontal networks between civil society actors, developed at national or at transnational levels. These networks on several occasions served as an important resource of knowledge and information exchange as well as a tool for sharing innovative practices. As is suggested by the Greek case, these networks are often developed in the area of transnational solidarity movements. A statement made by a member of the grassroots solidarity movement well illustrates these processes:

> 'In the context of the development of our knowledge to create solidarity cooperatives, we have been in contact with large international solidarity networks and academics from abroad. We did seminars to learn the basic administrative and financial tools of the Social and Solidarity Economy. They have taught us how to design and implement such employment actions.' (Greece, CSO)

The existing horizontal collaborations serve not only to transform knowledge and know-how but also to provide material support to be independent from the state, as suggested by a representative of a Swiss non-governmental organisation (NGO):

> 'We collaborate with many other associations, we organise events together, exchange on practices, funding ideas etc, we send us persons and support us on rooms location. As our activities rely on rooms and rooms are very expensive in both cities, sometimes associations give us rooms for free or for cheaper.' (Switzerland, CSO)

The third external enabler is the development of cooperative and social entrepreneurship culture. It enhances the effectiveness of integration programmes in several countries, in particular Italy, Finland, Switzerland and the United Kingdom. This favourable culture of collaboration enhances the emergence of new partnerships between CSOs on the one hand and cooperative and social entrepreneurship culture on the other hand. The enabling role of the social cooperative is well demonstrated by the remark made by an Italian CSO representative:

> 'In 2015 we started a training course for self-entrepreneurship and in 2016 a group of young people from different countries established a cooperative that deals with ethnic catering. Currently the cooperative is still active and soon they will open their own restaurant with a cooking workshop. This cooperative is practically a spin-off of our social cooperative and they are now following their path independently, it is the first catering cooperative in Campania managed by refugees and asylum seekers.' (Italy, CSO)

This can also be seen in the case of Danish networking organisations, which manage to build links between employers and MRAs or between states and MRAs. Thanks to this collaboration CSOs can decrease their dependence on public funding, as suggested by a CSO member from the UK who argued that social enterprise enabled them to "not hav[e] to be on the other end of funding applications all the time, grant dependent and things like that" (UK, CSO 6). Furthermore, thanks to the initiatives' links with cooperatives and social entrepreneurs, MRAs have a number of volunteering, mentoring or internship opportunities that are valuable in stimulating the autonomy and agency of MRAs, as has also been suggested in the following observations made by a Greek solidarity cooperative representative:

> 'We are trying to guide our members to create solidarity cooperatives to meet basic human needs. There the workers are equal, without hierarchies. For example, they are making a cooperative that has the purpose of providing food without intermediaries. They go to some

farmers and receive a small income in cash and also get agricultural products from their crops. Then they sell their agricultural products at low prices in the cities.' (Greece, CSO)

As further suggested, the involvement of MRAs in cooperatives contributes to their empowerment in the job market or during the establishment of their businesses, as illustrated by the following remarks made by several representatives of CSOs from Finland and Italy:

'Therefore, being an entrepreneur myself, we direct them to the right areas, networks and people. We help them to buy a new business or open their own.' (Finland, CSO)

'With this tool [internship], many asylum seekers have found work. An example of a success story is a refugee who has done an internship with a cooperative of services with which we often collaborate: not only was he hired, but he also became a member of the cooperative.' (Italy, CSO)

Internal enablers facilitating civil society support for labour market integration

Besides external enablers, there are factors defining the role of CSOs in the integration policies system. CSOs have the potential to enable the labour market integration of MRAs through their internal capacities in several ways. In comparison with other public services, CSOs offer services with: (1) a greater level of flexibility and a lower degree of bureaucratisation; (2) a more personalised approach; (3) broader networking capacity; and (4) CSOs support MRAs both socially and culturally. CSOs can facilitate integration to labour market through (5) direct employment. They provide MRAs with (6) sources of soft knowledge considering labour market integration and, finally, they are important as (7) reflexive actors in the policymaking process.

First, flexibility and a lower degree of bureaucratisation compared to the "stuck" (Denmark, CSO 9) public sector allow CSOs to account for the specific needs, aspirations and experiences of individual MRAs.

Second, this personalised approach is linked to the capacity of CSOs to grant MRAs some agency in their integration efforts and to determine their own path to integration. Compared to public services, CSOs frequently have stronger potential to understand the personal needs of MRAs and to foster their agency. The following observation from Switzerland illustrates this point: "The public office of integration and the social worker were supportive, but they have an institutional view of the social-professional integration that could represent a real restriction" (Switzerland, MRA 2). In addition to MRAs in general, this focus concerns more specific groups, such as youth and women migrants, as has been for example emphasised in the Finnish context: "Sometimes women have the need for their own group. There may be subjects that they want to discuss only among women or due to cultural or religious customs it may not be meaningful to participate in mixed groups" (Finland, CSO).

Third, CSOs enable labour market integration thanks to their networking capacity. CSO representatives function as brokers who help MRAs connect with public officials, employers, trade unions, politicians and even with (although very rarely) journalists. The importance of networks was remembered by a Danish CSO representative, for example:

> 'We see that building networks is the most important part of integration. We have programmes that pair refugees with Danish volunteers who support them in their everyday lives. There is no money involved so it's an equal relationship. But it makes refugees feel like they have a network of friends in Denmark.' (Denmark, CSO)

Fourth, the role of networking is not only social, providing MRAs with access to social networks which they could not access otherwise, but also cultural; CSO representatives ensure cultural mediation, supporting MRAs both culturally and linguistically. More specifically, CSOs can provide MRAs with information about national cultures and norms and assist them with translation. Therefore, CSO representatives connect actors who would otherwise remain disconnected. Furthermore, CSOs have the capacity to understand and perceive the needs of MRAs and articulate them towards the state, employers and other relevant external stakeholders. The complexity of this mediator work is well-illustrated in the following quotes:

> 'We go over all the basic information in the migrants' own language about Finnish working life: what are the responsibilities of the employer, what are the responsibilities of the employee, what is Finnish working culture like, why you need to be on time, what your contract should state, how salary is paid and generally how to behave in the workplace.' (Finland, CSO)

Fifth, and in a related way, the agency of MRAs in some national contexts is enhanced thanks to their involvement in CSOs, either through professional work or through volunteering, often participating in language counselling services. In the Finnish context, for example, CSOs work as important job providers. Moreover, in some national contexts (for example, Finland, the UK, Switzerland) migrants themselves actively establish organisations with explicit integration objectives or they participate in CSO activities, as illustrated by the following example from Greece:

'As a volunteer, I am the person in the reception in the ANKAA [which stands for equitable pathways towards education and employment] project. I help with the translation too from Farsi. Because I am unemployed right now it's better for me than sitting in the house, so I prefer to come to a place like this and help people. And at the same time, I am getting working experience as a volunteer, and I am improving my English.' (Greece, MRA)

Sixth, MRAs appreciate the psychological benefits which come with the personalised approach taken by CSOs. This personalised method can help foster the self-confidence of MRAs and prevent their alienation not only during the process of job searching but in integration more broadly. Several MRAs also appreciated that the non-profit ethos, differentiated from the public administration, helps to avoid the stigmatisation of MRAs commonly diffused among public officers, as is well exemplified with a story told by a migrant from Switzerland:

'The coaches don't just help you to improve your CV and your motivation letter. They help you also psychologically. If we have any kind of worries or problems you can count on them, they become your reference. You can talk openly with them and they will try to find a solution as quickly as possible. The association tries really to help every single woman. There is a personal approach that improve a feeling of self-confidence, which you lose when you arrive here, you easily forget that you have some competences and that you are qualified.' (Switzerland, CSO)

Seventh, several CSOs provide MRAs with valuable sources of soft knowledge considering labour market integration services and enhance their orientation on the labour market. More specifically, they provide MRAs with important, simple but not always available answers to the following questions: Where to go? What service to use? And whom to contact and how? Furthermore, CSOs help in the complicated and bureaucratised administration of work permits and work contracts. The value of CSO support is well demonstrated with the following remark made by a migrant living in Greece:

'Friends, if they know how to do something they will help, but when you go to an NGO or an organisation they can do the bureaucracy work for you, they can help you with a lot of paperwork, help you with things people don't know about, so they are not like friends, they have another value for me. Like this morning I had to do a tax clearance in order to open a bank account so I did it here with the accountants.

But if you go to another organisation for a tax clearance they will tell you to come back in three months.' (Greece, MRA)

Eighth, CSOs are important as reflexive actors in the policymaking process, providing input, although only taken into consideration accidentally rather than systematically, for policy change through advocacy. This role of CSOs is well illustrated with a remark made by a Greek CSO member, who pointed out: "We strive to influence public debate and public policy decisions from the smaller to bigger. So, it's more effective. We strive to have so much technical knowledge about every detail of the issue we want to change, so progressively it goes in our direction" (Greece, CSO 3).

In this vein, CSOs locate the importance of labour market integration in the broader context, articulating a more holistic vision of integration. Therefore, they remind us that labour market integration cannot work on its own, in a separate work-related bubble, but that labour market integration must also be developed hand-in-hand with broader social and cultural integration. In other words, CSOs can work as discursive shifters, as subjects who can potentially correct somewhat limited mainstream national integration policies where integration has a very narrow meaning, as well documented by the following quote: "We tried to change the narrative and not use the word 'indvandrer' (immigrant) and say 'nydansker' (new Dane) instead" (Denmark, CSO).

Civil society organisations and labour market integration: barriers

While CSOs act as important enablers of MRAs labour market integration, their position and role should not be idealised. The empirical evidence from seven European countries suggests that CSOs face several external barriers in their work and that, moreover, the nature of the CSO itself does not always favour integration processes, it can also undermine them.

External barriers hindering the role of civil society for labour market integration

CSOs, in their labour market integration initiatives, encounter several barriers: (1) limits of state funding and public policies; (2) subsidising of CSOs by public administrations; (3) the co-optation of the originally non-governmental nature of integration services by the state; (4) co-optation of the originally non-governmental nature of integration services by private business providers; (5) the distrust and suspicion of MRAs; (6) migrants' values, norms and cultural background; and (7) ignorance from policymakers.

The first barrier is related to public funding. Considering the instability, temporality and uncertainty of the state support of CSOs, the dependence on funding influences the very existence of CSOs. The resource dependence hinders the contribution of CSOs to labour market integration objectives. Several CSOs across all the examined countries suggested that the public funding they have recently received was temporal, precarious, uncertain and significantly affected by austerity measures and the changing political climate. These problems have even been perceived by migrants: "NGOs have programmes only for a few months services. NGOs are not for the long term" (Greece, MRA).

CSOs in all the analysed countries also face a hostile national political environment sometimes accompanied by the establishment of national and transnational anti-migration CSOs that further inhibits more systematic political support, evident in several countries and well-demonstrated by the following quotes from Italy and the Czech Republic:

'We moved from being considered as trustworthy actors providing solidarity, to being perceived as actors pursuing selfish interests. This is the result of the heavy political climate we face now in Italy.' (Italy, CSO)

'We are also worried about what will happen if some political subjects that are calling for the destruction of the civic sector will be successful in the election. … It is also uncomfortable to talk with possible donors who might have negative attitudes towards our work or who refuse to support us because of the negative reaction from the public.' (Czech Republic, CSO)

Moreover, due to the project-driven and dispersed nature of the funding, the integration initiatives provided by CSOs are undermined by the lack of coordination, notably where CSOs act as labour market integration service providers. In the context of missing coordination, the heterogeneous needs of MRAs are hardly being met. This is well illustrated here: "Almost every year charities have to design projects to fit the funding which means that if the following year they have to go for another funding source they have to treat their project in another way so it's … it's difficult to bring stability" (UK, CSO). Furthermore, the empirical evidence from all the explored countries suggests that the precarious nature of funding leads to situations in which accumulated know-how and evidence remains unused and not further developed after the termination of projects which CSOs initially established, as mentioned by a representative of a Finnish CSO: "We receive funding but it is not permanent and it changes from project to project and that is a challenge that we do not have permanent services to offer – projects and employees come and go and then we start again from the beginning" (Finland, CSO).

Moreover, the limited funding provided to the non-governmental sector can undermine the collaborative spirit within the sector itself; although CSOs in a variety of national contexts act primarily as collaborators in service provision and altogether strive for the same cause, they are occasionally constrained to become competitors who struggle over the limited volume of public funding. This increased competition also occurs due to the growing number of CSOs and is recognised as a danger by some CSO representatives:

'We must be very careful not to compete with other associations working in the field of professional integration. There is a risk for funding and there may be discrepancies.' (Switzerland, CSO)

'Until recently, what we had in mind was the picture of the associations working on their own, without any intention to collaborate with others because of a fear of competition; but, I think this is changing.' (Switzerland, CSO)

This competition can negatively impact the service quality provided by CSOs given the fact that they are constrained to invest more energy into the preparation of project funding proposals which are not necessarily in line with the know-how they develop in time. The uncertain funding not only influences the economic sustainability of CSOs but it also risks disrupting the continuity of their involvement in labour market integration services, as suggested by a remark made by a Finnish CSO representative who suggested that to "enable the continuation of [their] great results and good practices is a huge challenge, especially for small organisations that do not have constant funding" (Finland, CSO).

A second barrier is how the subsidising of CSOs by public administrations influences the agenda of NGOs, defines the (un)desired target groups, or determines the nature and spectrum of the provided services. As an interviewee from Denmark suggested: "I would be lying if I said that the government's priorities don't affect our work. If we want to be relevant as an organisation and have an impact on the government's work, we need to show them that we have the same priorities" (Denmark, CSO).

National funding can also be used as a tool to subsume integration services under the principles of migration securitisation. More specifically, access to integration programmes is conditioned by detailed monitoring of MRA participation in these programmes. Such monitoring can have other functions beyond simple compliance with accountability principles. More specifically, the CSOs' adherence to accountability principles risks being used as a tool for monitoring and surveillance of the migrant population. Therefore, integration initiatives run by CSOs can be instrumentalised as tools of surveillance.

Third, some CSOs mentioned the problem of co-optation of the originally non-governmental nature of integration services of the state. The process of co-optation results in the exclusion of CSOs from the arena they (co-)created and in which they operated. In other words, in cases of co-optation, CSOs would open a new path of integration policies, establish integration courses or start implementing mentoring services. However, once established, the provision of these services would lose state support and become secured exclusively by public administrations. The co-optation of ideas can sometimes be accompanied with the co-optation of CSO personnel – original NGO employees become state employees.

Fourth, the sphere of CSOs can sometimes similarly be co-opted and strategically misused by private business providers, as happened in the United Kingdom or Greece. This idea emerged notably in national contexts where the number of emergency ad hoc services introduced in response to the so-called 'migrant crisis' in 2014 attracted a number of actors with opportunistic business-driven interests rather than a non-profit spirit. For example, since 2016, their policy interest in the 'refugee crisis' intensified in the UK and many "new organisations which just repeated or copied the work of existing organisations" were set up (UK, CSO).

This co-optation can also be strongly developed in those national contexts where funding preferences prioritise established, usually bigger, and financially stable organisations; in particular, in the UK context, this means favouring even for-profit companies.

These companies would use the legal forms of the non-governmental sector in an opportunistic way and take advantage of public funding so as to pursue their business interests. Similarly, in these contexts, the stereotypical understanding of CSOs would be, though rarely, related to the suspicion that the free provision of services could work as a strategic tool to acquire clients for future profit activities, such as in the case of the Vietnamese community in the Czech Republic: "Other Vietnamese [other than the interview partner] do not trust services that are free. They suspect that free assistance have to be only false advertisement luring them into following paid services" (Czech Republic, MRA).

Fifth, the distrust and suspicion of MRAs would also suggest there are a series of sociocultural barriers influencing the interaction between CSOs and MRAs. These barriers prevent MRAs from stronger use of CSO services. These circumstances have been observed in relation to closed ethnic and national communities who have established their own networks that provide the same functions otherwise ensured by NGOs. These communities approach CSOs only rarely, perceiving them as formal organisations and often conflating their position with the position of the public service. Viewing CSOs as 'official' and 'formal' organisations, they struggle to develop trustful relationships. The conflation of CSOs with the state also occurs due to the low visibility of CSOs and the low familiarity of MRAs with the services provided by CSOs. In some cases, the fact that the service of CSOs is provided for free would further increase the distrust of some MRAs, who would understand the counselling as lacking expertise and being 'insufficiently professional', regardless of the know-how, experience and education of CSO volunteers and employers.

Sixth, the insufficient use of CSO services is also determined by culturally based personal honour; some MRAs would simply not approach CSOs as a matter of personal honour, perceiving a free service as a symptom of their own personal failure, as well demonstrated by a remark made by a refugee from Denmark: "I am not a charity case. I want to get a job on the basis of my qualifications. I don't want anyone to think that I am like a refugee and need free help" (Denmark, MRA).

Seventh, the success of integration programmes is hindered by the fact that NGOs are awarded very little recognition from policymakers, and their recognition remains only tokenistic, as observed in Czech Republic the United Kingdom. An example from the latter suggests that in these contexts, CSO representatives perceive their participation in decision-making processes as strictly formal, with no impact or space to influence existing policies:

'So within that discussion, you contribute and participate and all that, and you realise that your contribution is not valid. So yes, they give you the power to make the decision and to be engaged and hold but the recognition is not there, and it goes back to that point of just ticking the box.' (UK, CSO)

Internal barriers hindering the role of civil society for labour market integration

Labour integration can be also hindered by factors related to how CSOs operate: (1) processes of othering and objectification; (2) the lack of experience and know-how; (3) a 'CSOs' professional bubble'; (4) the implementation of accountability measures; (5) bureaucratisation and institutionalisation; and (7) resource dependence.

First, the effectiveness of integration services can suffer from the low engagement of MRAs in CSOs. Some CSOs would explicitly suggest that the key objective of NGOs is to provide professional services, regardless of the participation of MRAs in CSOs everyday activities. However, the low participation of MRAs can reinforce the processes of othering and objectification. The objectification of MRAs is apparent from the following comment: "When organisations organise events, they don't ask us what we want. Sometimes they just bring students who watch us like we are in the zoo. I don't feel like I am treated like a normal human being" (Denmark,

MRA 9). As part of this approach, MRAs are a priori understood as passive and somewhat incompetent actors with deficits. This approach hinders the development of autonomy and the independence of MRAs, and at the same time, it risks strengthening their dependence on CSO services or welfare systems more broadly. As the following quotes suggest, the provision of services can yield different outcomes; the risks of increasing dependence on CSO services and the related underdeveloped autonomy was perceived by MRAs as well as by CSOs:

> 'Operators tend to assist you in everything without leaving you autonomy. But when you leave the centre, you are not very able to get away with it alone. In fact, you move from 100 to zero in terms of support.' (Italy, MRA)

> 'Sometimes we do have to do quite a lot of things on their behalf. I have even had to write a CV on the behalf of someone who dictated it to me and then I wrote it. This is how it often goes in career counselling, even though it should not go this way.' (Finland, CSO)

Second, labour market integration services have been hindered due to the lack of experience and know-how of some CSOs, in particular those founded in an emergency context as a reaction to the so-called migrant crisis. As an interviewee from an Italian cooperative suggested, they had to reorient their agenda to integration work overnight, with staff with very little experience in the migration sector. As they suggested, previously they dealt with identification and expulsion centres:

> 'So the complete opposite of integration ... only business. ... The message that has always come to us is: "we only do what is required by the prefectures: if we integrate people, better, but it is not mandatory" ... fortunately we are all young people with clear beliefs and therefore we try to integrate.' (Italy, CSO)

The operational capacity of these newly established CSOs was further restricted (although not necessarily) due to limited networking capacities, undermining the possible role of CSOs as brokers mediating the relations between MRAs and employers or the public administration. This lack of experience also occurs because of the precarious position of CSOs, which exposes CSO staff to precariousness as well. This precariousness and personnel discontinuity hinders information exchange, knowledge transfer and the accumulation of expertise – much needed for efficient labour market integration.

Third, some CSOs and their employees tend to operate in a 'professional bubble', which prevents them from considering the individual situations of

MRAs holistically as well as understanding their sociocultural expectations. An inordinate focus on the professional identity of CSO social workers accompanied with excessive expertisation and prioritisation of technical skills can undermine the sociocultural potential of CSOs. Some professional service workers involved in integration programmes stressed that their organisation does not need to have MRAs at all costs, stressing that the 'professional' approach is a priority for them. By using the adjective 'professional', they stressed the fact that their workers possess all the necessary technical know-how, important to carry out everyday bureaucratic procedure related to permits or welfare support. Some MRAs would, however, perceive this strictly or primarily technical approach as insufficient, lacking a more in-depth understanding of their life histories and specific needs.

Fourth, the excessively professionalised ethos of CSOs is sometimes closely intertwined with the implementation of accountability measures, based on quantification and inadequate attention given to the nature of activities. The approach prioritising statistical evidence instead of experience can, for example, contribute to the fact that CSOs act as actors who extend the state's pressure on MRAs to get a job at any cost instead of considering the position and experience of MRAs:

'Like the government, all they [CSOs] talk about is labour market integration. I don't think they have ever asked me what I want to do. They don't know what my experiences and skills are. All they want me to do is get a job quickly because they think we will just stay home and live off welfare benefits.' (Denmark, MRA)

Fifth, the capacity of CSOs to understand the personal needs of MRAs and to foster their agency is marginalised by the pressures of bureaucratisation and institutionalisation. Similar to the excessive emphasis given to expert knowledge, the bureaucratisation and institutionalisation of CSOs undermine the flexible nature of organisations and foster their more or less deliberate reluctance to take into account the specific experiences and skills of individuals. Excessive bureaucratic requirements and formalisation of operational activities requested by funding bodies according to some CSOs risks channelling out personal capacities which could be potentially used for a more direct social work with MRAs.

Sixth, the previously mentioned dependence on external funding can influence the internal nature of CSOs and undermine the contentious and transformative character of CSOs. The dependence on funding can therefore marginalise critical voices within CSOs, leaving the contribution of CSOs towards integration to rest on individualised service provision rather than collective action. An excessive alignment with state integration policy, embracing a narrow understanding of integration, is apparent in Denmark, where refugee and asylum seekers commented that CSOs tend to repeat state discourses and simply put into practice state policies.

Conclusion

In this chapter, we argued that several CSOs are significant enablers in the context of labour market integration, often representing the key pillars of integration. We suggested that they not only directly enable MRAs' integration through their initiatives and everyday operations but that their role is at the same time potentially enabled by external actors and institutions. Although CSOs primarily stimulate integration processes and often manage to complement labour integration with a broader societal integration, they do not operate as enablers only.

The empirical evidence from seven European countries suggests that the functioning of CSOs is determined and hindered by external pressures and the integration objectives can also be undermined by some internal limits of CSOs. In other words, to sum up, CSOs' involvement in the labour market integration is facilitating and facilitated as well as hindering and hindered.

By providing mentorship, training programmes, volunteering or even direct employment, CSOs contribute to the development of the work skills and competencies of MRAs and provide platforms to enhance their agency and autonomy. Furthermore, CSOs overcome the lack of networks by acting as brokers and mediators in the relationship between MRAs on the one hand and the state or employers on the other hand. CSOs frequently either individually or collectively raise problematic situations of illegal employment practices, exploitation, human trafficking and underpaid wages. Last but not least, they help to mitigate and struggle against, often together with MRAs, the hostile context of a widely diffused xenophobic atmosphere.

The role of CSOs has also been hindered by external and internal barriers. CSOs struggle with unstable and uncertain funding provided by the states, which in some contexts impose the agendas of CSOs' services, their volume as well as the target groups. The dependence on public funding could limit the potentially contentious and transformative character of CSOs. The power of CSOs is also limited due to a lack of space provided to CSOs in decision-making processes. Moreover, CSOs' initiatives risk being co-opted by the public or private sectors. The integration potential of CSOs is further undermined by a series of sociocultural barriers influencing the interaction between CSOs and MRAs. Lack of experience and know-how on the one hand, as well as an excessive focus on technical skills, professionalisation and bureaucratisation, represent further barriers undermining labour market integration.

To conclude, notwithstanding some of the mentioned barriers, CSOs represent one of the key pillars of the integration process.

References

Alapuro, R. (2005) 'Associations and contention in France and Finland: Constructing the society and describing the society', *Scandinavian Political Studies*, 28(4): 337–399.

Čada, K. and Ptáčková, K. (2014) 'Between clients and bureaucrats: An ambivalent position of NGOs in the social inclusion agenda in Czech statutory cities', *Policy and Society*, 33(2): 129–139.

Dunleavy, P. and O'Leary, B. (1987) *Theories of the State: The Politics of Liberal Democracy*, London: Palgrave Macmillan.

Evers, A. (2005) 'Mixed welfare systems and hybrid organizations: Changes in the governance and provision of social services', *International Journal of Public Administration*, 28(9): 737–748.

Fagan, A. (2005) 'Taking stock of civil-society development in post-communist Europe: Evidence from the Czech Republic', *Democratization*, 12(4): 528–547.

Galera, G., Giannetto, L. and Noya, A. (2018) 'The role of non-state actors in the integration of refugees and asylum seekers', OECD Local Economic and Employment Development (LEED) Working Papers, No. 2018/02, OECD Publishing, Paris. Available at: https://dx.doi.org/10.1787/434c3303-en

Garkisch, M., Heidingsfelder, J. and Beckmann, M. (2017) 'Third sector organizations and migration: A systematic literature review on the contribution of third sector organizations in view of flight, migration and refugee crises', *Voluntas: International Journal of Voluntary and Nonprofit Organizations*, 28(5): 1839–1880.

Greenspan, I., Walk, M. and Handy, F. (2018) 'Immigrant integration through volunteering: The importance of contextual factors', *Journal of Social Policy*, 47(4): 803–825.

Han, J. (2017) 'Social marketisation and policy influence of third sector organisations: Evidence from the UK', *Voluntas: International Journal of Voluntary and Nonprofit Organizations*, 28(3): 1209–1225.

Henriksen, L.S., Smith, S.R., Thøgersen, M. and Zimmer, A. (2016) 'On the road towards marketization? A comparative analysis of nonprofit sector involvement in social service delivery at the local level', in S. Kuhlmann and G. Bouckaert (eds), *Local Public Sector Reforms in Times of Crisis*, London: Palgrave Macmillan, pp 221–236.

Jaworsky, B.N. (2016) *The Boundaries of Belonging: Online Work of Immigration-related Social Movement Organizations*, Basingstoke: Palgrave Macmillan.

Kalogeraki, S. (2019) 'A mixed method approach on Greek civil society organizations supporting migrants during the refugee crisis', *Journal of International Migration and Integration*, 21(3): 781–806.

Lester, E. (2005) 'A place at the table: The role of NGOS in refugee protection: International advocacy and policy-making', *Refugee Survey Quarterly*, 24(2): 125–142.

Matikainen, J. (2003) 'The Finnish Red Cross in refugee settlement: Developing the integration timeline as a tool for integration in the Kotopolku Project', *Journal of International Migration and Integration/Revue de l'integration et de La Migration Internationale*, 4(2): 273–295.

Mayblin, L. and James, P. (2019) 'Asylum and refugee support in the UK: Civil society filling the gaps?', *Journal of Ethnic and Migration Studies*, 45(3): 375–394.

Pries, L. (2018) *Refugees, Civil Society and the State: European Experiences and Global Challenges*, Cheltenham: Edward Elgar.

Rother, S. and Steinhilper, E. (2019) 'Tokens or stakeholders in global migration governance? The role of affected communities and civil society in the global compacts on migration and refugees', *International Migration*, 57(6): 243–257.

Ruiz Sportmann, A.S. and Greenspan, I. (2019) 'Relational interactions between immigrant and native-born volunteers: Trust-building and integration or suspicion and conflict?', *Voluntas: International Journal of Voluntary and Nonprofit Organizations*, 30(5): 932–946.

Salamon, L.M., Sokolowski, W., and List, R. (2003) *Global Civil Society: Dimensions of the Nonprofit Sector: An Overview*, Baltimore: Johns Hopkins University Press.

Saukkonen, P. (2013) 'Kolmas sektori: Vanha ja uusi', *Kansalaisyhteiskunta*, 4(1): 6–31.

Schrover, M., Vosters, T. and Glynn, I. (2019) 'NGOs and west European migration governance (1860s until present): Introduction to a special issue', *Journal of Migration History*, 5(2): 189–217.

Sunata, U. and Tosun, S. (2018) 'Assessing the civil society's role in refugee integration in Turkey: NGO-R as a new typology', *Journal of Refugee Studies*, 32(4), 683–703. https://doi.org/10.1093/jrs/fey047

Szczepaniková, A. (2009) 'Mezi státem a klienty – Nevládní neziskové organizace pracující s uprchlíky a migranty v ČR'. Available at: https://migraceonline.cz/cz/e-knihovna/mezi- statem-a-klienty-nevladni-neziskove-organizace-pracujici-s-uprchliky-a-migranty-v-cr

Vandevoordt, R. (2019) 'Eroding rights, crafting solidarity? Shifting dynamics in the state–civil society nexus in Flanders and Brussels', *Social Inclusion*, 7(2): 106–117.

Vandevoordt, R. and Verschraegen, G. (2019) 'The European refugee controversy: Civil solidarity, cultural imaginaries and political change', *Social Inclusion*, 7(2): 48–52.

Zimmermann, K., Aurich, P., Graziano, P.R. and Fuertes, V. (2014) 'Local worlds of marketization–employment policies in Germany, Italy and the UK compared', *Social Policy & Administration*, 48(2): 127–148.

6

Social partners: barriers and enablers

Simone Baglioni, Tom Montgomery and Francesca Calò

Introduction

Chapter 6 undertakes a study of the role that social partners and social dialogue can play in integrating migrants, refugees and asylum seekers in the labour market. Social partners play a key role in labour market dynamics as they contribute towards determining the policy and legal frameworks that shape labour markets, but also the social, political and economic trends in which labour markets are embedded (Auer, 2001). Therefore, an examination of social partners' understanding of the newcomers' capacities and their appreciation of the opportunities and challenges to be addressed is unavoidable in any research willing to understand how to facilitate unlocking the employment potential of migrants, refugees and asylum seekers.

When social partners are at stake with reference to migration and asylum, extant research has investigated primarily the role of unions (Penninx and Roosblad, 2000; Marino et al, 2015, 2017; Refslund, 2021) while scarcer attention has been paid to the employers' side (OECD and UNHCR, 2016; Adecco Group, 2017) and even fewer studies have investigated the role of social dialogue. Hence, our chapter fills a gap in the existing literature as it presents findings from a four-month-long process of fieldwork of interviews with social partners (gathering overall 123 interviews) complemented by an experts' survey which managed to collect responses from 293 additional social partners' representatives across our seven countries.

The debate surrounding migrants and refugees in European countries is often polarised around two dominant narratives. One that portrays newcomers as a burden for the public budget and the welfare state, casting them as people in constant need of support and services. Another which highlights their activity in the labour market and depicts them as potential competitors with the 'native' workforce (Berg, 2015; Ferrera and Pellegata, 2018). Within such polarised debates, social partners as well as 'hybrid' corporate actors such as social cooperatives and social enterprises have articulated a range of positions which sometimes appear to be diverging (Scalise and Burroni, 2020). For example, trade unions have been faced by the dilemma of including or excluding newcomers from their activities and membership when inclusion could be considered a 'betrayal' of native and traditional workforces exposed to the risk of 'social dumping' and further deregulation, or conversely, whether or not migrants could be considered as an untapped reservoir of labour solidarity whose recruitment may mitigate against well-established long-term declines in trade union density across the European (particularly young and precarious) workforce (Penninx and Roosblad, 2000; Mackenzie and Forde, 2009; Gorodzeisky and Richards, 2013; Gumbrell-McCormick and Hyman, 2013). On the other hand, employers have been supportive of migrants meeting the market-driven flexible and cyclical shape of labour demand, in particular (but not only) in agricultural and tourism seasonal work, as well as in personal and home care services or in the construction sector (Van Hooren, 2012; Berntsen, 2016). While social enterprises and the social economy have favoured migrants in part to respond to the same workforce needs in the service (for example social care) industry, but also to promote more innovative and inclusive business models and a new generation of entrepreneurs (Harina and Freudenber, 2020).

In the discussion that follows we present findings which demonstrate how social partners perceive and portray the contribution that extra-EU migrants, refugees and asylum seekers bring to European economies and societies, but also their ideas about the (still many) barriers and (few) opportunities that can be crucial in determining the transition to decent work for newcomers. In this chapter we elaborate common threads and contrasts that have emerged from the social partners' expert survey we have conducted to complement our in-depth interviews.

Methods

Underpinning the findings of this chapter is a research design that is committed to a mixed methods approach. The approach was operationalised through three key elements: (1) a review of the existing literature on social partnership and its intersection with the labour market integration of migrants and refugees across each country; (2) an online experts' survey of social partners conducted across each of the countries with the purpose of exploring the views, values, attitudes, expectations and behaviours of social partners, and how these vary across countries; and (3) semi-structured interviews with social partners across each of the countries designed to elaborate key issues of labour market integration with social partners, such as skills shortages that could be filled by migrants, tensions between migrant and native workers, the role of informal labour markets, the involvement of social partners in policy design, and the role of collective bargaining and social dialogue in the integration process. Through adopting this mixed method approach we were thus able to glean a complementary quantitative and qualitative insight into the barriers and enablers of labour market integration for migrants and refugees from the perspective of social partner organisations across Europe and the similarities and variations that exist across these distinct contexts.

Our questionnaire covered questions including the perception of migrants and refugees as an asset or burden, how social partners perceived the skills levels of migrants and refugees as well as questions relating directly to the issue of social dialogue and labour market integration. As with our survey questionnaire, the interview guide was designed to elicit responses from social partners that would provide a more comprehensive understanding of the issues explored in our online survey.

In terms of our sampling, each of the teams undertook the same process to construct their national samples of social partner organisations. Firstly, teams were asked to take into consideration the findings of our earlier work, reported in Chapter 1 of the book, and the sectors identified as having the potential to absorb migrant and refugee workers. Next, we asked teams to draw upon those sources from previous research to identify key actors in sectors which held potential for the labour market integration of migrants and refugees. We then asked teams to map large umbrella organisations (for exampe, trade union confederations, employer representative organisations, business federations, and so on) of social partners in each of their countries to assist in populating their national samples. Teams were asked to draw upon the membership of these large umbrella bodies to identify key individuals who could be potential research participants. These same samples were utilised by researchers across the research teams to recruit participants for both the online survey and the semi-structured interviews. Once the national samples were constructed teams were asked to contact those key individuals identified within social partner organisations to participate in our research.

Table 6.1 presents the experts' distribution across social partners' categories by country (although our survey was overall taken by 293 experts, we have decided to include in most of the analyses that follow only responses by those who had filled in at least 70 per cent of the survey, to allow us to report experts' views with a higher reliability degree given the complexity and length of the survey itself). Unions are the most popular category, with overall 110 experts responding to our survey (ranging from 28 in Finland to seven in Greece and Italy); employers' organisations are the second most frequent category with overall 46 expert-respondents (ranging from 16 experts having responded to the survey in Switzerland to one in Greece and the UK); but we have also captured overall seven experts from chambers of commerce; and finally we have 33 experts overall responding from a mix of categories including private companies, social enterprises, professional guilds and associations of precarious workers.

Table 6.1: Distribution of survey expert respondents by social partner categories (by country)

Social partners	Countries							
	Czech Republic	Denmark	Finland	Greece	Italy	Switzerland	UK	Total
Unions	19	18	28	7	7	10	21	110
Employers	7	4	12	1	5	16	1	46
Chambers of commerce	1	0	0	1	3	0	2	7
Mixed category*	12	3	0	6	8	7	0	33
Total	39	25	40	15	23	33	24	199

Note: We have included in the analysis only respondents who completed at least 70 per cent of the survey. * This category includes: private company (Denmark, Italy, Switzerland), social enterprises (Denmark, Greece, Italy), association of precarious workers (Greece), professional guild (Greece, Switzerland).

Newcomers' skills: an unlocked potential?

As a way to begin discussing the extent to which social partners appreciate the contribution that migrants provide to European labour markets and wider society, we can consider experts' responses to the question: 'What perception do you have of the skills levels of most migrants or refugees arriving in your country?'. As discussed by the literature, with reference to trade unions, the understanding that social partners have of migrants depends upon other factors such as the characteristics of migrants themselves and the experience that a given country has had with immigration. Table 6.2 provides a first piece of evidence to support such an assumption: results point to a different appreciation of newcomers depending on their (legal) status or reason for immigration. While two-thirds of social partners think that so-called economic migrants are either highly skilled or moderately skilled, the percentage goes down to less than one in every two for refugees. Conversely, only one in five respondents believe economic migrants do not possess meaningful skills, versus almost one in every two thinking the same for refugees. Such results resonate with a popular, albeit not evidence-based, assumption that those who migrate to seek a better life or to seek an economic advantage arrive with more skills than those who enter Europe to escape violence and persecution at home. Although evidence suggests that asylum seekers and refugees experience an extremely stressful situation which may hinder their wellbeing and capacity to work, the skills they have acquired in their earlier life and work do not disappear as they move forward. Hence, we should refrain from an aprioristic evaluation of people's skills on the simple basis of the reason for their arrival.

Table 6.2: Respondents' perception of newcomers' skills by type of newcomers

	Migrants	Refugees
Highly skilled	22%	7%
Moderately skilled	58%	45%
Low skilled	20%	48%
N	167%	161%
Total	100%	100%

However, we can also interpret such a sharp contrast in the appreciation of the skills of economic migrants and refugees as an awareness among social partners that refugees and in general migrants seeking international and humanitarian protection, due to the stressful and perilous circumstances under which they flee their home countries, might need more bespoke services of support and guidance to assist in properly preparing them to enter the labour market and progress in their employment.

We next turn to those perceptions of newcomers' skills across types of social partners. Table 6.3 presents our findings which consider four categories of social partners: trade unions, employers, chambers of commerce, and a residual category of other organisations, which is mainly composed of social enterprises and cooperatives. Although the different appreciation of economic migrants and refugees mentioned earlier occurs across all social partner categories, except for our 'other' category, which shows a more balanced appreciation between the two types of newcomers, there are some differences among social partners that warrant closer scrutiny. For example, trade unions appear to have a stronger appreciation of newcomers' skills than the other social partners: in fact, 29 per cent of experts from trade unions consider economic migrants to possess high skills while only 14 per cent of employers' organisations and chambers of commerce believe this to be the case, while slightly lower than that (9 per cent) believe the same among the residual 'other' category. Such a finding contrasts with extant studies that have critically pointed to the 'weak' attitude of unions towards migrants (Lucio and Perrett, 2009; Connolly et al, 2014). Although not openly challenging such an understanding, it does provide evidence that although unions may express concerns regarding social dumping, they appear to be the most open category among social partners towards migrants. Moreover, most respondents across the three categories consider economic migrants to be arriving with an existing set of skills (with 'moderately skilled' as the response item which scores highest across all social partners groups for economic migrants).

To what extent does such a picture change if we consider differences between countries? Social partners' appreciation of migrants' skills in fact

Table 6.3: Responses to the question 'What perception do you have of the skills levels of most migrants and refugees?'

	Unions		Employers		Chambers of commerce		Other	
	M	R	M	R	M	R	M	R
Highly skilled	29%	10%	14%	6%	14%	0%	9%	0%
Moderately skilled	54%	42%	64%	39%	72%	80%	55%	65%
Low skilled	16%	48%	22%	55%	14%	20%	36%	35%
N	92	90	36	36	7	5	22	20
Total	100%	100%	100%	100%	100%	100%	100%	100%

Note: M = migrants; R = refugees

needs to be contextualised, as at least four contextual aspects affect social partners' attitude towards migrants: (1) the role of trade unions in society, the more institutionalised and organised, the less inclined they are to opening up employment and their own ranks to newcomers; (2) the labour market structure and dynamics (which sectors are generating a higher demand for migrants and to what extent are these sectors unionised); (3) wider societal trends (consensual versus conflictual traditions, political polarisation, and so on); (4) characteristics of the migrants (type, origin and earlier experiences with unions) (Marino et al, 2015). Countries such as Italy, Greece and the Czech Republic, which have primarily attracted migrants to take up jobs requiring fewer qualifications, mainly in the agriculture, manufacture and the care sectors, or which are employed in the irregular economy, show a smaller share of social partners perceiving migrants as highly skilled individuals than in other countries. In Greece, our social partner experts have a particularly poor perception of the skillset of refugees: 43 per cent of social partners who responded to our survey consider refugees as being low skilled. While in countries that either have a long tradition of immigration such as the UK, or in countries where migrants have also been employed in skilled occupations, there is a far more developed appreciation of migrants' skills. For example, in the UK more than half of the social partners who responded to our expert survey consider both economic migrants and refugees as arriving with well-developed skills; and in Finland four out of ten experts consider migrants arriving with high skills and another five out of ten consider them bearing some skills.

The overall economic and labour market appreciation of newcomers among social partners is also revealed by another question of our expert survey which asked whether respondents considered migrants and refugees primarily an asset or a burden for their countries. Narratives of migration and asylum have abundantly speculated upon the cost of hosting migrants and in particular refugees, one example being the UK debate which involved consistent tropes regarding 'bogus asylum seekers' and 'scrounger migrants' which have affected not only British debates and immigration policies (Squire, 2016), but also the country's most important political decision of the century – that is, the exit from the European Union (Baglioni et al, 2019). However, our findings reveal that, overall, social partners across our countries do not subscribe to the anti-migrant rhetoric: almost eight out of ten respondents consider migrants an asset or more an asset than a burden for their countries, and one in every two has the same appreciation for refugees (hence, again, a clear difference appears in appreciation: favouring migrants versus refugees). If we consider cross-country variations, only in the Czech Republic is there a consistent share (one-third) of social partners among those who responded to our survey who consider newcomers as only being a burden, while in Denmark, Finland and Switzerland, a similar share of respondents considers refugees to be more of a burden than an asset (respectively 24 per cent, 41 per cent and 25 per cent of respondents) (data not shown here for sake of space).

If we consider how the same question scores across types of social partners (Table 6.4), our data reveal that, overall, trade unions, employers' organisations, chambers of commerce and other types of organisations have a similar relatively high degree of appreciation of newcomers, and in particular of economic migrants. But employers' organisations are those presenting the highest scores for responses considering refugees more as a

Table 6.4: Responses to the question 'Are migrants and refugees more of an asset or a burden for our societies?' by type of social partner

	Unions		Employers		Chambers of commerce		Other	
	M	R	M	R	M	R	M	R
Only an asset	29%	18%	14%	3%	29%	33%	19%	16%
More of an asset than a burden	51%	33%	61%	28%	71%	33%	52%	42%
Subtotal positive view	*80%*	*51%*	*75%*	*31%*	*100%*	*66%*	*71%*	*58%*
Only a burden	7%	7%	6%	8%	0%	0%	5%	11%
More of a burden than an asset	3%	25%	8%	36%	0%	0%	10%	5%
Subtotal negative view	*10%*	*32%*	*14%*	*44%*	*0%*	*0%*	*15%*	*16%*
Neither an asset nor a burden	10%	17%	11%	25%	0%	34%	14%	26%
N	94	94	36	36	7	6	21	19
Total	100%	100%	100%	100%	100%	100%	100%	100%

Note: M = migrants; R = refugees

burden than an asset, a finding which seems to suggest that although there are consistent examples of businesses and companies vocal in their support for labour market integration, including for the most vulnerable groups of newcomers, there is still room for improvement in the private sector for a full understanding of the potential which lies within refugees and asylum seekers that still remains unrealised.

Are newcomers disrupting national labour markets?

Much of the scepticism that social partners, and in particular trade unions, have shown towards migrants is related to the potentially disruptive effect that newcomers can have on the labour market of receiving societies (Marino et al, 2017). They can be perceived as representing a 'cheap' and docile workforce which can be employed at a lower economic and social cost than local or native workers (Krings, 2009). Hence, there is a fear that they may generate social dumping, reduce the already shrinking employment opportunities of the lower skilled local workforce, and contribute towards jeopardising the leverage of trade unions in wage negotiation and employment regulation dynamics (Lillie and Greer, 2007). In fact, evidence suggests that the potential negative impact of the entry of newcomers in a given labour market might be stronger in the period immediately following their entrance in the country, as they might be tempted or forced by restrictive regulations and inadequate integration opportunities to enter the irregular market/economy, might be available to work at lower-than-average salaries, and compete with local lower skilled workers (IMF, 2016). In the longer term, when newcomers stabilise their position, are more confident and, importantly, legally entitled to consider the wider range of jobs available, their competition effect upon locals declines substantially. Still, in the vulgarised, politically motivated, narrative of the effect of migrants on native workers, the fear of newcomers stealing jobs is strong in some political discourses and particularly right-wing populist narratives (Lucassen and Lubbers, 2012; Gorodzeisky and Semyonov, 2016).

Our expert survey asked if the arrival of migrants had created tensions in the labour market of the respondents' countries. Table 6.5 shows that social partner experts seem to share, at least to a certain extent, the idea that a tension exists between newcomers and native workers, and in fact almost one in every two of our respondents admit the arrival of newcomers has created tensions in the labour market (Table 6.5). Moreover, consistent with the literature (Holgate, 2005; Perrett et al, 2012; Connolly et al, 2014; Alberti and Però, 2018), trade unions appear to be the actor most concerned by such tensions between newcomers and the local workforce. However, experts' answers to such a question depend also upon the type of actor/sector they represent. As shown by the Finnish case, trade unions representing

Table 6.5: Responses to the question 'Has the arrival of migrants or refugees created tensions in the labour market in your country with native workers?'

	Migrants	Refugees
Yes	45%	43%
No	55%	57%
N	164	160
Total	100%	100%

sectors of the labour market with stronger concentrations of highly skilled workers tend to adopt a more liberal approach to immigration than those unions representing blue-collar employees or workers with fewer skills and educational levels. In the former case, the native workforce is protected by the requirements needed to enter these professions while in the latter workers are more exposed to competition. Such a perspective is similarly distributed across our countries, with the most concerned respondents being in the Czech Republic and those least concerned in Switzerland and the UK. The Czech case seems a particularly interesting one in this regard: the country's social partners recognise the role that immigrant workers play in an economy blessed by low unemployment rates and in need of a foreign workforce, still, trade unions show some concern about the tensions that the arrival of newcomers in local labour markets may bring. Such tensions appear most salient either for those foreign workers that operate through jobs agencies or those who take up highly qualified positions in the health sectors such as doctors and nurses from Ukraine.

Among the experts who answered yes to our question about the arrival of newcomers having created tensions in the labour market of their host country, Table 6.6 shows that the most pertinent reasons for such tensions to occur are related with the perceived competition for jobs brought by migrants, and connected to this aspect, the risk of lower wages. However, the causes of tensions are also considered to be the perceived cultural differences, and related to this aspect, the perceived religious differences. Yet, respondents recognise that tensions around migration issues can also originate from outside of the labour market, emanating from those tensions that result from the actions and rhetoric of political entrepreneurs seeking to gain political advantage by spreading fears and exploiting social vulnerabilities. In fact, the role of populist parties is recognised as a cause of tensions by one in every two respondents (Table 6.6). While the role of policymakers at various territorial levels is residually mentioned as an origin of those tensions related with labour migration.

When adopting a comparative cross-country view of the causes of increased tensions with reference to newcomers and the labour market, we

Table 6.6: Causes of tensions (this response item applied only to those who responded positively to the question on tensions in the labour market provoked by migrants)

Perceived competition for jobs	65%
Perceived cultural differences	64%
Populist parties	51%
Perceived lowering wages	44%
Perceived religious differences	40%
National policymakers	17%
EU policymakers	11%
Regional policymakers	5%
Local policymakers	1%
Total N	85

noticed a difference between countries in which the perceived competition between migrants and local workers for jobs is a salient issue (Greece, Italy, Switzerland and the UK) and those countries in which job competition is a relevant concern but not as important as perceived cultural differences (the Czech Republic, Denmark and Finland). Concerning the Nordic countries, we should bear in mind their well-established patterns of tripartite agreements that regulate every aspect of the labour market and the employment experience. The institutional strength of their social partners, and in particular trade unions, does effectively discourage social dumping, and therefore it is unsurprising that tensions regarding labour migration are more directed towards cultural and religious differences. While in countries with high unemployment rates and large irregular labour markets, such as Greece and Italy, but also in countries such as the UK and Switzerland with less powerful unions and, for the latter, a long-standing issue of contested cross-border workers, the concerns surrounding job competition and social dumping are dominant.

As vividly summarised by an employers' organisation representative interviewed in Greece:

> 'The role of immigrants in the Greek economy is certainly positive. Many small businesses would have been shut down if they had not immigrant workers willing to work hard and with relatively low wages. Also, many big companies might have left Greece and headed for another country in the Balkans with lower wages. However, we must not forget that the weak negotiating position of immigrants and refugees often leads them to the irregular economy. This is a negative consequence of their presence.' (Greece, Employers' organisation)

Finally, it is worth noting that only in the Czech Republic and Denmark – for different reasons – are EU policymakers considered to be stoking tensions on labour migration. In Denmark, perhaps this is due to the country's usually protective stance towards any attempt by the EU to Europeanise social policies, which are perceived as attempts to challenge its welfare state, its tripartite based labour market and industrial relations system, and its wage system. Moreover, in the Czech Republic, perhaps the identification of EU policymakers as sources of tension can be attributed to the country's reluctance to adhere to the EU system of quota distribution for asylum seekers and relatedly the EU's more open approach towards internal mobility and intra-EU migration.

Furthermore, in our expert survey we also gathered opinions about the tools to be used to mitigate the potential harmful effect of the competition between newcomers and native workers (Table 6.7). Unsurprisingly, social partners' traditional actions, such as social dialogue or increased trade union representation, are popular mitigating tools among respondents, but also employment inspections and minimum wages are viable options according to our social partners. In particular, the need to improve those tools and resources to implement workplace inspections appear to be salient measures in Italy and in Greece. In the former, further inspections could perhaps contribute towards reducing the massive use of irregular workers in the agriculture industry of Southern regions and the terrible consequences this has had on the lives of the immigrants involved. As elaborated by a trade union representative in Greece: "It is important to increase controls. Arbitrary actions exist when controls are not intense."

Measures that are often invoked by political parties and policymakers, such as entry quotas or entry restrictions, are rarely mentioned as being useful (with only 8 per cent of our expert respondents selecting these measures).

Table 6.7: Tools to mitigate competition between migrants and natives (this response item applied only to those who responded positively to the question about such a competition and multiple responses were allowed)

Social dialogue	60%
Employment inspections	41%
Minimum wages	40%
Greater union representation	40%
Migrant quotas	16%
Entry restrictions	8%
Other	8%
Total N	134

Barriers and enablers according to social partners' experts

Statistical data on the labour market integration of third country nationals in the EU shows the existence of a long-standing gap between migrants' and European citizens' employment rate given that the former score much lower than the latter (see Chapter 2 in this volume and Eurostat data on migration and labour market integration[1]). This gap is even more pronounced when women and young people are at stake. Such a gap speaks to an employment potential which remains largely unrealised for third country nationals. The social partner experts we have engaged with in our survey seem to be aware of the newcomers' employment potential situation as well as the need to address the employment gap, but they also appear to be acutely aware of the work that needs to be done for refugees rather than for economic migrants. Table 6.8 shows that almost half the respondents consider the potential of economic migrants relatively realised. In contrast, only one out of ten considers the labour potential of refugees to be fully realised. Six out of ten consider the employment potential of migrants to be only slightly realised, and one-third believe that refugees' labour market potential is still completely untapped.

When asked to indicate the most relevant causes preventing the full realisation of migrants or refugees' employment potential (Table 6.9), social partners point to language proficiency, but also legal and administrative hurdles that make getting into employment difficult for newcomers. In addition, a lack of effective mechanisms for the recognition of qualifications, a lack of services that support integration, skills mismatches, discrimination, cultural differences and poor knowledge about the labour market of the host country are all identified by our experts. However, only one in ten of our respondents focused upon economy related issues.

Consistent with the causes, the remedies (Table 6.10) point to the need to have more language classes provision, but also different migration

Table 6.8: Responses to the question 'Do you think that the employment potential of migrants or refugees is fully realised?'

	Migrants	Refugees
Fully realised	4%	1%
Somewhat realised	40%	8%
Slightly realised	42%	57%
Not realised at all	15%	34%
N	159	154
Total	100%	100%

Table 6.9: Responses to the question 'What are the most important factors that prevent the full realisation of migrants or refugees' employment capacities? (Please select every option that applies)'

Language issues	79%
Legal/administrative issues/immigration policy	61%
Lack of recognition of qualifications	55%
Lack of services to support integration	45%
Skills mismatch	44%
Discrimination	42%
Cultural differences	41%
Lack of knowledge regarding the national job market	37%
Economy related issues	14%
Total N	159

Table 6.10: Responses to the questions 'What are the most effective factors in facilitating labour market entry? (Please select every option that applies)'

Increase language services	118
Migration policies	87
Support for job search	77
Skills matching	73
Anti-discrimination policies	62
Job mentoring	59
Skills profiling	57
Anti-exploitation policies	53
CV preparation and interview	50
Volunteering opportunities	27
Total N	164

policies, given that, as we have shown in Chapter 3, current legislation makes it very difficult for third country nationals, and in particular for asylum seekers, to enter the labour market and gain regular, stable and decent employment. Social partners indicate that better job search support services, along with skills matching, skills profiling and job mentoring, could improve the employment situation of third country nationals. Furthermore, anti-discrimination and anti-exploitation policies (or a more effective implementation of these) would help too. Only a small proportion of respondents considered volunteering opportunities as something that could help third country nationals find employment.

Table 6.11: Responses to the question 'Are policies effective in filling skills shortages?'

Very effective	1%
Somewhat effective	15%
Slightly effective	43%
Not effective at all	33%
I am not aware of these policies	8%
Total N	148

The data presented thus far should be discussed while bearing in mind what social partners think about the existing policies operating in their countries to address skills shortages. In fact, if the employment potential of newcomers is far from being fully realised, in most countries there are skills shortages which migrants could contribute towards mitigating if they could be allowed to work or be properly supported/prepared for employment. Table 6.11 shows responses to the question about the effectiveness of policies to address skills shortages: one-third of the social partners we interviewed believe that such policies are not effective at all, and almost half consider such policies to be only slightly effective. Overall, only one out of ten considers policies to be effective. This result is consistent across the countries of our study, apart from Switzerland in which most survey respondents consider the country's policies in this area to be somewhat effective.

A configuration of ineffective policies to address skills needs which newcomers might address and an environment which is often legally and socially obstructive, with poor opportunities to have qualifications and skills recognised, can lead to a situation in which newcomers end up working in the irregular economy. As migrants enter such employment, they risk being trapped in such sections of the labour market, resulting in a large-scale waste of talent. In some countries, third country nationals may end up in precarious, and sometimes irregular, work. Social partners are aware of this scenario and in fact two-thirds of them consider newcomers to be more exposed than native workers to the health and safety risks (Guldenmund et al, 2013; Moyce and Schenker, 2018) often associated with those sections of the labour market (Table 6.12).

Finally, we must consider if social dialogue, often thought as the right tool to be used in labour migration regulation (ILO, 2014) is purposively used to improve migrants' labour market experience. Slightly less than one in every two respondents say that their organisation has been involved in social dialogue processes in the past five years in the specific field of migration. On the one hand, such a finding could be considered a positive sign given the difficult years trade unions have been experiencing in the past decades due to de-unionisation and changes in the labour market (Ebbinghaus and

Table 6.12: Responses to the question 'Do you think that the health and safety risks faced by migrants and refugees are higher than, the same as, or lower than the risks faced by the native workforce?'

Definitely a higher risk	34%
A slightly higher risk	33%
The same risk	32%
Definitely a lower risk	1%
A slightly lower risk	0%
Total	100%
N	145

Visser, 1999; Gumbrell-McCormick and Hyman, 2013). On the other hand, however, given the salient role immigration has played in public and political debates across Europe, the result (data not shown here) of less than one in every two respondents having being part of social dialogue processes on the topic tells us something about the real commitment that social and political actors have in resolving immigration issues. Moreover, there are no major differences across countries in these results, apart from Finland, where a lower share of respondents (one-third) declares having engaged in social dialogue processes while two-thirds had not.

When we investigate the reasons for the lack of social dialogue engagement on labour migration issues (Table 6.13), respondents point to either political issues (primarily the lack of political will to engage in social dialogue tout-court) or labour migration dialogue issues (policymakers across Europe consider migration a minefield which could threaten their re-election). But reasons for limited social dialogue development are also contingent to the specificities of third country nationals, most of whom are poorly or not unionised at all and therefore unions do not feel membership pressure to get involved, nor do they see an immediate advantage in spending resources to protect categories who are not among their members (Penninx and Roosblad, 2000). As shown in the Finnish and in the Czech cases, foreign workers often come from countries in which unions are not recognised and known as genuine tools of democratic participation and interest representation. On the contrary they are perceived as potentially dangerous bodies. Hence, when unions intervene on migration issues, they often tend to intervene to shelter their members from the potential of social dumping that newcomers represented rather than to advance migrants' rights, as mentioned earlier in the introductory section. Moreover, the causes of poor social dialogue engagement among social partners are contingent to the labour market segmentation, and the channelling of labour migrants into the irregular economy: it is only when migrant workers shift from precarious

Table 6.13: Responses to the question 'Which factors prevent the development of opportunities for social dialogue (negotiation and consultation between organised workers and employers which can often include policymakers, for example, collective bargaining) on migration and labour migration (if more than one, please select the three most important)?'

Lack of political will to strengthen social dialogue	32%
Lack of political will to resolve labour migration issues	32%
Weak unionisation specifically among migrants and refugees	29%
Weak unionisation generally	20%
Large informal/irregular sector/market	20%
Lack of will among employers to strengthen social dialogue	16%
Lack of will among employers to resolve labour migration issues	12%

legal and employment statuses into more stable ones that they eventually recognise the relevance of trade union membership.

Conclusion

Social partners across Europe are a crucial component in labour market regulation and in connected social, policy and economic dynamics. In some countries social partners are, along with political actors and institutions, part of well-established systems of bargain and negotiation which cover issues such as wages, working hours, and workers/employers' rights and entitlements applying to the entire country or sector of the economy in that country. In contrast, in other countries, social partners occupy a less central position due to economic or purely political dynamics, but still it is through their organisation that employment takes form: companies and business provide opportunities of employment, and unions try to interject in the employer–employee relationship with results that vary across countries. Hence, regardless of the influence and power they have in their societies, unions, employers' organisations, and cooperatives or social enterprises are the social and economic actors through which third country nationals can gain employment and as such we need to consider their perspectives when studying the causes that prevent newcomers from gaining access to full and decent employment, and the remedies that can be developed.

The responses of the experts we surveyed reveal that some of the key issues that had been discussed by extant studies, and in particular the dilemmas faced by unions vis-à-vis migrants, are still relevant. Our data also reveal an awareness among social partners of the higher (compared to local workers) risks that migrants face in terms of their health and safety due to the poor regulations which often confine newcomers to employment in the irregular economy, or to jobs requiring lower skills and which offer poorer prospects of progression.

However, our survey also reveals the appreciation that social partners have of migrants' skills, of their potential contribution to the wellbeing of our societies and economies, a potential which very often remains unrealised. This is due to reasons that are on the one hand pertinent to our society's regulation of migration and on the other hand connected with the characteristics of the migrants themselves (language proficiency, social capital, personal wellbeing and health). What we can take from this preliminary analysis of social partners is the need for both policymakers at various levels of government and social partners to commit to create further social dialogue opportunities. Too few cases of social dialogue have occurred across our seven countries in the field of labour migration, but social dialogue seems to us a (if not *the*) fundamental tool to begin proper efforts to resolve problems occurring in such a polarised domain of migration, and in what is even a more contentious one, that of labour migration. Rather than leaving space to single-actor claims and activities, even when these are very positive in terms of problem solving, we should encourage a more coordinated multi-actor effort based on dialogue and mutual understanding, as represented by social dialogue.

Note
[1] www.eurostat.eu

References

Adecco Group (2017) 'The labour market integration of refugees: A focus on Europe', White Paper 06/17, Adecco Group Publications. Available at: https://www.adeccogroup.com/wpcontent/themes/ado-group/downloads/labour-market-integration-of-refugees-focuseurope.pdf

Alberti, G. and Però, D. (2018) 'Migrating industrial relations: Migrant workers' initiative within and outside trade unions', *British Journal of Industrial Relations*, 56(4): 693–715.

Auer, P. (2001) *Changing Labour Markets in Europe: The Role of Institutions and Policies*, Geneva: ILO Publications Center.

Baglioni, S., Biosca, O. and Montgomery, T. (2019) 'Brexit, division, and individual solidarity: What future for Europe? Evidence from eight European countries', *American Behavioral Scientist*, 63(4): 538–550.

Berg, J.A. (2015) 'Explaining attitudes toward immigrants and immigration policy: A review of the theoretical literature', *Sociology Compass*, 9(1): 23–34.

Berntsen, L. (2016) 'Reworking labour practices: On the agency of unorganized mobile migrant construction workers', *Work, Employment and Society*, 30(3): 472–488.

Connolly, H., Marino, S. and Lucio, M.M. (2014) 'Trade union renewal and the challenges of representation: Strategies towards migrant and ethnic minority workers in the Netherlands, Spain and the United Kingdom', *European Journal of Industrial Relations*, 20(1): 5–20.

Ebbinghaus, B. and Visser, J. (1999) 'When institutions matter: Union growth and decline in western Europe, 1950–1995', *European Sociological Review*, 15(2): 135–158.

Ferrera, M. and Pellegata, A. (2018) 'Worker mobility under attack? Explaining labour market chauvinism in the EU', *Journal of European Public Policy*, 25(10): 1461–1480.

Gorodzeisky, A. and Richards, A. (2013) 'Trade unions and migrant workers in western Europe', *European Journal of Industrial Relations*, 19(3): 239–254.

Gorodzeisky, A. and Semyonov, M. (2016) 'Not only competitive threat but also racial prejudice: Sources of anti-immigrant attitudes in European societies', *International Journal of Public Opinion Research*, 28(3): 331–354.

Guldenmund, F., Cleal, B. and Mearns, K. (2013) 'An exploratory study of migrant workers and safety in three European countries', *Safety Science*, 52: 92–99.

Gumbrell-McCormick, R. and Hyman, R. (2013) *Trade Unions in Western Europe: Hard Times, Hard Choices*, Oxford: Oxford University Press.

Harima, A. and Freudenberg, J. (2020) 'Co-creation of social entrepreneurial opportunities with refugees', *Journal of Social Entrepreneurship*, 11(1): 40–64.

Holgate, J. (2005) 'Organizing migrant workers: A case study of working conditions and unionization in a London sandwich factory', *Work, Employment and Society*, 19(3): 463–480.

ILO (International Labour Organization) (2014) 'Fair migration: Setting an ILO agenda', report of the Director-General, Geneva.

IMF (International Monetary Fund) (2016) 'The refugee surge in Europe: Economic challenges', SDN/16/02. Available from: https://www.imf.org/external/pubs/ft/sdn/2016/sdn1602.pdf

Krings, T. (2009) 'A race to the bottom? Trade unions, EU enlargement and the free movement of labour', *European Journal of Industrial Relations*, 15(1): 49–69.

Lillie, N. and Greer, I. (2007) 'Industrial relations, migration, and neoliberal politics: The case of the European construction sector', *Politics & Society*, 35(4): 551–581.

Lucassen, G. and Lubbers, M. (2012) 'Who fears what? Explaining far-right-wing preference in Europe by distinguishing perceived cultural and economic ethnic threats', *Comparative Political Studies*, 45(5): 547–574.

Lucio, M.M. and Perrett, R. (2009) 'The diversity and politics of trade unions' responses to minority ethnic and migrant workers: The context of the UK', *Economic and Industrial Democracy*, 30(3): 324–347.

Mackenzie, R. and Forde, C. (2009) 'The rhetoric of the good worker versus the realities of employers' use and the experiences of migrant workers', *Work, Employment and Society*, 23(1): 142–159.

Marino, S., Penninx, R. and Roosblad, J. (2015) 'Trade unions, immigration and immigrants in Europe revisited: Unions' attitudes and actions under new conditions', *Comparative Migration Studies*, 3(1): 1.

Marino, S., Roosblad, J. and Penninx, R. (eds) (2017) *Trade Unions and Migrant Workers: New Contexts and Challenges in Europe*, Cheltenham: Edward Elgar. DOI https://doi.org/10.1007/s40878-015-0003-x

Moyce, S.C. and Schenker, M. (2018) 'Migrant workers and their occupational health and safety', *Annual Review of Public Health*, 39: 351–365.

OECD (Organisation for Economic Co-operation and Development) and UNHCR (United Nations High Commissioner for Refugees) (2016) *Migration Policy Debates: Hiring Refugees*. Available at: https://www.oecd.org/els/mig/migration-policy-debates-10.pdf

Penninx, R. and Roosblad, J. (eds) (2000) *Trade Unions, Immigration, and Immigrants in Europe, 1960–1993: A Comparative Study of the Attitudes and Actions of Trade Unions in Seven West European Countries*, vol 1, Oxford and New York: Berghahn Books.

Perrett, R., Lucio, M.M., McBride, J. and Craig, S. (2012) 'Trade union learning strategies and migrant workers: Policies and practice in a new-liberal environment', *Urban Studies*, 49(3): 649–667.

Refslund, B. (2021) 'When strong unions meet precarious migrants: Building trustful relations to unionise labour migrants in a high union-density setting', *Economic and Industrial Democracy*, 42(2): 314–335.

Scalise, G. and Burroni, L. (2020) 'Industrial relations and migrant integration in European cities: A comparative perspective', *Journal of European Social Policy*, 30(5): 587–600.

Squire, V. (2016) *The Exclusionary Politics of Asylum*, Cham: Springer.

Van Hooren, F.J. (2012) 'Varieties of migrant care work: Comparing patterns of migrant labour in social care', *Journal of European Social Policy*, 22(2): 133–147.

7

The 'back-stepper' and the 'career diplomat': turning points of labour market integration

Irina Isaakyan, Simone Baglioni and Anna Triandafyllidou

Introduction

There have been many studies on various forms, or proxies, of labour-market integration (De Beer and Schills, 2009; Bal, 2014; Berntsen, 2016). Among scholars and policymakers, there is a consensus on the economically integrated migrant as a well-paid professional who works in the area of his/her specialisation and rapidly progresses in his/her career (Baglioni and Isaakyan, 2019; Weinar and Klekowski von Koppenfels, 2020). However, there is limited knowledge about how migrants navigate complex new relations that underpin their labour-market accession, and how these people reflect upon their own experiences of integration. Living in precarious employment conditions in their new and often hostile societies, they make difficult choices and develop various coping strategies, while existing institutional practices and immigration laws often make their lives even more complicated (Oelgemoller, 2011; Marchetti, 2014; Koikkalainen and Kyle, 2016; Squire, 2017; Triandafyllidou, 2018; Marchetti et al, 2022).

It is within this context of everyday uncertainty, institutional bureaucracy and political instability that we seek to capture the biographic, or agentic, aspect of labour market integration. We want to look deeply into vulnerable and, at the same time, empowering lives of migrants and into the meanings they assign to their lived experience of (not) being integrated in their host societies. To achieve this, we use the method of narrative-biographic inquiry, which stresses the role of 'critical events' (Creswell, 2013) – or 'turning points' (Denzin, 1989, 2011) – in structuring people's lives and influencing their perceptions and self-positioning. To understand how migrants themselves understand and manage their own integration, we ask two questions. What are the most critical events that affect migrants' labour market integration? How do migrants respond to such challenges? The first question relates to the integration needs of migrants; while the second question connects to their own understanding of these needs and, consequently, to their coping strategies.

Through the prism of narrative-biographic research, our chapter looks at migrants, refugees and asylum seekers (MRAs) who arrived between 2014 and 2019 in seven European countries – notably, the Czech Republic, Denmark, Finland, Italy, Greece, Switzerland and the UK. These countries have been marked by significant post-2014 inflows of MRAs, who have very different migration experiences and backgrounds. We investigate, through the intersubjective yet critical lens, their initial labour market integration. Giving voice to the migrants themselves, we highlight their own experiences and understandings of the labour market integration process in the first years of immigration.

Our chapter has the following structure. The next section presents a critical literature review on integration and agency. In this section we elaborate on the basic concepts of 'integration', 'migrant agency' and 'migrant vulnerability', by illuminating their interconnectivity. We argue that integration of migrants is closely connected to their agency; while migrant agency, or 'navigation of social relations' by the migrant, is a dynamic, multidimensional process, which brings together an interplay of individual characteristics and structural forces such as gender, class and ethnicity (Triandafyllidou, 2018). Our starting point is, therefore, the 'integration–agency–vulnerability' nexus/triangle, which implicates the processual, multidirectional and dynamic nature of migrant agency in its difficult work towards achieving integration. The third section outlines the methodology and provides details of our sample. The fourth section discusses the main findings. It focuses on the main critical moments experienced by our informants in relation to their integration. These critical moments, or 'turning points' (Denzin, 1989, 2011; Creswell, 2013), throw light on integration challenges experienced by our informants and their emerging needs when they seek to enter and adjust to the host labour markets. In particular, we explore the role of such critical moments (or interrelated factor) of labour market integration as first job application (or labour market entrance), encounter with a biased administrator or official, and solidarity networking. We do not divide these critical encounters into barriers and enablers of integration for the following reason. We argue that integration is 'liquid' (or 'fluid') by nature, which means that one and the same event may affect integration both positively and negatively, depending on the circumstances and the work of migrant agency. In the fifth section, we develop an innovative typology of labour market integration: we present several types of migrants based on their perception of and responses to the challenges mentioned.

Integration, migrant agency and vulnerability

Squire (2017) defines migrants' agency as 'a conduct based on their ability to act consciously and to realize their migratory intentions'. As Triandafyllidou (2018) further explains, agency is their capacity for autonomous decision-making that takes place when they deal with various challenges of migration. Migrant agency manifests itself in the extent to which a person autonomously imagines a future migratory process, collects information, makes a cross-border movement, chooses his/her accommodation and professional or social activity in a new place, and/or forms a circle of new friends (Triandafyllidou, 2018). In other words, the agency of a migrant is revealed in his/her capacity to navigate the social environment of a new country and to become integrated in the host society and in the host economy. Moreover, the agentic potential of a migrant is realised through his/her labour market integration. Searching for a job, having your credentials recognised, negotiating your employment contract and fighting for your labour rights in a new country are indeed very challenging activities that require both autonomous decision-making and flexible networking on the part of the migrant. The labour market integration and migrant agency thus form a strong organic nexus.

Integration is generally understood by migration scholars and policymakers as 'the process of mutual adaptation between host society and migrants, implying a sense of mutual respect for values that bind migrants and their host communities to a common purpose' and mutual acceptance of each other (IOM, 2011: 51). At the core of this process is the reciprocity between migrants' needs and the hosts' actions (Penninx, 2018). This means that migrants should make an effort to learn and master the new culture while the hosts should try to understand the migrants' needs and provide a variety of cultural and economic accommodations to include the migrant in the host society as fully as possible. In theory, migrants should offer their skills to the host societies, who should provide the migrants with necessary accommodations such as adequate salaries and employment conditions that would match their professional qualifications.

Various studies show that success of labour market integration is generally associated for the migrant with employment in decent working conditions (De Beer and Schills, 2009; Bal, 2014; Bernstein, 2016). The International Labour Organization (ILO, 2020) defines 'decent work' as a mode of employment that 'delivers a fair income, security in the workplace, social protection for families, better prospects for personal development and social integration, freedom for people to express their concerns, and equal opportunity and treatment for all women and men'. The ILO (2020) further states that, only under these conditions, migrants' lives can be self-fulfilling.

In practice, however, such expected reciprocity is usually skewed, to a certain extent, towards the responsibility on the part of the migrant. In terms of labour market integration, the main task of finding employment and negotiating its conditions rests on the shoulders of the migrant and depends mostly on his/her capacity for independent and proactive decision-making (Penninx, 2018). The autonomy of the migrant's agency thus manifests itself in his/her decision-making in the conditions of minimum reciprocity with the host society. Studies show that a successful case of the migrant's decent work is an outcome of his/her agency because prolific conditions of employment at destination are usually achieved by migrants through difficult decisions and various hardships rather than given to them gratis (Bal, 2014; Bernstein, 2016; Baglioni and Isaakyan, 2019).

This further leads us to see another nexus – between migrants' agency and their vulnerability, or their openness to potential and real exploitation and harm, in the host labour market (Waite, 2009). In fact, within the context of minimum to null reciprocity, migrants as workers often become subjected to underpayment, unqualified employment, abusive employment relations and overall career downscaling and dissatisfaction (Waite, 2009; Piper, 2017; Piper and Whiter, 2018). While there are many established structural forces that support the vulnerability of migrants in the host labour market (Baglioni and Isaakyan, 2019). Scholars argue that legal provisions, labour market integration policies and discourses as well as civil society organisations and social partners provide migrants with a range of different opportunities, which differ across countries and migrant categories (De Beer and Schills, 2009; Bal, 2014; Berntsen, 2016). For example, 'economic migrants' are provided with opportunities that asylum seekers or irregular migrants do not have (Squire, 2017; Weinar and Klekowski von Koppenfels, 2020). Gender differences also create different structures of opportunity: thus women continue to lag behind men in their benefits from recruitment policies and become adversely affected by persistent cultural stereotypes about gender roles both in the family and in the economic system (Christou and Kofman, 2022). As a result, the childcare duties and educational disadvantages may become unsurmountable barriers for women-migrants in general and for refugee women in particular (Christou and Kofman, 2022). Alongside this, employment obstructions are added by disability. Thus not only more educated but also more physically fit migrants de facto have better employment opportunities at destination, while newcomers with medical conditions may have unrecognised healthcare needs that impede their successful employment (De Beer and Schills, 2009; Bal, 2014; Berntsen, 2016). Especially at the beginning of their immigration, migrants are, in fact, very vulnerable workers, who must confront their own vulnerability mostly on their own if they want to survive.

However, employment relations can be changed any time, and Waite (2009) gives credit to migrants' capacity for turning their own vulnerability into a factor enabling their independent decision-making and integration.

In fact, migrants' agency – or their decision-making about relocation and settlement (Squire, 2017) – is a highly interactive process of exploring complex social relations while 'navigating' towards, away from or past integration (Triandafyllidou, 2018). The dynamic and multidimensional nature of migrants' agency becomes especially apparent in their navigation towards labour-market integration, which often develops in non-linear ways (Katz et al, 2004; Triandafyllidou, 2018). Triandafyllidou (2018) argues that it is a 'fragmented' itinerary with different 'stops and intermediate milestones', where the journey can change its nature and direction and where there can be returns and new departures. Searching for work, migrants navigate complex administrative requirements, adapt to a new cultural context and identify job opportunities through formal or informal channels (Triandafyllidou, 2018).

During these phases of navigating the new country environment, there is an interplay between the migrant's initial hopes and expectations, actual conditions that she/he is faced with, and ways in which the migrant develops her/his agency and seeks to turn these conditions in his/her favour (Triandafyllidou, 2017, 2018). This process also involves an intense interaction between individual migrants, their families, and various structural and relational forces that shape migrants' trajectories and perceptions of integration (Carling and Schewel, 2017; Van Hear et al, 2017).

This interactive nature of migrant agency resonates with the fundamental argument of Anthony Giddens (2000) about the 'agency-structure' nexus, which implies an interactive – although not always reciprocal and symmetric – relationship between the individual and their environment. Migration scholars note that, while struggling with their hostile environments, migrants do not only make new forced decisions under the impact of various circumstances of their migration but also create new opportunities for themselves through these dynamics (King et al, 2017; Squire, 2017; Triandafyllidou, 2018). As generally noted by Norman Denzin (2011), some events that happen to people may change their lives entirely and create new circumstances. Such critical events may become the signposts of migrant agency.

The list of such events includes facing the loss of the significant other, graduating from the university, meeting a new person, undergoing a divorce or experiencing a difficult socioeconomic situation such as war or unemployment. During such encounters, people often have to change their habitual life plans and life routines and make new important decisions. The decision-making process – or the work of human agency – thus becomes altered or redirected towards new goals. For example, having lost a parent or a spouse, a person may suddenly enter a difficult economic situation and start thinking of new ways to earn money. Being affected by a war, political persecution or unemployment, an individual may start thinking about changing a living environment and emigrate. An encounter with a new colleague or stranger may lead to new social connections and, consequently, new opportunities for further decision-making. Thus people often change/ choose their jobs and places of residence, including new countries, based on the advice or information from people they occasionally meet. When such events lead us to make new decisions, make new choices and change our lives, they become our 'turning points' (Denzin, 1989, 2011).

Methodology

In the light of the discussion in the previous section, we would like to explore how migrants themselves understand the dynamics of their own labour market integration. To achieve this, we ask: What were the most critical events that helped the migrants understand their own needs? To what extent did the migrants feel 'able' to overcome emerging obstacles, mobilise their resources and achieve mobility in the labour market?

To answer these questions and to explore migrants' lived experiences of labour market integration, the SIRIUS research project consortium[1] has conducted 100 semi-structured narrative-biographic interviews with post-2014 MRAs in seven countries, namely: 16 interviews in Greece; 10 in Italy; 11 each in Switzerland, Finland and the UK; 14 in the Czech Republic; and 27 in Denmark. Fieldwork in Italy, Finland, Switzerland and the UK took place during the COVID-19 pandemic, which prevented the researchers from reaching out to a higher number of interviewees. In this context, an alternative and effective approach to obtaining the narrative-biographic data was its collection from secondary sources such as social media stories and published migrant biographies (De Fina and Georgakopoulou, 2012).

The choice of the countries has been determined by their political-institutional approaches towards welfare services, immigration and labour market structure. For example, Denmark is a country with a strong welfare system, which, however, has implemented a variety of flexible measures. On the other hand, Southern European countries have continued to rely upon more rigid labour market policies and have provided fewer social provisions from the welfare state (Eichhorst et al, 2009; Giugni, 2010; Simonazzi and Villa, 2010; van Aerschot and Daenzer, 2016).

The selected countries vary considerably in terms of their political-institutional approaches towards unemployment, welfare state and Europeanisation. On the one hand, these countries have some 'contingent convergence' of instruments, goals and outcomes in labour market regulations (Eichhorst and Konle-Seidl, 2008). On the other hand, substantial differences in their policymaking dynamics and policy implementation have led to the establishment of diverse employment policy regimes (Gallie, 2007a, 2007b, 2007c; de Beer and Schills, 2009; Rothgang and Dingeldey, 2009; Anxo et al, 2010).

The overall analytical framework is critical ethnography, which conveys a critical inquiry into the relationship between victimisation and empowerment (Creswell, 2013). In our case, it is the relationship between MRAs' vulnerability and their agency – the relationship between their insecurity (Waite, 2009) and autonomous decision-making (Squire, 2017; Triandafyllidou, 2018). As De Fina and Georgakopoulou (2008: 385) note, critical ethnography 'pays a close attention to both micro- and macro-levels but always take the local level of interaction as the place of articulation of phenomenon to be explained'.

Thinking about the crossroads of integration, migrant agency and meaningful biographic experience, we seek to find events that may change trajectories and self-positioning of migrants. The conducted semi-structured interviews lasted for 2–3 hours each and paid attention to the most critical moments in the lives of our informants. Using the narrative-biographic method, we specifically look into those 'turning points' (Denzin, 1989; Creswell, 2013), which challenged our informants by obstructing and/or enabling their integration and into the informants' reflections on those changes (including their perception of gender, class and race/ethnicity). We then examine consequences that those events have had for the dynamics of the informants' employment and develop a typology of their labour market integration.

The signposts of integration

Our findings show that the course of labour market integration never runs smooth. It is a complex trajectory, which has a few signposts. It stumbles over or gathers momentum from specific events, which may either disrupt or support it, depending on the external circumstance and the migrant's reaction to them. Such critical points that had challenged our informants and (re)directed their integration paths were their attempts to enter the job market upon destination, encounters with a biased administrator or official, and encounters with and accession to a solidarity network. Some of our female informants had also experienced their turning points during their pre-emigration years, when their countries of origin had been in a political turmoil and when disturbing events had been, consequently, intensified.

Entering the labour market

The first job at destination became a crucial event for all our informants, changing their perspectives on 'new life' and, to a certain extent, predetermining their further integration trajectories. Some of our informants entered the host labour market in the reciprocal conditions of informational transparency and with full respect to their human rights.

As migrant-newcomers, our informants were enjoying the right to work legally and to obtain regular employment in such instances. For their less fortunate counterparts, the only available choice was, however, no legal right to work, which meant employment in the irregular market. In either case, our informants admit having joined the labour market to occupy a position and fulfil tasks that were different from their previous professional experience back home. For example, Maria[2] entered the Czech Republic with a fake tourist visa – that is, without a formal permission to work. As an undocumented migrant, she had no other option than to take "the dirtiest job at a factory with the salary around CZK 32 per hour".

This turning point made the majority of our informants extremely disenchanted from European integration, at least, for some time. The emotional pain and the perception of integration as a difficult process were mostly associated with feeling 'useless' in terms of one's own professional experience – "as if no one needed your skills" (Finland, MRA). Failure with the recognition of credentials became an additional – aftermath – encounter that intensified the effect of the failed first job application. Although theoretically considered a key aspect of the labour market functioning, the existing mechanisms for the recognition of educational credentials and related skills acquired outside Europe prove to be cumbersome and inefficient in most European countries (Isaakyan and Triandafyllidou, 2019). As a result, our informants (many of whom were highly skilled migrants) were expected to start their employment at destination 'from scratch', as if they had had no prior work-related education or experience. In such a migrant-hostile milieu, even the interviewees with in-demand skills such as healthcare operators found it very problematic to secure qualified employment.

In such cases, their migrant agency did not suffice to find the way out because it was intertwining with the traditional segmentation of European labour markets. Within such socially stratified rhetoric, the majority of employment resources are de facto allocated on the grounds of an invisible, caste-like, division of workers (Lhuilier, 2005; Duffy, 2011). In this heavily discriminatory milieu, even highly skilled migrants frequently specialise in certain tasks and jobs that are usually not what they would expect, especially when such jobs score low in the socail esteem hierarchy (Duffy, 2011), while local populations are engaged in other – more desirable – domains of work (Duffy, 2011). Our informants thus had to take their first jobs in the sectors of personal care, domestic work, agriculture, house cleaning and garbage collection.

The revelatory perception of employment in Europe as 'extremely unfair' and 'intrinsically prejudiced' was compounded by the informants' encounters with administrators and immigration officials who held a personal anti-migrant bias in their decisions. For example, an informant from the Czech

Republic admits that, when she was filling in the job application forms, she was interested only in a job she would be qualified for. However, the civil servant suggested that she should apply for the 'cleaning maid' position. The informant was shocked and extremely upset by the cynicism and indifference of the official, admitting: "That civil servant did not actually care about what I was writing in the form. She just wanted me out of her office as soon as possible" (Czech Republic, civil servant).

Meeting the right person

However, the sad 'labour-market segmentation' story did have a happy ending for some migrants such as the meteorologist Mohammed, who lives in Greece. Struggling through a series of discriminatory encounters and personal biases of powerful people, he incidentally met a diasporic co-national, with whose support he quickly found a good job, thus terminating all his employment sufferings. As Mohammed notes, "[f]or the majority of migrants, their ethnic networks appear to be the main communication channel with the Greek labour market".

In this reference, scholars argue that networking is indeed a key condition for qualified and satisfactory employment in all EU countries (De Luca and Ambrosini, 2019). As the UK-settled migrant Danielle explains, "[g]ood employment is not just about finding a vacancy and applying for a job. It is all about networking". She concludes, however, that "it is not easy to create personal connections if you are not from here, if you have not been born in the host country". Linda, a migrant living in Finland, confirms the importance of authentic ties and the difficulty of searching for friends and other 'weak ties' with strangers (see Granovetter, 1983) as a substitute for the native networking that works in local communities:

> 'The way to work in Finland is to know a friend who will recommend you to the company that is looking for workers. In this way, you can work with them for a long time, and they will see how you work. This is important because they are afraid of signing a long-term contract with you in case you are not suitable for the work.' (Finland, MRA)

The interviews illuminate the contradictory nature of migrant networking. Although networks may help to alleviate the administrative bias and present the migrant as a trustworthy candidate for a good job, they are also of the segmentary nature: as 'national outsider' or 'people from not here' migrants are almost de facto located at the bottom of the networking hierarchy. While the 'small world' rule of paving your network road through friends (Granovetter, 1983) may in some cases work instantaneously, in others it can become a rather challenging activity, depending on the sociocultural conditions for migrant agency. Thus, for the Ukrainian migrant Lena, an encounter with a stranger became a positive critical moment of networking in the Czech Republic: the co-national man she met by chance became her boyfriend and immediately helped her to find a well-paid and secure job in a bar in Prague, with which she has been fully satisfied.

At the same time, the ethnic/diasporic 'network' encounters do not work as powerful turning points for all migrants. This is illuminated by dependent women-migrants from North Africa, who are still marginalised in their networking and, consequently, in their job search in Europe. They complain about constantly feeling the inadequacy of ethnic networking, which is contaminated by the scarcity of the childcare resources and the inadequacy of public services for migrant-women in the EU. For example, Zuleika, who has followed her husband in Denmark as a family migrant from Yemen to Denmark, explains that neither her husband nor her in-laws from the same household help her with the childcare. And since she has to spend most of her time at home, raising the children and looking after the house, she has no opportunity to search for a network. Above that, all her encounters with the diasporic network itself have made her feel as if she is 'falling behind'. They have made her feel that she was 'not good enough' to gain the network support. At the same time, such women admit that the networking strategy would have been more effective for them if they had no husband putting the brakes on their diasporic networking.

A call from the past

The importance of pre-emigration turning points that have changed the lives and prospective integration trajectories of some independent women-migrants became clear in the case of women-migrants coming from countries where there was a military conflict. Thus Lena, a former police officer with a law degree from Ukraine, was affected by the Crimean war in 2014, as a result of which she could not find a job at home. That war intensified various attitudes of prejudice prevailing in her home society, including sexist practices in employment. An encounter with a highly misogynistic team of prospective employers who were administering her job interview had persuaded her to leave Ukraine and to be happy with any job abroad. Among Syrian women the war and the relocation to Denmark became a catalyst in their marriage and eventually led them to divorce and to seek to take their lives in their own hands – an achievement that was particularly difficult in a foreign country. That turning point had made Lena more open to integration and, consequently, more flexible to the impact of various other encounters such as job market entrance and communication with officials at destination. Pre-emigration turning points thus make the migrant's agency more resilient at destination and more open to negotiating integration barriers.

The typology of the 'integrated migrant'

Having experienced all these turning points in their lives, our informants underwent significant changes both in their life perception and in their coping strategies. Some of them started to re-evaluate their priorities and aspirations and to look for more pragmatic ways to facilitate their integration. Based on their responses (both inner thoughts and actions) to the critical events discussed, our informants can be divided into two broad types of 'integrated migrant': (1) 'back-stepper' and (2) 'career diplomat' (or 'alternative/flexible careerist'). There are finer divisions within each type:

1. Back-stepper ('depot migrant', or 'migrant-in-waiting'):
   (a) proactive back-stepper (or 'new-skill-learner');
   (b) passive back-stepper (or 'depot dweller').

2. Career diplomat ('alternative careerist'):
   (a) re-skilled professional;
   (b) work–life balancer (working mother).

The back-steppers can be subdivided into 'proactive back-steppers' (or 'skill learners') and 'passive back-steppers'. While career-diplomats are further divided into: 're-skilled professionals' and 'working mothers' (or 'work–life balancers').

'Maids-in-waiting': stepping back to learn or to get lost?

All our informants agree that the degree to which you will be able to find satisfactory employment in emigration depends on your first job at destination and on the recognition of your credentials, the latter factors influencing (or 'contaminating') the former. Having encountered significant barriers for immediate qualified employment and understanding the difficulties of overcoming these barriers, many informants decided rather pragmatically to 'take a step back' and 'wait for a better chance' – or to 'wait for the second chance'. They thus agreed to take 'a very dirty manual job' through the irregular market – sometimes feeling helpless to change anything but sometimes pursuing the intent of 'buying in the time' that was necessary for their prospectively envisioned integration. They can be conceptualised as 'living-in-waiting', or 'depot-stationed'. The question is for how long they are intent on waiting and how soon they manage to move further.

The expected 'second chance' did not come to all back-steppers – but only to those who had invested in proactive planning and learning, which brings us back to the work of migrant agency as a proactive and well-planned process. While holding under-skilled jobs, some of our informants decided to use this employment as an opportunity to learn new skills such as the national language or additional career credentials and also to gather more information for locating the network. That is why they can be called the 'proactive back-steppers', or 'new-skill-leaners'. Some of them have even managed to build up alternative careers and thus to convert into 'career diplomats', pointing to the interconnectivity between and porousness within these two categories of migrant.

In many of such cases, our informants have accumulated new skills and knowledge through volunteering and as supported by local civil society organisations. The story of Diana, who now lives in Switzerland, proves that, for migrants, volunteering can become a valid surrogate of work experience and networking in the country of settlement:

> 'The volunteer work that I am now doing is closely connected to my area of professional specialisation. It gives me confidence that I am able to work in the field here in Switzerland. Now I have a good estimate of where and how I can further get a decent job with a decent salary.' (Switzerland, MRA)

Volunteering has thus become not only an important way to a new experience but also a path towards new personal networks. And such proactive back-steppers have often accumulated their news skills through ethnic/gender solidarity that penetrated established institutional practices. This is evident in the testimonies about immense support from municipal case workers of the diasporic origin provided to our female informants. Their testimonies also show that the personal bias of an official can be positive, and it can work in favour of the migrant, thus creating a very powerful turning point at the crossroads of ethnic/gender solidarity and institutionalisation.

However, volunteering can work only for those migrants who trust this strategy and invest in it to the fullest. Among our informants, there are also those who have been looking at volunteering with suspicion, viewing it as doing something denigrated, which is below their professional level. The lack of knowledge about and, consequently, the lack of trust in volunteering and related networking is what may actually keep the migrant from ascending to the alternative career. And this mistrust may steer the migrant's conversion into a depot-dweller, or a passive back-stepper, who lives in-waiting forever. Many of our informants in Finland admit 'having got stuck' in their depots, first waiting for their second chance and then giving up that hope. They complain about working as cleaning maids in cheap hotels or spa salons without any prospects for a positive change. They also admit having initially set unrealistic goals for their prospectively envisioned integration and having not invested in volunteering and proactive learning.

Alternative navigation, or growing to love

Angela, who had migrated to Finland, used to hear many stories about such depot-dwelling migrants. Afraid of this kind of conversion, she decided to explore the situation proactively as soon as she had realised that she could not easily find qualified employment as a medical doctor. She knew that she did not know the Finnish language very well, including the Finnish medical language. Having invested in language learning, she tried to apply for the medical assistant position, soon understanding that the job market in that sector was highly competitive for her. She had finally agreed to develop an alternative career – the career of a nurse.

That integration path was of course supported by her husband, who is a medical doctor himself and therefore has connections in the medical work sector. However, the main factor contributing to her re-qualification has been her pragmatic re-evaluation of her own skills and of the timing for their accumulation:

> 'I was told that the language demands are less stiff for nurses. I also felt more comfortable knowing that I would not be fully in charge of many things because prescriptions required irreproachable comprehension and communication skills in Finnish. Starting sceptically, I have eventually grown to love my new profession.' (Finland, MRA)

The worker and the woman: the equilibrium of integration

To what extent do material benefits and career aspirations remain important and to what extent can migrants be resilient when facing their full or partial loss? This is the question that seems logical in the light of the story about Angela's resilience. This question probably relates to our female informants from Syria who had to re-evaluate economic incentives for and moral benefits/damages from their immigration to Europe when dealing with such pre-emigration critical events as divorce and sometimes a consequent separation from children.

For example, Habiba, a Syrian refugee-woman, fled to Denmark after having divorced her violent husband. That divorce had significantly changed her attitude to life and made her more flexible as a work–life balancer. Such experiences of liberation from a long-term marital abuse are located at the crossroads between the woman's self-perception as "a wife who is falling behind" and her concurrent positive thinking of herself as "a free person who is entering the new world". The latter element of self-revelation has become a very strong factor of the women's labour market integration. The conflict between the envisioned professional qualifications and existing employment opportunities has been resolved through the consolidation of such women's pre-emigration abuse experiences and their new feeling of self-emancipation. The taken "first available job" has been perceived by Habiba and other Syrian women from the same sociocultural background as "still a very good opportunity to obtain a high level of social control over your life".

It is true that many skilled migrants view their 'forced' employment in a down-scaled sector with zero tolerance and repulsion, waiting for a better life chance. For example, Valerie (who lives in the UK) confesses that she "was forced, in a way, to accept the only job available, working in a beauty studio, providing waxing and other beauty treatments, and emotionally suffering from no career development". However, the informants like Habiba feel quite satisfied with such a job because it allows them to achieve and to sustain the initially envisioned work–life balance.

Conclusion: Liquid integration

Summing up, the course of labour market integration does not always run smooth, as our findings show. They illuminate the labour market integration of MRAs as a complex trajectory, which is oriented to specific signposts. Specific events may both disrupt and support it, depending on external circumstances and the migrant's reaction to them. Critical moments that have challenged our informants and (re)directed their integration paths are their experiences of first job at destination, encounters with prejudiced officials and encounters with solidarity networks.

When dealing with such turning points, our informants used the main strategies of stepping back (and waiting for a better chance) and re-skilling for an alternative career. On the basis of these two broad strategies, we can recognise the following four types of the 'labour market integrated migrant':

1. *Proactive back-stepper* who does not merely wait for his/her other chance but learns new skills, in order to foster the second chance, and shows pragmatic flexibility in re-evaluating his/her priorities.
2. *Passive back-stepper (depot-dweller)* who lives as if in the eternal depot, not actually waiting for the second chance but complaining about the denigrated employment.
3. *Career diplomat* who is a re-skilled – though, to a certain extent, downscaled – professional (as illuminated by the 'doctor-to-nurse' career descent).
4. *Career diplomat* whose overall work–life balance compensates for his/her employment insecurity (as illuminated by the careers of divorced working mothers from the Middle East).

The division of our informants into 'back-steppers' and 'career diplomats' shows that their integration differs in terms of their agency of investing. It is an investment in further integration that a turning point primarily disrupts or provokes. These turning points, that have detached some informants from their host societies, have actually stranded them away them from investing in integration – from learning new skills, from looking for new network connections, from trying volunteer work and from reconsidering their lives in general. The dirty work experience thus translates into integration for some migrants while into marginalisation for other. Labour market integration is thus an agentic category of skill/reflexivity investment.

Our analysis shows how integration is a dynamic process. People cross the borders through various interconnected channels of mobility and share their migratory experiences across different 'migrant' categories (Engbersen, 2018). Their labour market integration develops in interactions between policies, legal categories and frameworks on one hand, and their actions on the other – such actions include not only their effective actions but also how they feel about them and how they make sense of what happened to them. This is clearly visible in the polysemantic character of the turning points they face: one and the same critical event (such as first job or networking) can have different meanings for different migrants and, consequently, provoke different integration outcomes. Thus some 'maids-in-waiting' may endlessly wait for another chance and suffer from underemployment while others may actively invest in the accumulation of new skills and connections.

Second, the fluidity of labour market integration is seen in the porousness of its categories: proactive back-steppers can any time convert into career diplomats or depot-dwellers.

Third, integration is interconnected and sometimes moving back and forth rather than progressing in a linear way. Segmented labour markets prevent people from improving their professional situation and oftentimes it happens that their integration remains 'liquid' (Bauman, 2000) in the sense that migrants are kept in poor quality initial jobs, in-waiting for better opportunities but these do not always materialise even if migrants develop required new skills and solidarity networks.

Finally, integration experiences often become contaminated, like liquids that permeate across stratified areas. Thus, the effect of the 'first job application' becomes contaminated – or negatively affected – by the recognition of credentials or the gender/ethnic bias.

Notes

[1] For more information see www.sirius-project.eu
[2] Names of interviewees have been modified by the authors.

References

Anxo, D., Bosch, G. and Rubery, J. (2010) *The Welfare State and Life Transitions: A European Perspective*, Cheltenham and Northampton: Edward Elgar.

Baglioni, S. and Isaakyan, I. (2019) *Integrated Report on Individual Barriers and Enablers*, Work Package 6 Research Report, SIRIUS Project. Available at: https://www.sirius-project.eu/sites/default/files/attachments/Individual%20Barriers%20and%20Enablers.pdf

Bal, E. (2014) 'Yearning for faraway places: The construction of migration desires among young and educated Bangladeshis in Dhaka', *Identities*, 21(3): 275–289.

Bauman, Z. (2000) *Liquid Modernity*, Cambridge: Polity.

Berntsen, L. (2016) 'Reworking labour practices: On the agency of unorganized mobile migrant construction workers', *Work, Employment and Society*, 30(3): 472–288. https://doi.org/10.177/0950017015617687

Carling, J. and Schewel K. (2017) 'Revisiting aspiration and ability in international migration', *Journal of Ethnic and Migration Studies*, 44(6): 945–963. https://doi.org/10.1080/1369183X.2017.1384146

Christou, A. and Kofman, E. (2022) *Gender and Migration*, Cham: Springer-IMISCOE.

Creswell, J. (2013) *Qualitative Inquiry and Research Design: Choosing Among Five Approaches*, third edition, Thousand Oaks: SAGE.

De Beer, P. and Schills T. (2009) *The Labour Market Triangle: Employment Protection, Unemployment Compensation and Activation in Europe*, Cheltenham and Northampton: Edward Elgar.

De Fina, A. and Georgakopoulou, A. (2008) 'Analyzing narratives as practices', *Qualitative Research*, 8(3): 379–387.

De Luca, D. and Ambrosini, M. (2019) 'Female immigrant entrepreneurs: More than a family strategy', *International Migration*, (57)5: 201–205.

Denzin, N. (1989) *Interpretive Biography*, Thousand Oaks: SAGE.

Denzin, N. (2011) *Interpretive Autoethnography*, Thousand Oaks: SAGE.

Duffy, M. (2011) *Making Care Count: A Century of Gender, Race, and Paid Care Work*, New Brunswick: Rutgers University Press.

Eichhorst, W. and Konle-Seidl, R. (2008) 'Contingent convergence: A comparative analysis of activation policies', Working Paper, IZA DP No. 3905, Bonn: Institute for the Study of Labour.

Eichhorst, W., Marx P. and Tobsch V. (2009) 'Institutional arrangements, employment performance and the quality of work', Working Paper, IZA DP No. 4595, Bonn: Institute for the Study of Labour.

Engbersen, G. (2018) 'Liquid migration and its consequences for local integration policies', in P. Scholten and M. van Ostaijen (eds), *Between Mobility and Migration*, Cham: Springer-IMISCOE, pp 63–76.

Gallie, D. (ed) (2007a) *Employment Regimes and the Quality of Work*, New York: Oxford University Press.

Gallie, D. (2007b) 'Production regimes, employment regimes, and the quality of work', in D. Gallie (ed), *Employment Regimes and the Quality of Work*, New York: Oxford University Press, pp 1–33.

Gallie, D. (2007c) 'The quality of work life in comparative perspective', in D. Gallie (ed), *Employment Regimes and the Quality of Work*, New York: Oxford University Press, pp 205–232.

Giddens, A. (2000) *Runaway World*, London: Routledge.

Giugni, M. (ed.) (2010) *The Contentious Politics of Unemployment in Europe*, Basingstoke: Palgrave Macmillan.

Granovetter, M. (1983) 'The strength of weak ties: A network theory revisited', *Sociological Theory*, 1: 201–233. https://doi.org/10.2307/202051

ILO (International Labour Organization) (2020) *Decent Work*. Available at: https://www.ilo.org/global/topics/decent-work/lang--en/index.htm

IOM (2011) *IOM and Migrant Integration*, Geneva, IOM Press.

Isaakyan, I. and Triandafyllidou, A. (2019) 'European Union', in Federico, V. (ed.) *Legal Barriers and Enablers: Sirius WP 2 Report*. Available at: https://www.sirius-project.eu/sites/default/files/attachments/WP2_D2.2.pdf

Katz, C. (2004) *Growing up Global: Economic Restructuring and Children's Everyday Lives*, Minneapolis: University of Minnesota Press.

King, R., Lulle, A., Sampaio, D. and Vullnetari, J. (2017) 'Unpacking the ageing–migration nexus and challenging the vulnerability trope', *Journal of Ethnic & Migration Studies*, 43(2): 182–198.

Koikkalainen, S. and Kyle, D. (2016) 'Imagining mobility: The prospective cognition question in migration research', *Journal of Ethnic and Migration Studies*, 42(5): 759–776.

Lhuilier, D. (2005) 'Le sale boulot', *Travailler*, 2(14): 73–98.

Marchetti, S. (2014) *Black Girls: Migrant Domestic Workers and Colonial Legacies*, Boston: Brill.

Marchetti, S., Garofalo, G. and di Bartolomeo, A. (2022) 'Dilemmas around temporariness and transnational recruitment agencies: The case of migrant caregivers in Taiwan and Germany', *Journal of Ethnic and Refugee Studies*, forthcoming.

Oelgemoller, C. (2011) '"Transit" and "suspension": Migration management or the metamorphosis of asylum-seekers into "illegal" immigrants', *Journal of Ethnic and Migration Studies*, 37(3): 407–424.

Penninx, M. (2018) 'Old wine in new bottles?', in P. Scholten and M. Ostaijen (eds), *Between Mobility and Migration*, Cham: Springer-IMISCOE, pp 77–100.

Piper, N. (2017) 'Migrant precarity in Asia: "Networks of labour activism" for a rights-based governance of migration', *Development and Change*, 48(5): 1089–1110.

Piper, N. and Whiter M. (2018) 'Forced transnationalism and temporary labour migration: Implications for understanding migrant rights', *Identities*, 25(5): 558–575.

Rothgang, H. and Dingeldey, I. (2009) 'Conclusion: The governance of welfare state reform', in H. Rothgang and I. Dingeldey (eds), *Governance of Welfare State Reform*, Cheltenham and Northampton: Edward Elgar, pp 238–250.

Simonazzi, A. and Villa, P. (2010) '"La grande illusion": How Italy's "American dream" turned sour', in D. Anxo, G. Bosch and J. Rubery (eds), *The Welfare State and Life Transitions: A European Perspective*, Cheltenham and Northampton: Edward Elgar, pp 231–256.

Squire, V. (2017) 'Unauthorised migration beyond structure/agency? Acts, interventions, effects', *Politics*, 37(3): 254–272.

Triandafyllidou, A. (2017) 'Beyond irregular migration governance: Zooming in on migrants' agency', *European Journal of Migration and Law*, 19(1): 1–11.

Triandafyllidou, A. (2018) 'The migration archipelago: Social navigation and migrant agency', *International Migration*, 57(1): 5–19.

Van Aerschot, P. and Daenzer, P. (2016) *The Integration and Protection of Immigrants: Canadian and Scandinavian Critiques*, London and New York: Routledge.

Van Hear, N., Bakewell, O. and Long, K. (2017) 'Push-pull plus: Reconsidering the drivers of migration', *Journal of Ethnic and Migration Studies*, 44(6): 927–944. https://doi.org/10.180/1369183x.2017.1384135

Waite, L. (2009) 'A place and space for a critical geography of precarity?', *Geography Compass*, 3(1): 412–433.

Weinar, A. and Klekowski von Koppenfels, A. (2020) *High-Skill Migration: Between Settlement and Mobility*, Cham: Springer-IMISCOE.

8

The policy dimension: lessons learnt and ways forward

Maria Mexi

Introduction

The implications of the record migratory flows to Europe witnessed in 2015 and 2016 are still being felt today. Addressing migrants' labour market integration remains a long-standing challenge in many European countries. Migration and integration are complex processes that affect the security and welfare of a wide range of actors, from migrants to individuals and communities in both host and origin countries. This implies that migration responses are seldom simply about migration, but also about a slew of other public policy concerns, as migration and integration do not occur in a vacuum. Responses to migration and integration are embedded in national institutions, which can and often do vary among nations and evolve over time. The development of national, regional and international institutions and policies is primarily a political issue frequently reflecting electoral purposes; concurrently, policies and attitudes towards migrants are frequently founded, in some cases and at least in part, on prejudices and strong value-related emotions.

What can the analyses and case studies in this book tell us about the nature of, and methods for enhancing, policymaking ties between migration and integration considering these circumstances? There are two key insights. First, the case studies in the book have clearly underlined the necessity of paying attention to cross-country disparities in legal institutions (Chapter 3) that mediate the interrelationships between migration and integration public discourse, and policymaking. There are also significant disparities between countries in terms of the effects of welfare and labour market policies (Chapter 4), as well as the role of social partners (Chapters 5 and 6), all of which have consequences for how solutions to facilitate migrants' integration are created and may be structured. Recognising these distinct institutional settings is required before organising and supporting policy-relevant research in a way that is credible and useful for public discourse and policymaking processes.

Second, the fieldwork research conducted as part of the project shows that the COVID-19 pandemic has overshadowed policy debates on migration issues, yet it is inextricably linked with the present and future of migration governance within the EU and globally. The pandemic is affecting the health, social conditions, job prospects, language training of already vulnerable migrants, as well as their labour market and broader social integration. It is also highly affecting public opinion. When the COVID-19 pandemic began early in 2020, populists in Europe attempted to exploit the crisis for political gain, using migrants as scapegoats (Dayant, 2020). With vulnerabilities and inequalities worsening long after the end of the pandemic, there is a risk of a new backlash in public opinion against migrants similar to the one that European societies experienced during the post-2014 influx of migrants, refugees and asylum seekers. Therefore, understanding how European countries are able to work out an evidence-based way to deal with migration and asylum – rather than a prejudice-based one – is crucial for scientists, policymakers, stakeholders and society at large.

With these critical background insights in mind, this chapter identifies key lessons that can be drawn from the diversity of the country case studies investigated in the book and makes a number of observations for researchers, policy practitioners and other participants to help strengthen the links between integration and migration. We argue that these lessons can point to 'ways forward' in attempts to make migration and integration policy and public debates more research-informed. The ultimate goal is normative in nature, aiming to raise awareness about how, in the aftermath of the COVID-19 pandemic, we can sustain decent livelihoods for migrants and refugees, leaving no one behind. A fruitful strategy in that direction would be the development of a fully fledged normative agenda that specifies sound standards and an incentive system for all relevant stakeholders. At this point, we can only suggest where to look for the building blocks that will allow the starting steps to bring about the essential adjustments.

Key lessons and areas for action

Policy investments into the labour market and social integration of post-2014 migrants have long been considered as crucial for the long-term sustainability of the European workforce. Various empirical studies (for example, Kahanec and Zimmermann, 2009, 2016; Zimmermann, 2014; Blau and Mackie, 2016), before the outbreak of the COVID-19 crisis, had pointed to the economic opportunities of migration and, on this basis, suggest ideas of how Europe could achieve a fair and effective allocation of migrants that preserves European principles and European unity. While the current period is a very different situation than the one Europe faced during the so-called migration crisis of 2014–2015 (although it would be more appropriate to refer to a multilevel policy system crisis rather than a 'migration crisis'), these empirical findings must be taken into consideration in the vein of evidence-based policymaking by national and European policymakers in their efforts to establish a well-functioning integration policy in the post-COVID-19 era. Policymakers and civil society stakeholders can capitalise on several lessons learnt – first and foremost, the value of taking a step back, mobilising resources, and rethinking barriers and enablers fundamental to potential integration of migrants and ways to build durable multistakeholder synergies and results. There is a possible eruption of a second big migration crisis due to the economic consequences that COVID-19 will eventually leave behind (Marmefelt, 2020) and the accelerated climate change (Voegele, 2021) especially in developing countries in Africa and elsewhere. Therefore, crafting the next generation of integration policies at national and EU levels becomes of high importance in the post-COVID-19 recovery phase. In view of this, the following pointers to best practice have been put forward.

Integrating migrants' needs in post-COVID-19 recovery plans and strategies

In all the European countries studied in this book, the COVID-19 crisis has reinforced a number of key challenges migrants were facing even before the pandemic – such as language barriers and limited access to information, uncertainty related to their employment and legal status, ineffective administrative and legal structures, health insurance issues, the absence of a supportive family or community network, isolation, increased vulnerability and precarity in the face of work exploitation, a general atmosphere of xenophobia in society and (perceived) cultural barriers, and limited access to institutional support in situations of abuse (refer to Bagavos and Kourachanis, 2020; Collini et al, 2020; Mexi, 2020; Ndomo et al, 2020; Spyratou, 2020; Gheorghiev et al, 2021). More particularly, fieldwork in the seven countries analysed shows that the pandemic has exacerbated the vulnerable and precarious position of migrants especially by weakening their legal status (mainly temporary migrants), rights, opportunities and socioeconomic standing (Federico, 2018; SIRIUS Policy Brief No 2, 2019). Precarity has both immediate and future implications for migrants' labour market integration. As policymakers continue their efforts to address the adverse impacts of the COVID-19 pandemic, it is critical that migrants and refugees are integrated in recovery plans and strategies (Zenner and Wickramage, 2020) as full participants to ensure inclusive and sustainable recovery (European Economic and Social Committee, 2020). The next Multiannual Financial Framework (2021–2027), which has been paired with the Next Generation EU initiative that aims to assist member states with post-COVID-19 recovery is an opportunity to fund and design labour market policies that are attuned to the need of migrants. Our findings show that existing national policies do not adequately support and prepare the migrants for entry and integration into labour markets (see Chapter 4). For instance, job matching and career counselling services (offered as part of the integration programme) sometimes push migrants and refugees to jobs that are deemed low status (such as cleaning and driving), or which are otherwise perceived as suitable for non-natives (such as healthcare). We find that there is tension between public policy goals of trying to push migrants into work as quickly as possible, and finding jobs that match the ambitions and potential of individual migrants. In some cases, there were also indications that employment services case workers undervalued migrants' and refugees' potential to work in skilled jobs. In countries with strong active labour market policies, such as Finland, Denmark and Switzerland, the assistance was valued in some respects by the migrants, but also some degree of coercion was felt, in terms of being pushed into jobs deemed appropriate by case workers. This was particularly a problem in Denmark, where migrants felt the government's policy of 'jobs first' was pushing them into positions which did not reflect their education and skills. While some of this might reflect market demand for certain professions, which case workers are obliged to consider, it might also indicate a need for training case workers to value migrant skills.

Migrants need to be part – as a target population – of the next generation of labour market integration strategies and programmes, as this can contribute to the realisation of equality and social justice. In general, the eligibility of specific migrant groups to participate in labour market integration programmes should be expanded. The research discussed in this book has found that the eligibility varies from country to country, as do the availability of specific services. In some countries, such as the Czech Republic and Denmark, programmes are mainly offered to newly arrived refugees, while in others such as in Finland and Greece they are offered to all job-seeking migrants. In the United Kingdom, programmes are only offered to resettled refugees, which have been chosen in collaboration with the United Nations. Groups that could be included are:

- Asylum seekers who have not yet received their asylum decision. Because of the long wait for asylum decisions in many countries, extending eligibility for these programmes to asylum seekers with good prospects for a positive decision might allow more rapid integration, reducing the burden on public finances.
- Economic migrants: although they already have work, and do not necessarily have time to engage in integration training, many would like better access to language training, which would allow them better job opportunities.

- Parents who are caring for children sometimes miss out on integration programmes because they are not in the job market during their eligibility period, or do not have the time. More flexibility in the organisation of the programmes, or in the eligibility period, might improve access for this group (see Bontenbal and Lillie, 2019; SIRIUS Policy Brief No 3, 2019).

Furthermore, what the findings show is that to enhance responsiveness of policies, national authorities should involve all stakeholders, including municipalities, civil society and migrants and refugees in the planning, monitoring and implementation of a long-term integration strategy and programmes that will strengthen all aspects of integration, combat racism and xenophobic attitudes, and help all people recover from the pandemic (Human Rights Watch, 2021). The crisis, thus, provides an opportunity to value migrants for their crucial contribution to societies and economies, while reconsidering and tackling the structural barriers to their labour market integration.

Ensuring quality employment and fair working conditions for migrant workers

Migrants are significantly disadvantaged due to weaker protection of rights, precarious short-term contracts and weaker unionisation. Ensuring that new jobs are quality ones that allow migrants to enjoy a decent standard of living and contribute to their wellbeing and to a robust economy should lie at the core of an inclusive, rights-based and human-centric integration agenda. Job quality was already a concern before the COVID-19 crisis and even before the 2008–2009 global economic crisis. At the turn of the century, there was a political consensus in Europe, set out in the Nice Council Conclusions (December 2000), around the idea of quality work as a necessary element in delivering competitiveness and full employment. In 2010, following the adoption of the Europe 2020 Strategy, the European Commission's Communication identified better job quality and working conditions as one of the four key priorities for achieving the EU 2020 employment target. Yet, the fallout from the global economic crisis, and the internal devaluations and fiscal consolidation policies adopted, have led to an erosion of the European Social Model, and the notion of quality jobs appears to have taken a backseat since then (Vaughan-Whitehead, 2015; Lehto-Komulainen, 2018). Poor-quality jobs can lead to income insecurity, social exclusion, poverty in old age and poor physical and mental health. Concurrently, quality jobs are an essential feature of a well-functioning economy. Quality jobs give workers better job satisfaction, improved skills and greater motivation, which in turn lead to stronger, more productive and more innovative enterprises (OECD, 2014). This period of crisis in which we find ourselves is not only a threat but also an opportunity to lay the basis of a better socioeconomic model with a strong focus on migrants and their situation. Our findings show that the limited political will and capacities of state institutions, including local governments, to craft and implement enabling policies, along with weak governance arrangements and spaces for the co-construction of policy, have impacted the possibilities of designing and implementing collaborations to solve problems.

Strong multistakeholder dialogue and continued efforts are needed to put forward a Roadmap for Quality and Decent Employment with appropriate measures at the European and national levels and with specific targeted interventions to invest in quality and sustainable employment to counter the increase of in-work poverty, precariousness, poor working conditions and labour market segmentation currently facing migrants in several countries. Such a Roadmap should be course-altering, but also a catalyst for needed change. Policymakers need to empower migrants to advance decent working conditions and enhance jobs security, through prioritising such aspects in the European Labour Authority. In this context, it is also important that governments and social partners ensure that international labour standards (ILO, 2020a), the promotion and the realisation of Fundamental Principles and Rights at Work, other relevant international labour standards, and human rights more broadly – as a framework for ensuring decent work and inclusive integration – are at the centre of national responses and recovery plans in the post-COVID-19 era. More efforts are required to build and establish a common understanding about the necessity to promote equality of opportunity of treatment for migrant workers with regard to fundamental principles and rights at work and ensure – in accordance with internationally agreed normative standards, such as the widely ratified ILO Discrimination (Employment and Occupation) Convention, 1958 (No. 111) – that migrants are not being subject to discrimination, stigmatisation and harassment in their workplace based on their ethnicity, skin colour, country of origin, occupation or travel history (International Commission of Jurists, 2020).

Valuing the contribution of civil society organisations and establishing appropriate tracking and monitoring systems

Our research conducted before and during the pandemic has found that the third sector represents a key pillar in mitigating several of the integration barriers experienced by migrants (see Chapter 5), having an influence on policymaking both directly but also indirectly. In this case, civil society organisations' interventions can be used to 'legitimise' policy decisions that have become controversial and emotionally charged, but they can also be used to shift mindsets in the other way, making conversations more fact-based and less politicised. Depending on the institutional context, therefore, civil society action might be a critical and integrated component in the implementation of migration and integration policy.

The importance of civil society organisations has increased since 2014, though – as our findings show – disabling environments associated with their funding, weak initial conditions, assets and competencies have rendered some civil society organisations not only inherently fragile but also amenable to those populations at the bottom of the ladder in terms of endowments and capabilities. Chapter 5 findings provide strong evidence of noteworthy best practices about how civil society organisations are able to successfully address several of the challenges faced by migrants and act as effective actors in policymaking and agents of social change. Evidence also shows a positive appreciation on the part of migrants themselves for the service that civil society organisations provide and the role they play. Our fieldwork finds that civil society organisations work as important enablers of migrants' and refugees' labour market integration, especially in those areas not covered by public policies. More particularly, civil society organisations have been found to be important language course providers for post-2014 migrants and refugees, and thanks to their social, legal and administrative guidance, civil society organisations help migrants and refugee groups in overcoming ineffective administrative and legal structures. These activities are provided by the majority of civil society organisations across the seven countries. Several civil society organisations in these countries also assist migrants with the recruitment process, providing courses and advice on how to prepare for an interview, how to write a CV or how to draft a cover letter. Furthermore, civil society organisations assist migrants in their efforts to have their skills and qualifications recognised. Additionally, by providing mentorship, training programmes, volunteering or even direct employment, civil society organisations contribute to the development of skills and competencies of migrants and provide platforms to enhance their agency and autonomy. Overall, civil society organisations – the support of which is often vital as regards refugees and asylum seekers – have direct experience with and knowledge of the impact the recent crisis is having on so many people who are vulnerable in one form or another.

All in all, two key conclusions derive from these good practices: the first is that civil society organisations are an important bridge between migrants, public authorities, experts and employers. They must use that experience and knowledge to monitor and assess what is happening and work towards the articulation and development of inclusive integration that ensures every person's fundamental right to live a life of dignity and fully participate in society, and that allows migrants to overcome the sense of instability that is spreading everywhere and to regain control over their lives and futures. Ultimately, policy responses based upon robust monitoring, impact assessment and sex-disaggregated data can support more evidence-based economic policy measures. Recognising this particular role of civil society organisations in the wider migration and integration policy landscape requires, first and foremost, shaping enabling policy environments, so that civil society organisations do not end up working in silos. Civil society organisations that provide services to migrants experiencing exclusion are in a position to give a voice to the experience of the people they serve, a voice that tends to have few outlets for expression or influence in national public discourses, as our research finds – and these accounts can have an impact within and beyond country borders. A second conclusion is that the promotion of civil society organisations in decision-making structures – through channels of policy co-production – can be a significant tool for achieving social inclusion and cohesion with a strong focus on migrants, from local to European levels. While important, this also raises some issues, such as how to institutionalise civil society organisations in governmental structures; and how to establish permanent and effective mechanisms for civil society actors' participation in policy management, which should be treated cautiously so as to avoid the emergence of antagonistic relations between the civil society organisations and state actors. In this time of crisis recovery, the growth of the third sector often requires public policies to recognise the particularities and added value of the civil society organisations working with migrants in economic, social and societal terms (for example, forms of governance, outreach of vulnerable groups). As several civil society organisations heavily depend on public funding, it is worrying that many governments are currently reallocating funds to pandemic management and that this may mean that civil society organisations' budgets are likely to be trimmed and their operations will be adversely affected.

Enhancing migrants' representation and voice and promoting their labour market integration

EU and national leaders and parliamentarians must listen and engage actively with those migrants and refugees whose voices have been neglected and they have been systematically left out of labour market discourses and policymaking. Informal work arrangements and limited bargaining power can put migrants at higher risk of losing their jobs or seeing their pay cut during crises. Migrants need to be collectively and individually empowered through the support of their collective action and unionisation (ILO, 2020d). Enhancing representation and voice means enhancing the capacity of migrants to engage with various dimensions of the political arena, such as voice, contestation, advocacy, co-construction, negotiation, networking, and building and sustaining coalitions and alliances. Given the depth and duration of the COVID-19 crisis, employers' organisations and trade unions can play an essential role in the labour market integration of migrants. Migrant-led organisations need support to take equal part in decisions over rights at work, including representatives of migrant workers among stakeholders in the European Labour Authority, and by promoting migrants' representation in unions and collective agreements. Policy responses need to guarantee better the rights of migrants to freedom of association and collective bargaining which are crucial to negotiating fairer working conditions and addressing decent work deficits.

Strengthening social dialogue mechanisms can help to ensure the realisation of equity and social justice

Chapter 6 provides evidence for only a few cases of social dialogue having occurred across the seven countries in the field of labour migration, before the outbreak of the pandemic. Yet, social dialogue has an important role to play in building consensus on the necessary policy and legal reforms and ensuring social justice and decent work for all, especially in times of crisis recovery (Papadakis et al, 2020). Social dialogue processes and mechanisms are also critical to contributing to the realisation of inclusive rights-based integration for migrants, especially migrant workers in the informal economy in the agriculture industry of Southern regions who – as Chapter 6 findings show – are in extremely precarious situations, often not covered or insufficiently covered by formal social protection arrangements, and who lack voice and representation in social dialogue processes.

Strengthening social dialogue in this respect requires enhancing the capacity of state actors and workers and employers' organisations to take action on two fronts. First, the development of integrated strategies to support formalisation of work. This is crucial for the migrants who generally have difficulty finding employment in formal work. Meanwhile, the talent of many skilled migrants in the EU remains significantly underutilised, which is connected to problems relating to qualification recognition as well as prejudice in recruitment procedures. As a result, significant improvements in integration policies, particularly in the areas of education and training, will be required in order to better utilise the potential that migrants bring, while also contributing to economic growth and sustainable development.

Second, addressing the entire range of priorities to improve migrants' labour market integration prospects. As our fieldwork and interviews with social partners show (see Chapter 6), social partners in all seven countries studied stress the need to have more language class provision for migrants, but also different migration policies, given that legislation makes it very difficult for third country nationals, and in particular for asylum seekers, to enter the labour market and gain regular, stable and decent employment. Social partners consider also that better job search support services, along with skills matching and skills profiling, and job mentoring, could improve the employment situation of third country nationals. Furthermore, enhancing the agency of migrants through information campaigns, enriching capacities of migrants to represent themselves in trade unions and supporting trade unions to be more open to migrants and to effectively overcome language and cultural barriers have also been found to be critical aspects of an inclusive integration policy. Additionally, anti-discrimination and anti-exploitation policies (or a more effective implementation of these) would help too. In general, the consequences of the COVID-19 crisis, and especially its devastating impact on the livelihoods and incomes of migrant workers and enterprise owners, add even greater urgency to the promotion of sustainable formal employment opportunities in European economies (International Organization of Migration, 2020). Coordination among social partners, inclusion of migrants' associations in social dialogue activities (currently, in some countries, for example Italy and Greece, the participation of migrant associations in such activities is relatively marginal) can help voice their need beside the important role played by the third sector.

Prioritising social investment and economic stimulus to support inclusive rights-based policies

Social innovation and investment, especially at the local level, has a positive, preventive impact on the health and wellbeing of migrants and refugees, ensuring long-term savings for public budgets and improving the labour force's skills (Patuzzi, 2020). This may include, *inter alia*, the introduction of common social standards at the EU level,[1] emphasising that inclusive societies are more resilient societies and recognising that inclusive growth is not only about the most effective ways of promoting growth, but also about closing the gaps between those who are powerful and better off and those who are poor and excluded. National recovery policies and incentive packages should prioritise social investment programmes that foster innovation while targeting migrant workers and enterprise owners. In this area, national policymakers should act proactively and exploit the new knowledge generated through EU peer learning and the use of existing EU governance frameworks that promote the exchange of best practices and provide guidance to member states – particularly the Open Method of Coordination mechanisms and venues for collaboration. These are vital tools for pushing for support of innovative migrant-focused social and employment policies, along with considering how integration benchmarking architectures can effectively mature into national and local policymaking tools to promote the integration of migrants.[2] More broadly, as the socioeconomic effects of the pandemic can lead to declining wages and deteriorating working conditions overall (ILO, 2020b), the economic support measures provided to address these effects should ensure that migrants are not left out and that economic stimulus is not only available to nationals. Civil society organisations and human and civil rights movements should be aware of this danger and put resources into advocacy supporting migrants' rights.

Building socially responsive interventions and systems of support that are inclusive of migrant workers

Given the depth and duration of the COVID-19 crisis and its impact particularly on vulnerable groups (especially refugee women; see ILO, 2020c), the resilience of social protection systems must be improved to enable them to provide protection to the entire population in need. The evidence in Chapters 3 and 4 shows that unemployment benefits are another important element for understanding the legal barriers and enablers or best practices for the labour market integration of migrants and refugees. Noteworthily, Switzerland and Italy are the countries that present fewest restrictions in accessing unemployment benefits: all are entitled to such benefits in the same way as nationals, except undocumented migrants and asylum seekers who are not allowed to work in Switzerland. Moreover, in Greece, refugees, beneficiaries of subsidiary protection and long-term economic migrants can access the unemployment register and receive all benefits and services in the same way as Greek citizens do, whereas asylum seekers can do so only after having completed the application procedure. This is somewhat similar to the situation in the United Kingdom, where refugees and beneficiaries of subsidiary and national temporary protections are treated equally with British citizens, but long-term economic migrants must be granted indefinite leave to remain in the United Kingdom, unlike asylum seekers. Similarly, in the Czech Republic solely refugees, beneficiaries of subsidiary protection and long-term economic migrants are entitled to unemployment benefits. Concurrently, in Denmark, only refugees and long-term economic migrants holding a permanent residency permit can receive unemployment benefits, while, in Finland, unemployment benefits are made conditional upon permanent residency, which excludes asylum seekers and short-term economic migrants. Overall, while many countries have extended social protection coverage to nationals, migrants have been found to be less likely to be covered on par by social protection mechanisms because of discrimination and the type of jobs they have (ILO, 2020e). Including migrants in social protection measures and other risk-pooling mechanisms, including cash transfers and social health protection, in parity with nationals, is crucial to preventing them from experiencing further downward slips and ensuring equity and solidarity in financing. Further effort should also be encouraged in the provision of child and elderly care services to ease migrant women's entry into the labour market – this is important for countries such as the Czech

Republic, Greece and Italy where the gender gap is still large and not only for migrants, but also for natives.

In general, as a best practice, our findings call for stepped-up social protection interventions, especially for those who have suffered more from the health emergency, which would represent a promising path towards reducing social and labour market exclusion for migrants and inequality, as well as acting as a basis for labour market inclusiveness during recovery.

Recognising migrants' skills and their positive contribution to post-COVID-19 recovery

Our research conducted before the COVID-19 crisis shows that, although migrants and refugees have a variety of skills, they often encounter difficulties in the countries that host them to gain recognition of their qualifications, skills and diplomas acquired in their home countries (see Chapter 4). In particular, as a good practice, only Denmark, Switzerland and Italy (with the exception of asylum seekers) are open to the recognition of foreign qualifications; yet, in Italy the recognition process, being long and complex, substantially jeopardises the legitimate expectations of migrants. The United Kingdom recognises exclusively qualifications from selected countries of origin, on the basis of a common table of conversion. In the Czech Republic and Greece, the formal equalisation of qualifications is substantially undermined by the requirement of the official certificates issued by competent authorities, which is an unreasonable requirement for refugees and asylum seekers who often escape their countries in chaotic circumstances or whose countries' administrations have collapsed through conflict and violence. In between lies Finland, where it is not diplomas but proof of citizenship that is required, as to allow for fair conversions (again, a requirement that is very difficult to fulfil for refugees and asylum seekers). Noticeably, in all countries where this is allowed, migrants must specifically apply for recognition and, in the most favourable of cases, such as in Finland, this is done during the permit application process. Considering the digital and green transformations,[3] as well as the demand for new skills and jobs, there is an urgent need to address the barriers to recognising migrants' contribution and skills, as this issue is expected to have significant negative effects on countries' growth capacity well into the future, as indicated several times in the book case studies.

Since the outbreak of the pandemic, migrants have been at the frontlines in many of the occupations that have proved essential to the effective delivery of the COVID-19 response, that is, in medical professions and emergency services, food retail, logistics and agriculture (Baglioni et al, 2020; PICUM, 2020). On average, in the European Union, 13 per cent of all key workers are migrants (Fasani and Mazza, 2020), while countries such as the United Kingdom, Italy and the Czech Republic depend on foreign-born workers in the critical sector of healthcare services (OECD, 2019). As countries emerge from the pandemic, issues of migrants' skills and qualifications should acquire importance and be dealt with vis-à-vis the much-needed contributions that migrants can continue to provide to our societies and economies, ensuring long-term recovery. European countries and institutions have a strong interest in investing in migrant-inclusive labour markets and in embedding the structural contribution of, and reliance on migrants, including refugee groups, in national skills-related policy design. Recognition of prior home country education and experience, both in terms of formal recognition of certificates and employer recognition in recruiting, should improve. Visible in all the seven countries was a perceived need by migrants to start their education from the beginning again, because of a devaluing of foreign qualifications. More should be done to convert foreign qualifications into domestic equivalents, and to promote to employers the value of these qualifications. Programmes at education institutions designed to bring foreign qualifications up to local standards should be considered. Looking ahead, we found a strong consensus on the normative and pragmatic reasons and potential value of integrating migrants into European labour markets among the different stakeholders, which underline the awareness of the issue (see also ILO, 2020f). It remains to be seen whether such consensus could be taken as an opportunity for building a more inclusive, rights-based, integration agenda and shaping a future that avoids repeating the errors of the past.

Conclusion: Moving forward

To change the realities of migrants and refugees in European labour markets, a comprehensive approach is required that addresses the interconnection of migration and integration policies and other policy areas, as well as the interrelatedness of the institutional context and the roles of various policy and civil society actors. Overlooking issue complexities and interdependence can lead to policy failures and poor governance, with consequences for the position of migrants in host societies and labour markets.

All actors must acknowledge that migration and integration are complicated processes that need attentive and multifaceted policy responses. This may appear to be a simple argument, but it seems to be increasingly disregarded in public policy debates, which are frequently focused on immediate 'solutions' and responses to what are often difficult policy quandaries. This means that much more has to be done to establish such shared understandings, which necessitates ongoing communication among the main stakeholders.

Structure and actors both matter at the same time. The political and socioeconomic institutional environment can significantly affect the success of specific initiatives targeted at closing gaps, limiting the transferability of certain experiences and lessons between countries and across time. This is not to say that learning cannot occur across borders, but rather that each intervention must be adapted to the appropriate institutional setting.

It is also necessary to re-establish integration on domestic and European agendas by prioritising pragmatic and creative responses and evaluating integration outcomes. The political disagreements and crises that arose during the previous years must be replaced by a reinvigorated debate on larger aims. The lack of consensus and divergent interpretations of common goals that lead and support policy improvements will continue to be an impediment to developing successful and long-term policies in Europe. Against this background, it is vital to strengthen the linkages between research and policymaking so that diverse actors understand and grasp the intricacies surrounding migration and integration, as well as particular measures and interventions, and the real and perceived (controversial) implications on identity, culture and security. This necessitates a collaborative strategy that may foster the formation of more effective collaborations between the research and policy communities, as well as suitable norms and incentives for all key parties to participate. We believe that this chapter and book will serve to create further ideas about how this might be done in practice, in a way that promotes migrants' sustainable livelihoods and inclusive labour markets.

Notes

[1] Important social standards are quality and sustainable employment, adequate income support throughout the life cycle and universal access to quality and affordable care, social, health, housing, education and life-long learning services (see Social Platform, 2016).
[2] See, for example, https://www.mipex.eu/
[3] See, for example, INSEAD (2021).

References

Bagavos, C. and Kourachanis, N. (2020) 'Labour market integration of migrants, refugees and asylum seekers: Lessons learnt and best practices report on Greece', WP7 SIRIUS report. Available at: https://www.SIRIUS-project.eu/index.php/news/SIRIUS-greek-team-newreport-key-findings-and-covid-19-impact-labour-migration

Baglioni, S., Calò, F. and Lo Cascio, M. (2020) 'Covid-19 and labour migration: Investigating vulnerability in Italy and in the UK', *Quaderni di Economia del Lavoro*, 111: 109–129.

Blau, F.D. and Mackie, C. (eds) (2016) *The Economic and Fiscal Consequences of Immigration*, Washington, DC: A Report of the National Academies.

Bontenbal, I. and Lillie, N. (2019) 'Policy barriers and enablers', WP3 SIRIUS report. Available at: https://www.SIRIUS-project.eu/publications/wp-reports-results

Collini, M., Federico, V. and Pannia, P. (2020) 'Policy recommendations: Italy', WP7 SIRIUS report. Available at: https://www.SIRIUS-project.eu/news/SIRIUS-italian-team-newresearch-report-policy-recommendations-and-covid-19-impact-migrant

Dayant, A. (2020) 'Covid-19 and migration: Europe must resist a populist pill', Lowy Institute Blog. Available at: https://www.lowyinstitute.org/the-interpreter/covid-19-and-migration-europe-must-resist-populist-pill

European Economic and Social Committee (2020) 'EESC proposals for post-covid-19 crisis reconstruction and recovery: The EU must be guided by the principle of being considered a community of common destiny'. Available at: https://www.eesc.europa.eu/en/documents/resolution/eesc-proposals-post-covid-19-crisisreconstruction-and-recovery-eu-must-be-guided-principle-being-considered-community

Fasani, F. and Mazza, J. (2020) 'Immigrant key workers: Their contribution to Europe's covid-19 response', IZA Policy Paper No 155, April. Available at: https://www.iza.org/publications/pp/155/immigrant-key-workers-their-contribution-to-europescovid-19-response

Federico, V. (2018) 'Legal barriers and enablers', WP2 SIRIUS report. Available at: https://www.SIRIUS-project.eu/publications/wp-reports-results

Gheorghiev, O., Hoření, K., Švarcová, M., Numerato, D. and Čada, K. (2021) 'Policy recommendations: Czech Republic', WP7 SIRIUS report. Available at: https://www.SIRIUSproject.eu/index.php/news/SIRIUS-new-report-covid-and-labour-migration-czech-republic

Human Rights Watch (2021) 'World report 2021: Events of 2020'. Available at : https://www.hrw.org/world-report/2021

ILO (International Labour Organization) (2020a) 'ILO standards and covid FAQ: Key provisions of international labour standards relevant to the evolving covid-19 outbreak, v. 2.1'. Available at: https://www.ilo.org/wcmsp5/groups/public/---ed_norm/---normes/documents/genericdocument/wcms_739937.pdf

ILO (2020b) 'ILO monitor: Covid-19 and the world of work', third edition. Available at: https://www.ilo.org/global/topics/coronavirus/impacts-and-responses/WCMS_743146/lang--en/index.htm

ILO (2020c) 'ILO monitor: Covid-19 and the world of work', fourth edition. Available at: https://www.ilo.org/global/topics/coronavirus/impacts-and-responses/WCMS_745963/lang--en/index.htm

ILO (2020d) 'Protecting the rights at work of refugees and other forcibly displaced persons during the covid-19 pandemic', ILO Policy Brief, 19 June. Available at: https://www.ilo.org/global/topics/labourmigration/publications/WCMS_748485/lang--en/index.htm

ILO (2020e) 'Social protection for migrant workers: A necessary response to the covid-19 crisis', ILO Brief, 23 June. Available at: https://www.ilo.org/secsoc/information-resources/publications-andtools/Brochures/WCMS_748979/lang--en/index.htm

ILO (2020f) 'Protecting migrant workers during the covid-19 pandemic', ILO Policy Brief, 30 April. Available at: https://www.ilo.org/global/topics/labour-migration/publications/WCMS_743268/lang-- en/index.htm

INSEAD (2021) 'Global talent competitiveness index: Fostering green and digital jobs and skills crucial for talent competitiveness in times of COVID-19'. Available at: https://www.insead.edu/newsroom/2021-global-talent-competitiveness-index-fostering-green-and-digital-jobs-and-skills-crucial-for-talent-competitiveness-in-times-of-covid-19

International Commission of Jurists (2020) 'The impact of covid-19 related measures on human rights of migrants and refugees in the EU', Briefing paper, 26 June. Available at: https://www.icj.org/eu-the-impact-of-covid-19-on-human-rights-of-migrants-and-refugees/

International Organization of Migration (2020) 'Migration factsheet no. 6 – the impact of covid-19 on migrants: Synthesis analysis drawing on IOM's world migration report series'. Available at: https://www.iom.int/sites/default/files/our_work/ICP/MPR/migration_factsheet_6_covid19_and_migrants.pdf

Kahanec, M. and Zimmermann K.F. (eds) (2009) *EU Labor Markets After Post-Enlargement Migration*, Berlin: Springer.

Lehto-Komulainen, K. (2018) 'Creating good quality jobs: If not now, then when?', *Social Europe*. Available at: https://socialeurope.eu/creating-good-quality-jobs-if-not-now-then-when

Marmefelt, T. (2020) 'Covid-19 and economic policy toward the new normal: A monetary fiscal nexus after the crisis?', Policy Department for Economic, Scientific and Quality of Life Policies Directorate-General for Internal Policies. Monetary Dialogue Papers, European Parliament. Available at: https://www.europarl.europa.eu/thinktank/en/document.html?reference=IPOL_IDA%282020%29658193

Mexi, M. (2020) 'Policy recommendations on the labour market integration of migrants: Switzerland', WP7 SIRIUS report. Available at: https://www.SIRIUS-project.eu/news/SIRIUSswiss-team-new-report-covid-19-and-migration-and-policy-recommendations

Ndomo, Q., Bontenbal, I. and Lillie, N. (2020) 'Policy recommendations on the labour market integration of migrants: Finland', WP7 SIRIUS report. Available at: https://www.SIRIUSproject.eu/index.php/news/SIRIUS-new-report-effects-covid-19-labour-migration-finland

OECD (Organisation of Economic Cooperation and Development) (2014) *Employment Outlook 2014*. Available at: https://www.oecd-ilibrary.org/employment/oecd-employment-outlook2014_empl_outlook-2014-en

OECD (2019) 'Recent trends in international migration of doctors, nurses and medical students'. Available at: https://www.oecd-ilibrary.org/social-issues-migration-health/recent-trends-in-internationalmigration-of-doctors-nurses-and-medical-students_5571ef48-en

Papadakis, K., Mexi, M. and Cauqui, R. (2020) 'Peak-level social dialogue as a governance tool during the covid-19 pandemic: Global and regional trends and policy issues', Research brief, Geneva: International Labour Organization. Available at: https://www.ilo.org/wcmsp5/groups/public/---ed_dialogue/--- dialogue/documents/briefingnote/wcms_759072.pdf

Patuzzi, L. (2020) 'Driving migrant inclusion through social innovation: Lessons for cities in a pandemic', Migration Policy Institute Europe and International Organization for Migration. Available at: https://www.migrationpolicy.org/research/migrant-inclusion-social-innovationcities-pandemic

PICUM (2020) 'Non-exhaustive overview of European government measures impacting undocumented migrants taken in the context of covid-19', March–August. Available at: https://picum.org/wp-content/uploads/2020/10/Non-exhaustive-overview-of-Europeangovernment-measures-impacting-undocumented-migrants-taken-in-the-context-of-COVID19.pdf

SIRIUS Policy Brief No 2 (2019) 'Labour markets, post-2014 migrants and refugees in Europe: Evidence and thoughts for better integration'. Available at: https://www.SIRIUS-project.eu/publications/policy-briefs

SIRIUS Policy Brief No 3 (2019) 'Migrant labour market integration programmes: Policy lessons from the SIRIUS research project'. Available at: https://www.SIRIUSproject.eu/publications/policy-briefs

Social Platform (2016) 'EU social standards: Ensuring every person's fundamental right to live a life in dignity and fully participate in society', Position Paper. Available at: http://www.socialplatform.org/wp-content/uploads/2016/06/SP-position-paper-on-EU-social-standards.pdf

Spyratou, D. (2020) 'Policy recommendations, Greece country report: Impact of the covid19 crisis on labour market integration', WP7 SIRIUS report. Available at: https://www.SIRIUSproject.eu/index.php/news/impact-covid-pandemic-and-migrant-labour-greece-SIRIUSsolidarity-now-report-out-today

Vaughan-Whitehead, D. (ed) (2015) *The European Social Model in Crisis: Is Europe Losing its Soul?*, Geneva: International Labour Office.

Voegele, J. (2021) 'Millions on the move: What climate change could mean for internal migration', World Bank Blogs. Available at: https://blogs.worldbank.org/voices/millions-move-what-climate-change-could-mean-internal-migration

Zenner, D. and Wickramage, K. (2020) 'National preparedness and response plans for covid-19 and other diseases: Why migrants should be included', Migration Data Portal, 14 May. Available at: https://migrationdataportal.org/blog/national-preparedness-andresponse-plans-covid-19-and-other-diseases-why-migrants-should-be

Zimmermann, K.F. (2014) 'Migration, jobs and integration in Europe', *Migration Policy Practice*, IV(4): 4–13.

Index

References to figures appear in *italic* type;
those in **bold** type refer to tables.

A

Act of Immigration, Denmark 64
active labour market policy (ALMP) *see* ALMP (active labour market policy)
administrative guidance and support
 from civil society organisations 85, 90–91, 144
 as enabler for employment 112, **113**
advocacy, by civil society organisations 83
agency and autonomy of MRAs 84, 86–87, 121, 122–125, 126, 127, 147
Agency Italia Lavoro Spa 71
'agency-structure' nexus 124
ALMP (active labour market policy) 55, 56, 57, 59, 76–77
 Denmark 141
 Finland 65–66, 141
 Greece 68, 69
 Italy 71
 stigma and employer participation 60–61
 Switzerland 141
 UK 73–74
 see also labour market integration
Alpa, G. 50
alternative careerists 130, 132
assimilationist model of citizenship 57, 58
Asylum, Migration and Integration Fund 86
asylum seekers
 future labour market integration policies 141
 international comparison
  mean annual number of first decisions on applications 24, *25*
  mean annual number of first residence permits per 1,000 persons 24, *26*
  ratio of positive to total first instance decisions 24, *25*
 legal frameworks 41, 43, 51
 see also MRAs (migrants, refugees and asylum seekers)

B

back-steppers 130–131, 133

C

career diplomats 130, 131, 133
Carrera, S. 57
Centres for Support of the Integration of Foreigners, Czech Republic 63–64
chambers of commerce
 MRAs and the labour market 103, **104**
 skill levels of MRAs 105, **106**, 107, **107**
child care, future policy for 148–149
citizenship models 57–58
civic education 65, 71
civil society organisations (CSOs) 2, *3*, 5–7, 98, 148
 accountability 97
 anti-migrant organisations 92
 competition between 93
 cooptation of by private business 94
 cooptation of by the state 93–94
 Czech Republic 84, 85, 92, 94, 95
 Denmark 84, 85, 87, 89, 91, 93, 95, 97–98
 Finland 84, 85, 88, 89, 92, 93, 96
 funding issues 86, 91–92, 97–98
 future policies for 143–145
 Greece 68, 84, 85, 86–87, 89–90, 90–91, 92, 94
 Italy 70, 84, 85, 87, 88, 92, 96
 labour market integration barriers 91–98
 labour market integration enablers 85–91
 methods 84–85
 MRAs' distrust of 94–95
 networks between 86–87, 89
 othering and objectification by 95–96
 'professional' culture of 96–97
 roles and services 6–7, 83–84, 98, 144
 Switzerland 72–73, 84, 85, 87, 88, 89, 90, 93
 United Kingdom 73, 84, 85, 87, 89, 92, 94, 95
Collini, M. 71
conservative welfare state regimes 58, 59, 60, 68, 72, 75, 77
COVID-19 pandemic 1–2, 139, 142, 145, 147
 integration of migrants' needs in post-COVID-19 recovery planning 140–142
 migrants as key workers during 149–150
 socioeconomic impacts of 147–148
critical ethnography 126
critical events *see* labour market integration of MRAs, turning points
CSOs (civil society organisations) *see* civil society organisations (CSOs)
cultural differences, as barrier to employment 112, **113**

Index

cultural mediation, by civil society organisations 89
Czech Republic 2, 3–4
  civil society organisations 84, 85, 92, 94, 95
  health service's dependence on migrant workers 150
  key statistical analysis and overview
    asylum seekers, mean annual number of first instance decisions 25
    asylum seekers, mean annual number of first residence permits per 1,000 persons 24, 26
    asylum seekers, per 1,000 persons 23–24, 24
    asylum seekers, ratio of positive to total first instance decisions 25
    educational attainment level of foreign nationals 20, 21, 23
    employability indicators 29
    employment rates of foreign nationals 22, 23
    foreign-born population and shifts in size of labour force 17, 17, 18, **18**
    as a labour absorbing economy 27–28, **28**
    labour market participation of foreign nationals **18**, 20, 22
    net migration rate 23, 23
    population change, foreign-born population and overall population 14, 14, 15
    share of foreign nationals to total population 19, 20
  labour market integration
    LMI policies, and welfare regimes 56, 59, 61, 62–64, **75**, 76, 77, 141, 148–149
    turning points in 121, 125, 127–128, 129
  legal framework 39, 42, 51
    labour market access 43
    language proficiency and courses 46, 63, 64
    recognition of qualifications 44–45, 149
    retirement benefits 48
    self-employment 49, **49**
    unemployment benefits 48, **48**
    vocational education and training 46, **47**
  NGOs (non-governmental organisations) 64
  social dialogue 115
  social partners **104**
    attitudes towards MRAs 107
    MRA disruption of the labour market 108–109, 110, 111
    perception of skill levels of MRAs 106

D

De Fina, A. 126
decent work 122, 123
decommodification of labour 57, 58–59, 61, 68, 76–77
demographic characteristics, international comparisons 12
  foreign-born population and shifts in size of labour force 16–19, 17, **18**
  population change, foreign-born population and overall population 13–16, 14, 15
Denmark 2, 3–4
  ALMP (active labour market policy) 141
  civic education 65
  civil society organisations 84, 85, 87, 89, 91, 93, 95, 97–98
  'employment first' integration policy 64, 65
  key statistical analysis and overview
    asylum seekers, mean annual number of first instance decisions 24, 25
    asylum seekers, mean annual number of first residence permits per 1,000 persons 24, 26
    asylum seekers, per 1,000 persons 23, 24
    asylum seekers, ratio of positive to total first instance decisions 25
    educational attainment level of foreign nationals 20, 21, 23
    employability indicators 29
    employment rates of foreign nationals 22, 23
    foreign-born population and shifts in size of labour force 17, 17, 18, **18**
    as a labour absorbing economy 28, **28**
    labour market participation **18**, 19, 22
    population change, foreign-born population and overall population 14, 15, **15**
    share of foreign nationals to total population 19, 20
  labour market integration
    LMI policies, and welfare regimes 56, 59, 61, 64–65, **75**, 76, 77, 141, 148
    turning points in 121, 125, 129, 132–133
  legal framework 39, 42, 51
    language proficiency and courses 45, 65
    recognition of qualifications 44, 149
    retirement benefits 48
    self-employment 49, **49**
    unemployment benefits 47, **48**
    vocational education and training 46, **47**

157

NGOs (non-governmental organisations) 65
social partners **104**
  attitudes towards MRAs 107
  MRA disruption of the labour market 110, 111
Denzin, Norman 124
depot dwellers 130, 131, 132, 133
depot migrants 130
discrimination 47, 73
  as barrier to employment 112, 113, **113**

E

economic migrants
  future labour market integration policies 141
  legal frameworks 41, 50–51
  see also MRAs (migrants, refugees and asylum seekers)
economic stimulus policies 147–148
educational attainment level of foreign nationals 20, *21*, 29
  and employment rates 21–22, *23*, 25–26
elderly care services, future policy 148–149
employability of MRAs, international comparisons 12–13, 26
employability indicators, structural analysis of 28–30
employment opportunities 27–28, **28**
employers 6, 73, 102
  ALMP programme participation 60–61
employers' organisations 101, 116
  perception of skill levels of MRAs 105, **106**, **107**, 107–108
  perceptions of MRAs and the labour market 103, **104**
  see also social partners
employment
  decent work 122, 123
  employment opportunities
    gender differences in 123
    international comparison 27–28, **28**
  employment rate of MRAs
    and gender 25–26
    impact of COVID-19 pandemic on 1–2
    OECD data 1
  health and safety risks 114, **115**, 116–117
  informal/precarious 114, 116–117
    Greece 68
    Italy 70, 72
  quality employment and fair working conditions policies 142–143
  right to work 43, 74, 127
  social partner experts' perceptions of barriers and enablers **112**, 112–116, **113**, **114**, **115**, **116**

'employment first' integration policy, Denmark 64, 65
entrepreneurial culture, and civil society organisations 87
Esping-Andersen, G. 58, 59, 76
ethnic networks 128–129
EU (European Union)
  common immigration policy 39
  Europe 2020 Strategy 142
  TFEU (Treaty on the Functioning of the European Union) 39, 42
  United Kingdom exit from 107
European Economic and Social Committee Section for Employment, Social Affairs and Citizenship 86
European Labour Authority 143, 146
European Migration Forum 86
European Social Fund 86
European Social Model 142
exclusionist model of citizenship 57, 58
expert-responders, social partners
  barriers and enablers to MRAs' employment **112**, 112–116, **113**, **114**, **115**, **116**
  perceptions of MRAs and the labour market 103, **104**

F

families, as source of social welfare in Greece 59, 68
family reunification rights 41
Federico, V. 41, 50
Finland 2, 3–4
  ALMP (active labour market policy) 65–66, 141
  civil society organisations 84, 85, 88, 89, 92, 93, 96
  key statistical analysis and overview
    asylum seekers, mean annual number of first instance decisions 24, *25*
    asylum seekers, mean annual number of first residence permits per 1,000 persons 24, *26*
    asylum seekers, per 1,000 persons 23, *24*
    asylum seekers, ratio of positive to total first instance decisions *25*
    educational attainment level of foreign nationals *21*, *23*
    employability indicators 30
    employment rates of foreign nationals 22, *23*
    foreign-born population and shifts in size of labour force 17, *17*, 18, **18**, 19
    as a labour absorbing economy 27–28, **28**
    labour market participation **18**, 19, 20, *22*
    net migration rate 22, *23*

population change, foreign-born
  population and overall population *14*,
  15, **15**
 share of foreign nationals to total
  population 19, *20*
labour market integration
 LMI policies, and welfare regimes 56,
  59, 61, 65–67, **75**, 76, 77, 141, 148
 turning points in 121, 128, 132
legal framework 39, 41, 42, 51
 labour market access 43, 44
 language proficiency and courses
  45–46, 67, 132
 recognition of qualifications 45, 149
 retirement benefits 48
 self-employment 49, **49**
 unemployment benefits 47, **48**
 vocational education and
  training 46, **47**
racism 66
social dialogue 115
social partners 103, **104**
 attitudes towards MRAs 107
 MRA disruption of the labour
  market 108–109, 110
 perception of skill levels of MRAs 106
vocational education and training 67
foreign-born population/foreign
  nationals 12
 activity rates 20, *21*
 demographic characteristics
  population change 13–16, *14*, **15**
  shifts in size of labour force 16–19,
   17, **18**
 educational attainment level 20, *21*
 employment rates 21–22, *22*, *23*
 labour market participation 20, *22*
 see also MRAs (migrants, refugees and
  asylum seekers)
Fundamental Principles and Rights at
 Work 143

G

Galera, G. 84
gender
 differences in employment
  opportunities 123
 and employment rates 25–26
 future policies to decrease participation
  gap 148–149
Georgakopoulou, A. 126
'ghetto effect,' and legal statuses 39, 40–42
Giddens, Anthony 124
GIO (Growth Potential Indicator for
 Occupations) 29
GIS (Growth Indicator for Sectors) 29
global economic crisis 2008–2009 142
Global Vector AutoRegression Model
 (GVAR) 27

Greece 2, 3–4
 ALMP (active labour market
  policy) 68, 69
 anti-migrant sentiment 68
 civil society organisations 68, 84, 85,
  86–87, 89–90, 90–91, 92, 94
 families, as source of social welfare 59, 68
 informal/precarious employment 68
 key statistical analysis and overview
  asylum seekers, mean annual number of
   first instance decisions *25*
  asylum seekers, mean annual number
   of first residence permits per 1,000
   persons 24, *26*
  asylum seekers, per 1,000
   persons 23, *24*
  asylum seekers, ratio of positive to total
   first instance decisions 24, *25*
  educational attainment level of foreign
   nationals 20, *21*, *23*
  employability indicators 29
  employment rates of foreign
   nationals *22*, *23*
  foreign-born population and shifts in
   size of labour force 17, *17*, 18, **18**, 19
  as a labour absorbing economy 27,
   28, **28**
  labour market participation **18**, 19,
   20, *22*
  net migration rate 23, *23*
  population change, foreign-born
   population and overall population 14,
   14, **15**
  share of foreign nationals to total
   population 19, *20*
 labour market integration
  LMI policies, and welfare regimes 56,
   59, 62, 67–69, 74–76, **75**, 77,
   141, 149
  turning points in 121, 125, 128
 legal framework 39, 42, 51
  labour market access 43
  language proficiency and courses 46
  recognition of qualifications 44–45,
   149
  retirement benefits 48
  self-employment 49, **49**
  unemployment benefits 47–48, **48**
  vocational education and
   training 46, **47**
 National Integration Strategy 68–69
 NGOs (non-governmental
  organisations) 68, 75
 Public Employment Service (OAED) 69
 social dialogue 147
 social partners 103, **104**
  MRA disruption of the labour
   market 110, 111
  perception of skill levels of MRAs 106

Growth Indicator for Sectors (GIS) 29
Growth Potential Indicator for Occupations (GIO) 29
GVAR (Global Vector AutoRegression Model) 27

H

health and safety risks in employment of MRAs 114, **115**, 116–117
Hobsbawm, Eric 40

I

ILO (International Labour Organisation) 122
  Discrimination (Employment and Occupation) Convention, 1958 (No. 111) 143
individuals 2, *3*, 7–8
informal/precarious employment of MRAs 114, 116–117
  Greece 68
  Italy 70, 72
International Organization for Migration 86
International Protection Act L.4636/2019 43
IOA (Input-Output Analysis) 29
irregular migrants
  legal framework 51
  see also MRAs (migrants, refugees and asylum seekers)
Italy 2, 3–4
  civic education 71
  civil society organisations 70, 84, 85, 87, 88, 92, 96
  health service's dependence on migrant workers 150
  informal/precarious employment 70, 72
  key statistical analysis and overview
    asylum seekers, mean annual number of first decisions 24, *25*
    asylum seekers, mean annual number of first residence permits per 1,000 persons *26*
    asylum seekers, per 1,000 persons 23, *24*
    asylum seekers, ratio of positive to total first instance decisions *25*
    educational attainment level of foreign nationals 20, *21*, *23*
    employability indicators 30
    employment rates of foreign nationals *22*, *23*
    foreign-born population and shifts in size of labour force 17, *17*, 18, **18**
    as a labour absorbing economy 28, **28**
    labour market participation **18**, 19, 20, *22*
    net migration rate 22, *23*
    share of foreign nationals to total population 19, *20*
  labour market integration
    LMI policies, and welfare regimes 56, 59, 62, 69–72, 74–76, **75**, 77, 148, 149
    turning points in 121, 125
  legal framework 39, 41, 42, 51
    labour market access 43, 44
    language proficiency and courses 46, 71
    recognition of qualifications 44, 72, 149
    retirement benefits 48
    self-employment 49, **49**
    unemployment benefits 47, **48**
    vocational education and training 46, **47**
  NGOs (non-governmental organisations) 70, 75
  'Salvini decree' 70
  social dialogue 147
  social partners 103, **104**
  MRA disruption of the labour market 110, 111
  perception of skill levels of MRAs 106
  vocational education and training 71

J

job search support 141
  ALMP programmes 60
  civil society organisations 6, 85, 144
  Denmark 65
  as enabler for employment 112, 113, **113**

L

labour absorbing economies 27–28, **28**
labour market access, legal frameworks 42–44, **44**
labour market integration 1–2
  barriers and enablers, international comparisons 12, 19
  asylum seekers, mean annual number of first residence permits per 1,000 persons 24, *26*
  asylum seekers, mean annual number of first instance decisions 24, *25*
  asylum seekers, per 1,000 persons 23–24, *24*
  asylum seekers, ratio of positive to total first instance decisions 24, *25*
  educational attainment level of foreign nationals 20, *21*, *23*
  employment rates 21–22, *22*, *23*
  labour market participation 20, *22*
  net migration rates 22–23, *23*
  share of foreign nationals to total population 19, *20*

160

Index

barriers and enablers, social partners' perceptions of **112**, 112–116, **113**, **114**, **115**, **116**
LMI (labour market integration) policies 139–140, 150–151
and welfare regimes 55–61, 76, 78, 138
macro level of analysis 2, *3*, 3–5
meso level of analysis 2, *3*, 5–7
methodology 61–62
micro level of analysis 2, *3*, 7–8
migrants' voice and representation 145–146
turning points in 120–122, 133–134
  entering the labour market 126–128
  meeting the right person 124–125, 128–129
  methodology 125–126
  migrant agency and vulnerability 122–125
  pre-emigration turning points 129
  typology of 'integrated migrants' 130–133
see also ALMP (active labour market policy)
labour market participation 16
demographic characteristics 16, 17, **18**
international comparison 20, *22*
Labour Office, Czech Republic 63
language proficiency and courses 45–46, 55, 63, 64, 65, 67, 71, 73, 74, 112, **113**, 132, 147
legal framework 45–46
provision of by civil society organisations 6, 83, 85, 89, 144
legal frameworks 2, *3*, 4–5, 38–40, 50–52, 138
legal status, and the ghetto effect 40–42
rights, work and integration 42–50, *44*, *45*, **47**, **48**, **49**
legal peripheries 39
liberal welfare state regimes 58, 59, 60, 72, 73, 75, 77
LMI *see* labour market integration
local market access restrictions 8–9

M

Maggini, N. 71
Marcuse, P. 51
Martin, C. 61
mentoring 6, 85, 94, 98, 113, 144, 877
migrants *see* MRAs (migrants, refugees and asylum seekers) introduction and overview
migrants-in-waiting 130–131
migration governance 39–40
  comparative analysis 4–5
see also legal frameworks
migration rates, international comparison 22–23, *23*

Ministry of Labour, Italy 71
MRAs (migrants, refugees and asylum seekers)
  agency and autonomy of 84, 86–87, 121, 122–125, 126, 127, 147
  introduction and overview 1–9
  share of foreign nationals to total population 19, *20*
  social partners' perceptions of skill levels of 104–108, **105**, **106**, **107**
see also employability of MRAs, international comparisons; employment; foreign-born population; labour market access, legal frameworks; labour market integration
Multiannual Financial Framework (2021–2027) 140–141
multicultural model of citizenship 57, 58

N

narrative-biographic inquiry 120–121, 126
National Integration Strategy, Greece 68–69
networking 128–129
new-skill-learners 130
Next Generation EU 140–141
NGOs (non-governmental organisations) 64, 65, 68, 70, 75
Nice Council Conclusions (December 2000) 142

O

Occupational Structure Similarity (OSS) 29
officials, discriminatory and prejudiced attitudes amongst 127–128
Open Method of Coordination 147
OSS (Occupational Structure Similarity) 29
othering and objectification, by civil society organisations 95–96

P

Pannia, P. 41, 50
parents with child care responsibilities, future labour market integration policies 141
participation *see* labour market participation
policy discourse analysis 5
policy frameworks 2, *3*, 5, 8–9
'post-liberal' welfare state regimes 72
'post-socialist' welfare state regimes 59
psychological support provided by civil society organisations 90
Public Employment Service, Italy 71
Public Employment Service (OAED), Greece 69

Q

qualifications, recognition of 44–45, 72, 127, 147, 149
  and civil society organisations 85, 144
  as enabler for employment 112, **113**
  future policies 149–150
  legal framework 44–45, *45*
quality jobs, future policies for 141–142

R

recruitment process 6, 85, 144, 147
refugees
  legal frameworks 41, 42–43, 50
  see also MRAs (migrants, refugees and asylum seekers)
re-skilled professionals 130
retirement benefits 48
right to work 43, 74, 127
Roadmap for Quality and Decent Employment 143

S

SAI (Sistems di Accoglienza e Integrazione), Italy 70
'Salvini decree,' Italy 70
Scotland 46, 74
Sectoral Structure Similarity (SSS) 29
self-employment rights, legal framework 48–50, **49**
SIRIUS - Skills and Integration of Refugees, Migrants and Asylum Apllicants in European Labour Markets (Horizon 2020 EU project) 2, 62, 125
Sistema di Protezione per Richiedenti Asilo e Refugiati (SPRAR), Italy 70
Sistema di Accoglienza e Integrazione (SAI), Italy 70
skill levels of MRAs (migrants, refugees and asylum seekers)
  future policies 149–150
  social partners' perceptions of 104–108, **105**, **106**, **107**, 117
skills shortages, social partners' assessment of policy effectiveness 114, **114**
social cooperatives 101, 116
  perception of skill levels of MRAs 105, **106**, 107, **107**
  see also social partners
social democratic welfare state regimes 58–59, 60, 64
social dialogue 7, 101, 103, 111, 114–115, **116**, 117, 146–147
social dumping 102, 105, 110, 115
social enterprises 87, 101, 102, 116
  perception of skill levels of MRAs 105, **106**, 107, **107**
  see also social partners

social investment policies 147–148
social partners 6, 7, 101–102, 116–117, 138, 146–147
  experts' perceptions of barriers and enablers 112, 112–116, **113**, **114**, **115**, **116**
  methods 102–103, **104**
  MRAs' disruption of national labour markets 108–111, **109**, **110**, **111**
  perceptions of MRAs' skill levels 104–108, **105**, **106**, **107**, 117
social protection systems 148–149
Sohn, J. 40
SPRAR (Sistema di Protezione per Richiedenti Asilo e Refugiati), Italy 70
Squire, V. 122
SSS (Sectoral Structure Similarity) 29
State Integration Programme, Czech Republic 63
subsidiary protection beneficiaries, legal frameworks 41, 42–43, 50
Swank, D. 61
Sweden 3
Switzerland 2, 3–4
  ALMP (active labour market policy) 141
  civil society organisations 72–73, 84, 85, 87, 88, 89, 90, 93
  key statistical analysis and overview
    asylum seekers, mean annual number of first instance decisions 25
    asylum seekers, mean annual number of first residence permits per 1,000 persons 26
    asylum seekers, per 1,000 persons 23, *24*
    asylum seekers, ratio of positive to total first instance decisions 25
    educational attainment level of foreign nationals 20, *21*, *23*
    employability indicators 29–30
    employment rates of foreign nationals 22, *23*
    foreign-born population and shifts in size of labour force 17, *17*, 18, **18**, 19
    as a labour absorbing economy 27, 28, **28**
    labour market participation **18**, 19, 20, *22*
    net migration rate 22, *23*
    population change, foreign-born population and overall population *14*, 15, **15**
    share of foreign nationals to total population 19, *20*
  labour market integration
    LMI policies, and welfare regimes 56, 59, 62, 72–73, **75**, 76, 77, 141, 148
    turning points in 121, 131

162

Index

legal framework 39, 41, 42, 51
  labour market access 43, 44
  language proficiency and courses 46, 73
  recognition of qualifications 44, 149
  retirement benefits 48
  self-employment 49, **49**
  unemployment benefits 47, **48**
  vocational education and training 46, **47**
social partners 103, **104**
  attitudes towards MRAs 107
  MRA disruption of the labour market 108–109, 110
  policies to address skills shortages 114

T

tertiary education level of MRAs 20, *21*
trade unions 6, 7, 101–102, 114–115, 116, 145, 146, 147
  perceptions of MRAs and the labour market 103, **104**
  disruption of the labour market 108–109, 111
  skill levels of MRAs 104, 105–106, **106**, 107, **107**
  see also social partners
Triandafyllidou, A. 122, 124
turning points in labour market integration 120–122, 133–134
  entering the labour market 126–128
  meeting the right person 124–125, 128–129
  methodology 125–126
  migrant agency and vulnerability 122–125
  pre-emigration turning points 129
  typology of 'integrated migrants' 130–133

U

UN agencies, Greece 68
UN High Commissioner for Refugees 86
undocumented migrants
  legal framework 42
  see also MRAs (migrants, refugees and asylum seekers)
unemployment benefits 148
  legal framework 47–48, **48**
United Kingdom 2, 3–4
  ALMP (active labour market policy) 73–74
  civil society organisations 73, 84, 85, 87, 89, 92, 94, 95
  exit from the European Union 107
  health service's dependence on migrant workers 150
  'hostile environment' immigration policy 74, 76

key statistical analysis and overview
  asylum seekers, mean annual number of first instance decisions 25
  asylum seekers, mean annual number of first residence permits per 1,000 persons 24, *26*
  asylum seekers, per 1,000 persons 23, *24*
  asylum seekers, ratio of positive to total first instance decisions 25
  educational attainment level of foreign nationals 20, *21*, *23*
  employability indicators 30
  employment rates of foreign nationals 22, *23*
  foreign-born population and shifts in size of labour force 17, *17*, 18, **18**, 19
  as a labour absorbing economy 27, 28, **28**
  labour market participation **18**, 19, 20, *22*
  net migration rate 22–23, *23*
  population change, foreign-born population and overall population 14, *14*, **15**
  share of foreign nationals to total population 19, *20*
labour market integration
  LMI policies, and welfare regimes 56, 59, 61, 62, 73–74, **75**, 76, 77, 141, 148
  turning points in 121, 125, 128, 133
  legal framework 39, 42, 51
  labour market access 43
  language proficiency and courses 46, 74
  recognition of qualifications 44, 149
  retirement benefits 48
  self-employment 49, **49**
  unemployment benefits 48, **48**
  vocational education and training 46, **47**
negative narratives about MRAs 106–107
social partners
  MRA disruption of the labour market 108–109, 110
  perception of skill levels of MRAs 106

V

van Oorschot, W. 60
VAR/VEC framework 27
vocational education and training 67, 71
  ALMP programmes 60
  and civil society organisations 83, 85
  legal framework 46, **47**
  LMI (labour market integration) policies, and welfare regimes 55
volunteering 113, 131
vulnerability of MRAs 121, 122–125, 126

W

Waite, L. 123
welfare regimes 5, 57–60
  future provisions 148–149
  see also LMI (labour market integration) policies, and welfare regimes
women
  future policies to increase labour market integration 148–149
  gender differences in employment opportunities 123
  work-life balancers 132–133
'work-first' policy approach 4
working conditions and benefits, non-discrimination in 47
work-life balancers 130, 132–133